M000206921

Latina Leadership

Writing, Culture, and Community Practices
Steve Parks and Eileen Schell, *Series Editors*

Syracuse University Press's Writing, Culture, and Community Practices series is distinguished by works that move between disciplinary identity and community practices to address how literacies and writing projects empower a population and promote social change.

Other Titles in Writing, Culture, and Community Practices

The Arkansas Delta Oral History Project:
Culture, Place, and Authenticity
    David A. Jolliffe, Christian Z. Goering,
    Krista Jones Oldham, and James A. Anderson Jr.

Writing Suburban Citizenship: Place-Conscious
Education and the Conundrum of Suburbia
    Robert E. Brooke, ed.

LATINA
Leadership

Language and Literacy Education across Communities

Edited by
Laura Gonzales and
Michelle Hall Kells

Syracuse University Press

Copyright © 2022 by Syracuse University Press
Syracuse, New York 13244-5290

All Rights Reserved

First Edition 2022

22 23 24 25 26 27   6 5 4 3 2 1

∞ The paper used in this publication meets the minimum requirements of the American National Standard for Information Sciences—Permanence of Paper for Printed Library Materials, ANSI Z39.48-1992.

For a listing of books published and distributed by Syracuse University Press, visit https://press.syr.edu.

ISBN: 978-0-8156-3744-8 (hardcover)
       978-0-8156-3730-1 (paperback)
       978-0-8156-5531-2 (e-book)

Library of Congress Cataloging-in-Publication Data
Names: Gonzales, Laura, editor. | Kells, Michelle Hall, editor.
Title: Latina leadership : language and literacy education across communities / edited by Laura Gonzales and Michelle Hall Kells.
Description: Syracuse, New York : Syracuse University Press, 2022. | Series: Writing, culture, and community practices | Includes bibliographical references and index. | Summary: "This notable collection of ten essays by Latina educators features personal stories of mentorship and leadership, and serves as a resource for teachers and activists seeking to meet the language and literacy needs of their students and communities"— Provided by publisher.
Identifiers: LCCN 2021016605 (print) | LCCN 2021016606 (ebook) | ISBN 9780815637448 (hardcover) | ISBN 9780815637301 (paperback) | ISBN 9780815655312 (ebook)
Subjects: LCSH: Hispanic Americans—Education. | Hispanic American women college teachers—Social conditions. | Educational leadership—United States. | Mentoring in education—United States. | Language and education—United States.
Classification: LCC LC2669 .L337 2022 (print) | LCC LC2669 (ebook) | DDC 371.829/68073—dc23
LC record available at https://lccn.loc.gov/2021016605
LC ebook record available at https://lccn.loc.gov/2021016606

Manufactured in the United States of America

Para Camila y para todas nuestras hijas,
madres, abuelas, tías, y hermanas

Contents

Illustrations

Foreword

Our Personal Academic Literacy and Language Journeys

Cristina Kirklighter

While working on my dissertation in the 1990s, I noticed that many personal-essay scholars (mostly white males) valorized Michel de Montaigne as the "father of the personal essay." Back then, I devoted my second chapter to this Frenchman of the 1500s so that I could "join the conversation." I also devoted the last two chapters to Paulo Freire, Ruth Behar, and Victor Villanueva.

Recently, my mother gave me a beautiful mahogany hand carving of an ancestral Maya scribe writing on a scroll. It was given to her by her uncle's wife years ago. Well before Montaigne, Maya scribes were documenting the histories of their times, often through personal accounts from them and others. Now I often look at this wood carving for inspiration in my personal writing. I just finished reading *The Journey of Crazy Horse* (2005) by Joseph M. Marshall III, a Lakota writer whose sources were Lakota storytellers, some of them his relatives. As Marshall states in his introduction, "The biographic narrative is an attempt to unfold the life of Crazy Horse as a storyteller would" (xxii). Why did he write this biography in this way? Here is part of his explanation: "A wealth of cultural information and historical knowledge has not been available to non-Indians because of a basic suspicion on the part of many Lakota (and other indigenous peoples). The suspicion exists because too many non-Indian noses are turned up at the thought that oral tradition should be considered credible" (xix–xx).

As Latinas/Chicanas, we may be familiar with the power of testimonios from our Indigenous ancestors. Mónica González Ybarra demonstrates in her chapter how testimonios subvert how we have been conventionally taught to research and write in academia and instead help us navigate our insider/outsider positions by telling our stories and encouraging testimonistas to become coresearchers. Christine Garcia, by interviewing Christina Cedillo and Tanaya Winder, pays homage to the testimonios of Gloria Anzaldúa's authentic and decolonial ways of writing and speaking.

As I read the manuscript to write this foreword, I realized how these academic women writers were reclaiming an ancient oral and written tradition that would have made academic research and writing so much more powerful, accurate, knowledgeable, and honest if it only had been implemented by us and those like us long ago. However, we were the latecomers—not by choice, but by exclusion. We are here now, and with our arrival come great responsibilities to make the necessary corrections to academic research and writing. The damage to ourselves, our people, our ancestors calls for nothing less.

We are lucky, though, in taking up this call to reimagine research and writing as healing, for, as Tanaya Winder says in Christine Garcia's chapter, "The Chingona Interviews," we are not alone: "Whenever I am writing something that feels *real* in the utmost sense of realness (present, authentic, actually existing), I never feel that it is just me writing. I always feel as if my ancestors and Creator are speaking, writing, and singing *through me*" (her emphasis).

As I read (and you will read) these chapters, the collective voices of the authors are "real" and connected as if the authors are one and the same. I don't mean there are not different identities, different experiences, different source mentors, but there is something connectively real in what the authors in this collection have to say—much more so than with authors tied to formulaic nonpersonal academic writing. I won't call the latter traditional academic writing, for it does not mirror the traditions of the authors collected here. It is in fact a violation of these traditions.

In the next few pages, I want to describe just a few examples of this "realness" based on the authors' connectedness. I hope to encourage readers to experience these women writers' synchronicity in reading about their personal academic journeys. Synchronicity is the way our ancestors viewed their connected interactions with others, not as mere coincidences of connectedness but instead as synchronous moments of connectiveness with others.

The most significant synchronous moments in these chapters focus on the authors' multiple identities and the journeys they take their readers through in disclosing their identities tied to other identities. In the personal academic essay, the journey with its many discoveries, as in life, is everything. Why are so many of us subjected to academic-imposter syndrome? One of the major reasons is that few in academia know who we really are with our multiple identities, and most, sad to say, do not really care (Kirklighter, Cárdenas, and Wolff Murphy 2007). However, we care, as demonstrated in this collection, and one day we know that those who are suffering from imposter syndrome will read this book and find themselves in the identities described. The voices in this book will say in synchronous ways, "We know who you are, and you are not an imposter, just as we are not imposters. You belong here."

How do I know this will happen? I know this from a book I coedited with Diana Cárdenas and Susan Wolff Murphy more than a decade ago, *Teaching Writing with Latino/a Students: Lessons Learned at Hispanic-Serving Institutions*. I knew it was an important book for Latinx students, but I underestimated its significance to their identities as they read about themselves and their teachers in this book. Some teacher-writers in the book reveal how similar they were to their students when they were students. Readers would approach my coeditors and me at conferences, via email, or via phone and tell us how much they saw themselves in the book and realized they were not alone in going through these experiences as Latinx students. The authors cared enough to research and write about Latinx student experiences: who they were and where they came from. In other words, these students belonged in higher education because somebody cared, and they were not alone in their academic identities. They were not imposters. They belonged here.

This book you are about to read, of course, is much more personal. What makes it distinctive is that the focus on journeying identities reveals the healing processes for the writers that inevitably will affect the healing processes of the readers.

My favorite sentence in Ana Milena Ribero and Sonia C. Arellano's chapter that poignantly speaks to this book is the following: "Practices of comadrismo seek to feed the soul as well as the CV." As they say, mentoring a comadre brings spiritual satisfaction. The ingredients (or, as they say, themes) for feeding this spiritual soul are "kinship, fuerza, network of care, empathy, collaboration, paying it forward, and tangible support." Unfortunately, in many instances Latinas in academia are deprived of these vital ingredients by their white "colleagues" and sometimes by colleagues of color who choose the easier but soul-deprived assimilation recipe.

We often hear and read how Latinas and other academics of color struggle to belong not only in academia but within their own familias. What I see in Ribero and Arellano's organic comadre dialogues is a belongingness they created in both their respective familias and their new academic familias. The themes they created between themselves in academia are not disconnected from what many Latinas witnessed and learned in their familias.

Given the miniscule numbers of Latinas in the field of rhetoric and composition, it takes a high dose of courage to implement these feminist familial cultural themes that speak to who we are and what we value. It takes courage to be a Latina feminist committed to antiracism. But courage need not be associated with a solitary virtue or act. Its power, as Ribero and Arellano show us, is collaborative and rooted in comadrismo.

Although part one of the book, "Identity and Self-(Re)Identification," is probably the part most focused on identity, the theme of identities runs through all the chapters. Latina immigrants Blanca Gabriela Caldas Chumbes and Laura Gonzales show us in their chapters how they traverse multiple identities from both the countries they emigrated from and the United States. Their chapters most vividly demonstrate how transnational identities can be a "messy process" yet also quite enlightening and transformative.

Transformation is impossible without disconnection/fragmentation and knowledge/understanding, desconocimiento and conocimiento. Immigrant academics often offer profound insights on the ways their contradictory identities eventually offer a wholeness of the self once they embrace the complexities of their identities and can disregard how others construe and misrepresent those identities. After reading these chapters, I realized how their journeys are so helpful not only for Latinx/Chicanx academic immigrants but also for the Latinx/Chicanx daughters of immigrants as we work to understand our parent/parents.

Lorena Gutierrez, as the daughter of Mexican immigrants, captures the feelings of being in-between and not belonging either to her parents' cultures or to academia. I am a daughter of a Honduran immigrant, so this chapter strongly resonates with me. We grew up in these lands, not in our parents' lands. As children and adults, we help our parents navigate through these lands. We become English professors when our parent/parents struggle with English. Although we grew up in these lands, as Garcia discovers in her interviews with Cedillo and Winder, we carry over from our parents and grandparents their identities and beliefs—some of them ancient ancestral traditions that academics and others might deem to be myths or superstitions but that are very real in our familial backgrounds. We know that these backgrounds, although at odds with conventional academic ways of being, hold great value to ourselves, students, and others we interact with. These identities are carried forth in our bloodlines and from our ancestors, as Winder, a Native American, talks about in her interview with Christine. Latinxs/Chicanxs who have Indigenous lines carry these knowledges and practices within them either consciously or unconsciously.

Sometimes, as in Michelle Hall Kells's experiences, these ways come not necessarily through bloodlines but when family members marry into these bloodlines. They become family, and their cultures blend and shape their families' ways of thinking and living. However, not all family members are so accepting, as Michelle realized as a child when her grandfather rejected his young daughter for having a relationship with a mexicano. Witnessing racism against family members is so intimate and heartbreaking, as Michelle describes, yet when one rejects this path and instead chooses the path of those who embrace family members, it can shape one's identity as a family member and later as an academic. As a daughter of a southern white man from Tennessee, I saw how some southern families embrace racist, anti-Black rhetoric, and, like Michelle, I chose another path. Michelle, who has spent an academic lifetime recovering the histories of Latinx/Chicanx leaders, including Vicente Ximenes, Hector P. García, and now the women strikers of the Empire Zinc Mine strike in the 1950s, knows how her personal and academic identities were shaped long ago when her aunt married her tío. The injustices within the familia carried over into her work for justice in her academic life. Personal experiences at a young age have a way of following us in our journeys.

Our academic identities can be shaped and recalled in our encounters with those we teach and mentor. It can drive our chosen topics of research, our service, and our teaching. We see this most prevalently in the chapter by Aja Y. Martinez and the chapter by Stefani Baldivia and Kendall Leon.

Aja Y. Martinez takes readers through a detailed account of a student–teacher conference between crafted composite characters: a graduate student instructor, Alejandra Prieto, and a first-generation and first-year student, Rick Ramirez. As the teacher, Alejandra attempts to guide Rick to an awareness of how race, class, and difference "were shoved under [her] nose" as a first-year graduate student. Yet by the end of the conference Alejandra realizes that, like her student, she had not been ready for this awareness when she first started college. Rick was not ready to question but instead wanted to belong in academia. Timing and circumstances are everything in our journeying identities, as Alejandra came to realize in her essay journey. Alejandra's student, Rick, was instrumental in helping her see this. It is a valuable lesson for teachers to understand that discussing with our students our awakenings to academic and other injustices related to

Chicanxs/Latinxs must come with reminders of our own past experiences when we were not yet ready to awaken.

Cristina D. Ramírez, a descendent of many educators in El Paso, Texas, carried forth this legacy when she began teaching at Henderson Middle School in El Paso. As a border student who eventually became a border teacher, Cristina went from being a teacher who taught to state standards to a teacher who developed a mestiza pedagogical approach. She realized the power of knowing her students' and their familias' identities by introducing books and written assignments that spoke to her students' lives. As a border teacher, she knew that speaking the language of her students' parents and engaging in community outreach with them were critical mestiza pedagogies grounded in strengthening the identities of both a border teacher and her students. Later, when she became an academic, she discovered that little had been written on women political activists and journalists during the Mexican Revolution. In researching this topic, she discovered female mentor identities whom few had written about. Another mestiza identity emerged as she sought to recover these buried women's contributions and histories.

Stefani Baldivia and Kendall Leon, as first-generation Chicana scholars and archivists, developed ways to mentor students at their campus, California State University at Chico, by helping them write themselves into their institution's identities. Dissatisfied with the stock institutional narratives devoid of Latinx student identities, Stefani and Kendall had students research and interview members of campus organizations they belonged to. Their goal was to give these students a sense of belongingness and empowerment. I'm sure Kendall, formerly an undergraduate at this same campus, felt little connection with this institution's identities. Sometimes our motivation for a Chicanx approach to teaching our students stems from what we did not have as students. We wish not to engage in these practices done to us and therefore alleviate for others the pain of neglect in our own past identities.

Our identities in academia as Latina doctoral students and early career professors are often under assault, as Raquel Corona and Nancy

Alvarez discuss in their narratives of their time at the same institution. When under assault, we respond in ways others might perceive as "loca," or crazy. As both Raquel and Nancy reflect, we're affronted when others mistake our identities by assuming we cannot be instructors or professors. These others assume we are not worthy of our identities, or they see so few of us in such positions that they assume we cannot possibly hold them. They assault our identities when they question why others recognize our accomplishments and reward us, as both authors attest to in their experiences with their student peers. And it is not enough that we are assaulted in academia with such assumptions and accusations, but sometimes we are attacked on the home front as Latina/Chicana women seeking a career and delaying marriage and domestic commitments. We are "locas," as they say, for pursuing higher education. However, Raquel and Nancy offer a silver lining to all of this craziness when they discuss two of their graduate mentors. These mentors showed they cared by asking them a simple question about how they were doing. They encouraged Raquel and Nancy to go to conferences, knowing they would meet Latinx graduate students and professors like them. Because these mentors cared, they went the extra mile so that Raquel and Nancy could attend the conferences. Most of all, they helped shape Raquel's and Nancy's identities to help fight against the real craziness of academia.

As I bring this foreword to an end, I touch the mahogany wood carving of my ancestral Maya scribe. It is a synchronous moment like the many synchronous moments I have shared with this collection's contributors as I wrote this foreword. Now it is your turn, reader, to participate in this synchronicity.

References

Kirklighter, Cristina, Diana Cárdenas, and Susan Wolff Murphy, eds. 2007. *Teaching Writing with Latino/a Students: Lessons Learned at Hispanic-Serving Institutions.* New York: State Univ. of New York Press.

Marshall, Joseph M., III. 2005. *The Journey of Crazy Horse: A Lakota History.* London: Penguin Books.

Acknowledgments

This collection was a labor of love and resistance built collaboratively with all of our contributors, to whom we are eternally grateful. We also thank Eileen Schell and Steve Parks, series editors, and Deborah Manion, acquisitions editor at Syracuse University Press, for their support of this project. We have tremendous gratitude toward the Cultivating New Voices among Scholars of Color Program of the National Council of Teachers of English for bringing us together and inspiring this work.

Latina Leadership

Introduction

Reflection, Resistance, and Resilience in Latina Leadership

Laura Gonzales and Michelle Hall Kells

According to the National Center for Education Statistics, in 2016 Latinx faculty amounted to only 5 percent of all full-time faculty in US higher education, while 82 percent of all full professors across disciplines in academia identified as white (non-Hispanic) (Harris and González 2020, 3). As Ana Milena Ribero and Sonia C. Arellano note in chapter 1 in this volume, this lack of representation for all Latinx faculty and for Latina-identifying faculty specifically is reflected in rhetoric and composition and related fields: "It appears that in the last twenty years rhetoric and composition has become less—not more—diverse." In addition to Latinas lacking representation within our many academic homes, the "Latina" identity as a whole tends to be conflated and flattened in academia. Academia's insistence on a bifurcation between Latinas' academic identity and our local communities, families, and home literacies as well as the conflation of race and ethnicity under the ambiguous label *Latina* often erase Latinas' histories and the multiplicity of experiences embedded under a single label. This broad label can also further a flattening of identity that contributes to an erasure of Latina leadership efforts in and beyond the academy.

In a recent presentation at New Mexico State University, Cherokee scholar Qwo-Li Driskill explained that academics make a mistake when we separate community work from our academic endeavors. As Driskill elaborated, "We are here [in academia] because of liberation

1

movements, and we are part of them" (2019). Therefore, our academic spaces, publications, and conversations have always and will always be tied to community contexts, historical movements, and the lives of our students. This collection, as a discussion of Latina mentorship and leadership in academia, is no exception.

In our disciplinary contexts, Latina leaders have long been at the forefront of justice-driven efforts, particularly in relation to education and community engagement. As Kendall Leon explains in "Chicanas Making Change: Institutional Rhetoric and the Comisión Femenil Mexicana Nacional" (2013), Latinas have always drawn on the strength of our communities to survive in academia, for "within the university, we are often [further] limited by what we study and the bodies we inhabit—and those of the theorists we cite. Just like the city drawing boundaries around the neighborhood I grew up in, we are living the same ghettoization and disjuncture in our field: communities cannot teach us about institutions; the theories of only some people are applicable to all; and if we identify ourselves as Rhetoric and Composition scholars of color, it necessarily means we are given the authority to write about and care about only certain topics or issues" (168). In short, as Leon insinuates, Latina leaders, both within and beyond academia, have consistently seen connections among our embodied realities, lived experiences, historical contexts, surrounding communities, and the work we do in our professions and in our classrooms. These connections and overlaps are often reduced and erased in academic contexts that value disciplinary production over activist, community-driven labor. This collection, then, is a space to showcase connections (and differences) between Latinas in both K–12 and university contexts, to thread together narratives of experience, resistance, resilience, vulnerability, and growth as they take place across spaces, communities, and time. Academia was not made for or with Latina scholars, so Latinas' presence in academic spaces can be disruptive.

In her discussion of a "pedagogy of love," J. Estrella Torrez intentionally connects community and classroom activism through the revolutionary work of educators: "As revolutionaries, educators respond to and engage with sociohistorical politics, and are responsible for guiding emerging generations into a shared and collective future" (2015, 101). Through a Chicana feminist orientation, Torrez then illustrates the many ways in which Chicanas and Latinas in academia, across institutional settings, communities, and disciplines, can embody a pedagogy of love that can transform entrepreneurial, capitalist-driven institutions into spaces for activism and revolutionary love. Indeed, as Torrez also argues, across disciplinary contexts Latina leaders shape and sustain institutional, educational, and community-driven practices, methodologies, and pedagogies. Yet, as we argue in this collection, the scarcity of scholarship specifically about the work of Latina leaders in K–16 literacy education remains largely unaddressed. Thus, through the work of our contributors, this collection seeks to establish a space to focus on the narratives, scholarly lives, pedagogies, and educational activism of established and emerging Latina leaders in K–16 educational environments. We believe that sharing these narratives can both highlight the ongoing work of Latina leaders in academia and our surrounding communities and push for added coalitional action among Latina leaders.

We build on the work of other Latina leaders and on scholarship that has showcased the labor and power of Latina academics in K–16 settings, including *Latino/a Discourses: On Language, Identity, and Literacy Education* (Kells, Balester, and Villanueva 2004). Featuring established and emerging Latina leaders who offer a constellation of cross-talk and a rich range of perspectives, our collection seeks to center and privilege the unique voices and perspectives of an increasingly marginalized segment of K–16 educational practitioners. Although previous work has discussed the role of Latinas in literacy education and in rhetoric and composition more broadly, this collection focuses specifically on the histories and narratives of Latina leaders in education (broadly defined) as they are presented by Latina leaders themselves. Thus, in keeping with this focus, we want to share our own narratives and perspectives on the emergence of this collection before providing an overview of its organization and the contributors we are fortunate enough to share it with.

Laura

During the National Council of Teachers of English (NCTE) conference in Atlanta, Georgia, in 2016, Michelle and I left the conference center and took a walk in surrounding downtown Atlanta. We had just spent several hours getting to know our new cohort of fellows and mentors for the Cultivating New Voices among Scholars of Color (CNV) program, a biannual fellowship supported by NCTE that seeks to increase diverse leadership representation in and beyond NCTE. As a new fellow in this program, starting my fellowship year shortly after the outcome of the presidential election of 2016 and navigating my first year on the tenure track, I felt incredibly privileged to be in the presence of peers and mentors who understood the challenges I was facing as a new Latina faculty member at a white, English-dominant institution. I'll never forget a question Michelle asked me during our walk:

"Who are your senior Latina mentors?"

I immediately mentioned Sara Proaño, then director of the Language Services Department at the Hispanic Center of Western Michigan University, the woman who had completely shaped my career and my orientation to community engagement by welcoming me to her organization. I also mentioned J. Estrella Torrez, an associate professor in the Residential College of the Arts and Humanities at Michigan State University, who humanized academia for me by welcoming me to her community and teaching me about community engagement, what she called "the secret to surviving academia as a scholar of color." I went on to name several other mentors who have shaped our professional organizations. I also mentioned my mom, the woman who taught me at a young age to look up at the sky rather than stare down at the ground whenever I was feeling frustrated and scared. We then discussed groundbreaking Chicana leaders such as Gloria Anzaldúa and Cherríe Moraga as well as academics who have shaped my career and my scholarship, including Gabriela Ríos, Casie

Cobos, Sara P. Alvarez, as well as Tracey Flores and Aja Y. Martinez and the other contributors to this book. In this conversation, I also mentioned that while I have benefited greatly from my Latina mentors, I am also fortunate enough to be mentored by coalitions of African and African American, Indigenous, Asian/Asian American, and Pacific Islander women who brought me into academia and continue to fuel my soul and my career. As Natasha N. Jones describes in "Coalitional Learning in the Contact Zones" (2020), "Women of color have long envisioned shared learning that prioritizes coalitions" (518). Pointing to the work of the Combahee River Collective, Jones explains that "coalitions require an acknowledgement of interrelatedness and interconnectedness" (518), particularly as women of color work to acknowledge and leverage our many privileges as we build coalitions to combat systemic oppression.

Through our conversation, Michelle and I realized that although I have been privileged to receive mentorship from many Latinas, this mentorship has often been lateral and infused with strength from nonacademic areas such as our communities and families. Mentorship, at least for me as a Latina academic from Bolivia, stems from the people who ground me and expands beyond disciplinary and institutional boundaries. I continue hanging on to this conversation and to Michelle's question now as I continue navigating academic challenges while relying on the mentorship of my community, both within and beyond academia.

This collection stemmed from Michelle's idea to make space for Latina mentors (both established and emerging) to discuss their experiences in academia, a space to recognize women who invest tremendous amounts of material, intellectual, and emotional labor into their scholarship, their students, and their surrounding communities. Over time through the work of our contributors, the collection has evolved into a reflection of Latina experiences across several contexts and layers, incorporating stories of childhood resilience, growth, and constant (re)evaluation of identities and privileges. Mentorship is complicated, both in definition and in practice, and I'm grateful to have a space where the complexities and nuances of mentorship and

Latinidad more broadly can be illustrated through threaded stories and conversations.

Michelle

Mestizaje

Tengo alma
mestiza
adentro un cuerpo
infinito, una frontera–mezcla peligrosa.
This body, stretching across dusty borders, huérfanos.
The grandmother who wrapped my imagination in a red rebozo,
My father, a shadow speaking
Spanish, la lengua de mis antepasados, los ancianos.
La lengua de la sombra
weaving
memories of Tepeyac,
eating mangos y duraznos,
Ripe, fleshy earth
painted brown, my body a mural,
faded stories, dark gifts,
mis hijos, uvas
regalos de la tierra.

Michelle Hall Kells

In the summer of 1969 as I sat piled in the back of an old station wagon with mis tíos y mis primos driving down back roads of the San Joaquin Valley from Manteca to Sacramento, the radiator overheated, stranding us in the July heat in the fields. A patrol car approached with its cherry-red light flashing and came to a stop. I had no reason before this moment to believe that the presence of a law enforcement officer was anything but a good thing. The officer inspected the scene, my uncle enveloped in a cloud of steam spewing from beneath the hood. I do not know what words were exchanged between the officer and my uncle, but I could feel the tension and concern in my aunt's face as the California Highway Patrol officer paced around the car.

He paused, staring in the wide-open windows at three young children and me in the back seat, my aunt quietly avoiding
He seemed perplexed, pausing and staring at me, an elev
girl in the homemade white eyelet dress my aunt had sew
imagined then, in some kind of childish wishful thinking,
come to rescue us, bring us water, or offer to drive us to
town. Certainly, he would use his radio to call a tow tru
officer did not offer to help my uncle. And he left us th
hundred-degree heat, miles from a gas station or phone. M
nothing as he got back into the car, waiting for the boilin
is only in reflection that I later came to realize what I had witnessed.

I witnessed many things that summer of 1969: taking communion
with corn tortillas, listening to Spanish folk songs at the little Catholic
church in Manteca, swimming in the pesticide-infused waters of the
San Joaquin River, and watching farmworkers standing in the sun
holding signs for the United Farm Workers' grape strike. In *Claiming
Home, Shaping Community: Testimonios de los Valles* (2017a), editors
Gloria H. Cuádraz and Yolanda Flores, along with the contributors to
their powerful anthology, give testimony to their journeys from the
rural communities of the San Joaquin and Imperial Valleys to becoming scholars, teachers, and leaders in the University of California system. In their introduction to the volume, Cuádraz and Flores assert,
"Testimonio, as a genre, is about the claiming of 'lived experience.'
In staking this claim, those who testify bear witness to the dehumanizing processes to which their communities have been or are being
subjected. Testimonio is inherently political, a vehicle to counter the
hegemony of the state and to illuminate the repression and denial of
human rights" (2017b, 5).

The inspiration for this current collection in many respects began
for me in those formative childhood moments of emerging political
consciousness and nascent cultural identification. As a left-leaning liberal academic, I have come to recognize the limits of academic discourse in confronting the entrenched realities of institutionalized
racism and sexism in every facet of life in the United States. As a

1960s-era feminist who launched her first protest at Fair Oaks Elementary with the girls in Mrs. Summer's fourth-grade class and then celebrated the heady occasion of meeting Gloria Steinem while in college in 1980 at California Polytechnic University, Pomona, I have to acknowledge the failures of second-wave feminism and the post-civil-rights-era women's movement in advancing issues of social justice and equal access. Not unlike the patrol officer driving off and leaving mis tíos on the side of the road, the historical political abandonment of women of color in the academy is irrefutable. These recurring themes of institutionalized racism have informed my teaching, research, and scholarship for the past twenty years.

The scarcity of voices of Latina scholars, especially Latina scholars at tenure-line and research-intensive institutions, was first evidenced to me fifteen years ago while editing *Latino/a Discourses: On Language, Identity, and Literacy Education* (Kells, Balester, and Villanueva 2004). During my experience of serving as a mentor for NCTE's CNV program, the need for an anthology foregrounding the voices and testimonios of Latina leaders became increasingly evident to all of us: Laura Gonzales, Lorena Gutierrez, Blanca Caldas, and Mónica González Ybarra. We began imagining this book in November 2016 as the presidential election was in full swing. In Atlanta for the NCTE CNV institute, we wept together at the outcome of the election and the virulent resurgence of white nationalism dominating the national discourse—in our communities, our homes, our classrooms, our local and national media. We envisioned a collection that would break down the false binary between K–12 and college-level literacy education and foreground the stories and testimonios of Latina leaders navigating the complex and often hostile territory of the US academy and doing the work of language and literacy education across communities. We made the bold decision that the act of bearing witness to these journeys of struggle, loss, achievement, and success represents a position of strength as well as vulnerability. For sharing the powerful and healing experience of working together on this book, I will remain indebted and grateful to my coeditor Laura for her leadership and dedication to the vision. While putting the book together, I lost the two matriarchs

of my family. There are still no words to describe how death exca-
vates the soul. To be a daughter without a mother is to be inexorably
orphaned. My mother and my grandmother were inseparable for eighty
years. And in the end, my grandmother, at 101 years old, preceded my
mother in death by only six months. Each could not live without the
other. I take this as the abiding theme tying this anthology together:
we cannot live without each other. In the stories, the words, and the
testimonios of my colleagues, I am reminded of the durability of the
heart lines that connect us as women across time and space.

Chapter Overview

It's important to note that in inviting contributions to this collection,
we did not preimpose a set of themes or a set structure for authors to follow. We did not pick contributors who we thought would present their
experiences in particular ways. There was no set formula. We instead
invited contributors who currently work in K–16 settings and who, we
knew, have powerful and important experiences to share about their
journeys to becoming and being educators in those settings. Our goal
was to listen to their stories making connections between K–12 and
college-level Latina educators and illustrating the ways in which these
often separated sectors are inherently connected and fueled by Latina
discourses, practices, and communities that stretch beyond academia.
Through collaboration and conversation with our contributors, we
then decided to arrange the collection in three parts.

Part one, "Identity and Self-(Re)Identification," includes four
chapters with stories about the many pathways to both claiming and
reclaiming our roles as Latinas in academia. We begin this part with
Ana Milena Ribero and Sonia C. Arellano's essay "Advocating Comadrismo: A Feminist Mentoring Approach for Latinas in Rhetoric and
Composition." In discussing comadrismo as a "trusting kinship relationship" that "functions among women with deep commitments to
antiracist work," Ribero and Arellano illustrate how a feminist model
for Latina mentorship and leadership can be deeply rooted in Latinidad while also learning from and extending the intersectional work
of women-of-color feminists. Following Ribero and Arellano, in the

remainder of part one Blanca Caldas, Laura Gonzales, and Lorena Gutierrez grapple with questions such as: What does it mean to be a "Latina"? What terms do we use to describe ourselves and our communities, particularly as we work within institutions that were made neither for us nor with us? How does the work that we do as Latinas in academia build on the labor of other women of color in and beyond the academy, including our own families and communities? And, perhaps most importantly, how do we recognize and embrace our responsibility as Latinas who "made it" into the academy in the first place? Through these questions, the chapters in part one illustrate tensions, resistances, and lessons that Latina scholars, teachers, and community members face as we grapple with our own identities in the face of white, English-dominant institutions.

Although many conversations about Latinidad and about the experiences of Latinas in academia are built on stories of our own lived experiences, many of the contributors to this collection make important links between their own experiences and those of other Latina mentors. Part two, "Research, Recovery, and Learning from Our Histories," thus includes three chapters in which authors connect their own experiences in academia to historical roots and movements that have shaped the spaces in which Latina voices can be heard and recognized in contemporary contexts. From considering the role that university archives may play in recognizing (or perhaps erasing) Latina experiences to exploring the ways through which Latina icons such as Gloria Anzaldúa continue to shape contemporary Latina experiences and praxis, the second part of this collection cohesively makes a statement about the power of our Latina identities to shape scholarship across institutions, fields, and interests. Some may claim that sharing experiences of Latinidad does not "count" as "real" research, but the authors of this part provide us with intricate models of how a Latina perspective on research can fuel change at both institutional and community levels. Through the research examples shared in part two, we make a statement about the power of connecting our lived experiences and histories with the spaces that we seek to establish for our current and future students.

Part three, "Pedagogies and Mentorship within and beyond Academia," includes four chapters that collectively illustrate the importance of working across and beyond disciplinary and institutional boundaries when discussing Latina experiences. Ranging from graduate student experiences in a rhetoric-and-composition program to methodologies for teaching in English education programs, the chapters in this final part of the collection showcase what Latinas have known and continue to practice: that mentorship comes in many forms, relies on communal knowledge and reciprocity, and extends from our relationships with each other as Latinas and with the people who support us. Latina mentorship, as the contributors have shown us, cannot be contained to a particular field or contexts. There simply aren't enough of us to limit our resources and networks to a single discipline or field of study. As this collection illustrates, Latina mentorship is instead grounded in our collective vision and in our willingness to move beyond boundaries both to seek and to offer support.

Looking Forward

Countless studies, programs, and institutional initiatives across and beyond the United States seek to provide models or instructions for incorporating the experiences of historically marginalized people into contemporary curricula and research praxis. This collection does not seek to contribute to these efforts because it is not a space to provide "guidelines" or "how-to" protocols for supporting and recognizing Latinas in academia. Rather, this collection is a space for a group of Latinas to share for themselves and for each other what it is that we collectively see as Latina mentorship. The narrative here is intentionally polyvocal and, at times perhaps, even contradictory. As our contributors illustrate, Latina experiences are anything but monolithic. We come from different places, have different histories, and embody the spaces in which we live and work in radically different ways. Thus, this collection is an attempt to listen to and help our colleagues and communities listen to the experiences, stories, and expertise of Latina leaders, who have too often been excluded from the tables at which decisions and policies are designed and implemented. Our goal is to foster habitats for cultivating new leaders, new scholarship, and new connections with one another and with our histories, working toward extending conversations and relationships that not only are sustainable but are also sustaining and generative. We thank our readers for taking a seat at our table and joining us in this discussion.

References

Cuádraz, Gloria H., and Yolanda Flores, eds. 2017a. *Claiming Home, Shaping Community: Testimonios de los Valles.* Tucson: Univ. of Arizona Press.
———. 2017b. Introduction to *Claiming Home, Shaping Community: Testimonios de los Valles,* edited by Gloria H. Cuádraz and Yolanda Flores, 3–33. Tucson: Univ. of Arizona Press.
Driskill, Qwo-Li. 2019. "Weaving Together Rhetoric, Poetics, and Decolonial Resistance." Public lecture, New Mexico State Univ., Las Cruces, Apr. 19.
Gutiérrez y Muhs, Gabriella, Yolanda Flores Niemann, Carmen G. González, and Angela P. Harris, eds. 2020. *Presumed Incompetent: Race, Class, Power, and Resistance of Women in Academia.* 2nd ed. Logan: Utah State Univ. Press.
Harris, Angela P., and Carmen G. González. 2020. Introduction to *Presumed Incompetent: Race, Class, Power, and Resistance of Women in Academia,* 2nd ed., ed. Gabriella Gutiérrez y Muhs, Yolanda Flores Niemann, Carmen G. González, and Angela P. Harris, 1–14. Logan: Utah State Univ. Press.
Jones, Natasha N. 2020. "Coalitional Learning in the Contact Zones: Inclusion and Narrative Inquiry in Technical Communication and Composition Studies." *College English* 82, no. 5: 515–26.
Kells, Michelle Hall, Valerie Balester, and Victor Villanueva, eds. 2004. *Latino/a Discourses: On Language, Identity, and Literacy Education.* Portsmouth, NH: Heinemann.
Leon, Kendall. 2013. "Chicanas Making Change: Institutional Rhetoric and the Comisión Femenil Mexicana Nacional." *Reflections* 13, no. 1: 165–94.
Torrez, J. Estrella. 2015. "Translating Chicana Testimonios into Pedagogy for a White Midwestern Classroom." *Chicana/Latina Studies* 14, no. 2: 101–30.

Part One

Identity and Self-(Re)Identification

1

Advocating Comadrismo

A Feminist Mentoring Approach for Latinas
in Rhetoric and Composition

Ana Milena Ribero and Sonia C. Arellano

Abstract

This article outlines comadrismo as a culturally specific mentoring approach for Latinas in rhetoric and composition. The authors discuss the value of mentoring practices based on a kinship relationship and explore seven themes that constitute comadrismo mentoring—kinship, fuerza, networks of care, empathy, collaboration, paying it forward, and tangible support. Grounded in the literature on mentoring in rhetoric and composition, this article draws on the experiential knowledges of Latina academics to argue that scholars must attend to the specific needs of Black, Indigenous, and people-of-color women in order to recruit and retain diverse voices in the discipline.

Authors' Note

This article came about as we reflected on our trajectory as Latinas in academia. During our time as doctoral students, we were able to be

The editors are grateful to *Peitho: Journal of the Coalition of Feminist Scholars in the History of Rhetoric and Composition* for allowing us to reprint this groundbreaking article in our collection as a framework for Latina mentorship. Some changes have been made to conform to Syracuse University Press style guidelines and for consistency with the other chapters in this volume.

there for each other and had the privilege of being mentored by fierce Latinas. This experience highlighted for us the importance of Latina kinship bonds in academia—a predominantly white institution. Once we moved into our first tenure-track jobs, we no longer had the face-to-face help of our Latina mentors or of each other, but the networks we had created earlier continued to enrich us, sustain us, and allow us to persist. Our Latina academic ancestors influenced the types of scholars, teachers, and mentors we became.

The response to the article has been tremendous, both after we presented a paper on comadrismo at the Cultural Rhetorics Conference in 2018 and after the article's initial publication in *Peitho* the following year. We have heard from many other Latinas, sometimes with tears in their eyes, about how much they related to our framework for mentorship, whether they had experienced this sort of mentorship or they felt as if it was what was missing in their own academic careers.

In "Advocating Comadrismo," we argue for a type of mentorship that is specific to Latinas: one that recognizes that even though Latinxs are not monolithic, it helps to have mentors who speak from a Latina positionality in a predominantly white and male profession. Throughout this edited collection, we see how diverse Latinas are in our backgrounds, research, experiences, and even looks. However, we also see the commonalities we often share.

In the introduction to this collection, Laura Gonzales mentions that her mom taught her to "look up at the sky rather than stare down at the ground when [she] was feeling frustrated and scared." Throughout this collection, we see where Latinas look during such times. As reflected in the three parts of this book, Latinas look inward to examine and learn from embodied experiences; we look outward to family, community, and culture that ground us; and we look to Latina thinkers, activists, and educators who came before us and who continue to influence us. The Latinas in this collection look toward places and people to see ourselves, our ways of being, and our knowledges valued. This collection is a practice of comadrismo and reminds us of the need for more scholarship on Latina experiences in academia.

Advocating Comadrismo: A Feminist Mentoring Approach for Latinas in Rhetoric and Composition

In *Presumed Incompetent* (2012), the groundbreaking collection about BIPOC women academics,[1] Angela P. Harris and Carmen G. González argue that despite the increasing diversity of the US university student population, white men and women continue to occupy the overwhelming majority of full-time faculty positions at colleges and universities (1). Furthermore, they state, the numbers of BIPOC women decrease with rising academic rank, with only 3.4 percent of full professors in 2007 being BIPOC women (2).

Unsurprisingly, we can see these national trends reflected in the discipline of rhetoric and composition. While our discipline is exceptionally inclusive of white women, BIPOC women continue to be only minimally represented, as a cursory look at our major journals and conference programs can attest. Indeed, taking CCCC[2] membership as a measure (a data set that is not without its limits), it appears that in the past twenty years rhetoric and composition has become less—not more—diverse. In his 1999 article in *College Composition and Communication*, Victor Villanueva admonishes the discipline's dire representation of people of color. He writes, "We can do better than 7% among our teachers and scholars of color, better than a representation that is statistically insignificant in our journals" (652). By 2017, the number of CCCC members identifying as other than "white–non-latino/hispanic/Spanish" had decreased to a staggering 5.23 percent. The breakdown among different demographic categories was as follows: 0.32 percent identified as "American Indian or Alaska Native"; 1.09 percent identified as "Asian, including Asian Indian or Pacific Islander"; 1.72 percent identified as "Black/African American"; 1.47 percent identified as "Latino/Hispanic/Spanish"; and 0.63 percent

---

1. BIPOC means "Black, Indigenous, and people of color" and is a nuanced term that emphasizes the particularly devastating forms of oppression experienced by Black and Indigenous peoples.
2. Conference on College Composition and Communication.

identified as "two or more races."[3] While these demographic data are not intersectional (for example, they do not show what portion of those 5.23 percent identify as female, queer, etc.), we can infer that the number of BIPOC women in the discipline is quite low.

As Latinas in academia, we live these numbers every day. At our universities, we are often the only Latina in the room and one out of just a handful of BIPOC women in the department. We are very aware that we may be the only BIPOC women professors that our undergraduate and graduate students will ever meet. This lack of diversity reproduces itself, with fewer students of color choosing the discipline, fewer scholars of color entering the profession, and fewer faculty of color publishing articles and monographs that address issues of race and racism. Consequently, Latinas in academia may feel alone, with little to no culturally relevant guidance on how to succeed in graduate school and on the tenure track. Without many allies in tenured and administrative positions, BIPOC women in academia may also "find themselves 'presumed incompetent' as scholars, teachers, and participants in academic governance" (Harris and González 2012, 1).

This article, a collaboration between two Latina feminists in rhetoric and composition, contributes to the conversation about how to increase representation of BIPOC women in the discipline. While we agree with Villanueva that we need more representation of writers of color in our journals as well as a continued critical engagement with race and racism in our conferences and publications (1999, 652), we add that more purposeful feminist mentorship of students and junior scholars of color is also a necessity.

Fatima Chrifi Alaoui and Bernadette Calafell write that even though mainstream research on mentoring in academia shows the importance of mentoring relationships to academic career success, the assumption of a white middle-class mentoring model leaves the needs of BIPOC women academics unattended. They write, "Specifically, women of different historically marginalized groups may have

---

3. These numbers are unofficial but otherwise accurate.

different needs and expectations from a mentoring relationship than other women may have" (2016, 62). Within the discipline, we therefore need better mentoring practices for BIPOC women inasmuch as we care about recruiting and retaining diverse academics. In this article, we forward comadrismo as a feminist mentoring practice that attends to some of the needs and expectations of BIPOC women academics. With a long history of practice (Camacho 2012; Comstock 2012; Scholz 2016), comadrismo refers to a feminist reciprocal relationship among women. As a mentoring model, comadrismo is built upon a trusting kinship relationship and functions among women with deep commitments to antiracist work. We argue that comadrismo as a culturally specific mentoring model can help provide Latinas in rhetoric and composition with the holistic support they need to succeed in academia. Furthermore, comadrismo can help diversify our discipline not only by helping retain BIPOC women in our field but also by encouraging those women to center antiracist feminist work in their teaching and writing.

In what follows, we ground comadrismo in the conversation about mentoring in rhetoric and composition and demonstrate that we have much to learn from how mentoring is discussed and practiced in other disciplines. We then provide a brief review of the concept of comadrismo, a term rooted in Latin American feminist community practices. Finally, we outline the characteristics of comadrismo as a mentoring model. We base this model of mentorship on our personal experiences as Latina scholars in a purposeful move to value the experiential knowledges of underrepresented populations and dispute the hegemony of objectivity. In an attempt to avoid essentialism, we frame our discussion of comadrismo as a dialogue in order to highlight the diversity of our perspectives and experiences as Latinas in academia.

We hope this article provides some specific ideas about what mentoring Latinas in rhetoric and composition can entail. We have also written this article in a way that readers may take from it what works best for their particular circumstances. In other words, while we present comadrismo as a mentoring model among Latinas, we also believe that some or all of what we propose here may be useful to people of different positionalities. Additionally, we encourage others to consider what types of mentoring practices that challenge the white middle-class norms may work best for their positionalities. Our aim is not only to provide practical tools but also to engage the discipline in a conversation about how to better mentor BIPOC women—an important piece in the work of diversifying and decolonizing rhetoric and composition.

Understanding Latina Mentoring Relationships in Rhetoric and Composition and Beyond

Mentoring has long been a concern for scholars in rhetoric and composition, with some attention to mentoring women and people of color. Overall, the scholarship illustrates the variety of approaches to mentoring in the discipline as scholars have argued for mentoring that is contextually situated and attentive to the inherent power dynamics in this complex practice. For example, Jenn Fishman and Andrea Lunsford problematize the idea of mentoring, expressing their ambivalence to the concept as it replicates structures of power and requirements for assimilation (2008, 22). They propose that mentoring is sometimes practiced as a form of control, with even the ways that we talk about mentoring—for example, the use of the clunky term *mentee* to describe those being mentored—invisibilizing the agency of students and junior faculty (28).

Indeed, mentoring can often seem bent on shaping the scholar to the white-dominant academy and not on transforming the institution into a space that values minoritized ways of knowing and being in the world. For example, in *Women's Ways of Making It in Rhetoric and Composition* (2008), which is often referred to as the landmark text on women in the discipline, Michelle Ballif, Diane Davis, and Roxanne Mountford recommend that junior faculty "pursue the study of languages, especially Greek and Latin," "learn more classical rhetoric," "publish like crazy," and "act professional at all times, be confident and assertive, yet gracious and collegial" (86–89). This advice takes on an assimilationist stance that can be particularly devastating for women and academics of color who feel that they are unable and/ or unwilling to perform the "meritocratic" competitive academic culture. To challenge assimilationist models of mentorship, scholars of mentoring in rhetoric and composition have theorized feminist, critical, and activist mentoring in order to advocate for underrepresented scholars in the discipline (Okawa 2002; Kynard and Eddy 2009; Van-Haitsma and Ceraso 2017).

Pamela VanHaitsma and Steph Ceraso provide a possible alternative to power-laden mentoring through horizontal mentoring—a mentoring strategy that embodies the ethos of "making it together" (2017, 215) through the rejection of the traditional hierarchical relationship of "mentor and mentee." Yet the authors also recognize the limitations of horizontal mentoring or of any individual attempt to remedy the structural inequalities of the university: "Many of the challenges facing early-career academics are the result of structural and material forces that individual strategies simply cannot undo" (228). Their research highlights the reasons why structural critique, advocacy, and activism should be part of any critical mentoring practice.

Kathryn Gindlesparger and Holly Ryan's reflections on their "failing" feminist mentor group illustrate how conflict and change can be important parts of feminist mentoring. They write, "Feminist mentoring is acute, rhetorical, and must be carried out on a variety of fronts, with different mentors for different projects (there are different mentors for different needs). We must be adaptable and open to change and even dissolution if that is to the advantage of those involved" (2016, 67). In their article, the authors make a distinction between mentoring with the goal of fostering professional advancement (e.g., publishing) and mentoring for professional identity development (e.g., going from the position of graduate student to that of writing program administrator), implying that these two realms of an academic's life are mutually exclusive. This separation, however, seems to stem from the authors' positionality as white, middle-class scholars—a position that the authors acknowledge. For academics of color, however, professional identity is closely related to professional advancement. As Ersula Ore poignantly describes, "From the moment I step into the building I am marked an outsider. Regardless of external signifiers of a teacherly *ethos* . . . I am still assumed to be a student. My black body in these clothes, in this space, denies me any other identity" (2016, 9). For BIPOC women minoritized in and out of academic spaces, our abilities to teach and research are directly affected by the ways in which our bodies and identities are perceived.

A mentoring model for BIPOC women in the discipline must account for the obstacles along intersecting lines of race and gender that we face in white-dominant academia. On this there is much to be learned from scholarship on mentoring people of color in rhetoric and composition. For example, Carmen Kynard and Robert Eddy forward "critical mentoring" as a vital retention practice for students and academics of color and as a practice that helps "[undo] the toxic effects of racism on individual students and on ourselves" (2009, W35). Critical mentoring teaches students and academics of color that there are various paths to success in academia and that assimilation into white hegemonic norms is not the only option. Diverse models of success can be particularly valuable for Latinxs in academia (Cavazos 2012). In her doctoral dissertation,[4] Alyssa Guadalupe Cavazos (2012) suggests that mentoring can help students to trouble dominant narratives about what it takes to succeed in white-dominant academia. Rather than a singular trajectory, Latinx graduate students and junior faculty must see many and diverse examples of Latinx success in academia that move beyond assimilation and adherence to white-normative academic culture. Mentoring of Latinx students and junior faculty must reflect that Latinx academics can succeed on our own terms. For this to happen, Cavazos (2012) argues, it is important for there to be more Latinx faculty in our discipline rather than a tokenized few.

Mentoring of people of color in rhetoric and composition can be the sort of activist practice that works against the hegemony of whiteness in English studies and in academia. Gail Y. Okawa (2002) notes that advocacy must be an important part of mentoring as activist

---

4. Cavazos's dissertation is the only text that specifically approaches mentoring of Latinx academics in rhetoric and composition, yet it does not deal with issues of gender identity or other intersections.

practice. It is not enough to mentor students on how to enter the white academy. Activist mentors must intervene in the name of their students in cases of injustice and help them navigate the white institution with the goal of transforming it into the type of structure that does not privilege whiteness. This sort of mentoring, however, is time consuming and laborious, and it creates an undue burden on faculty of color, who may themselves be struggling to survive as professionals in the white institution (Kynard and Eddy 2009). Because of the invisible emotional labor that mentoring programs create, Ballif, Davis, and Mountford (2008) call on scholars and administrators in rhetoric and composition to consider who is taking on a disproportionate amount of the labor in mentoring programs aimed toward underrepresented populations. Additionally, they ask scholars and administrators to create practices that remedy the disproportionate distribution of labor along lines of race and gender.

While much can be gleaned from scholarship on mentoring people of color and other underrepresented populations in rhetoric and composition, an intersectional approach to mentoring in the discipline remains largely underdeveloped. Specifically, the discipline needs to theorize an approach to feminist mentoring for Latinas. We now look to scholarship outside our discipline, particularly in education, that discusses successful Latina mentoring in higher education and addresses the conditions that facilitate Latina success at the PhD and junior-faculty levels.

The importance of interconnectedness is evident in scholarship about Latina mentorship. For Latinas, success in higher education comes *with* community and *for* community. Moreover, mentoring relationships provide support by valuing personal experience as epistemic. The work of education scholar Juan Carlos González (2006) demonstrates these points by analyzing the academic socialization experiences of Latina doctoral students to understand how support systems aid student success. González found that while Latinas were negatively and positively affected by a variety of factors (e.g., earlier schooling experiences, institutional support systems, financial support, tokenism, assimilation, and cultural isolation), their success often depended upon finding and creating "networks of resistance" that allowed them to "integrate with similar minded scholars who supported and encouraged their resistance" to normative academic socialization (359).

One such network is described by Lucila Ek and her colleagues (2010), who illustrate how Latina junior faculty in education formed a pretenure support group that provided a space for transformational resistance and "*muxerista* mentoring" in preparation for promotion and tenure. They describe muxerista mentoring as a process that values BIPOC women epistemologies and lived experiences and, as a result, validates the difficult experiences Latinas face in academia (545). Additionally, in facilitating the retention of BIPOC women, muxerista mentoring "establishes a feeling of cooperation instead of competition" and facilitates professional support and growth (548). Comadrismo as a mentoring practice echoes the muxerista ethos of resistance and cooperation, as we see networks and connections among Latinas as crucial to our success in predominantly white institutions. Cooperation among Latinas ensures that our experiences and knowledges are valued and that our successes also benefit our communities. Muxerista mentoring demonstrates how we work in solidarity with other Latina academics and nonacademics for the welfare of our community and to lift each other up as we labor in a society that continues to bring us down.

Mentoring among Latinas always involves a practice of resistance, and critical consideration of intersectional identities is key to building mentoring relationships. In other words, Latina mentoring relationships are necessarily political and personal. For example, Rebeca Burciaga and Ana Tavares discuss a pedagogy of sisterhood, which they define as "a purposeful friendship rooted in political activism" that eventually evolves into a "pedagogical strategy that sustains [them] in academia" (2006, 133). They claim that the relationship they developed working together on an anthology challenged the isolation and individualism valued in academia, which is why they see creating sisterhood as an act of resistance and survival (138). Moreover, Burciaga and Tavares look to and learn from BIPOC women in academia who have challenged patriarchal structures: "Our learning in this supportive environment among feminist scholars is organized differently from that of the classroom—we become central to the curriculum in creating our own pedagogy" (138). Such a sisterhood created and influenced by BIPOC women provides a learning approach to facilitate Latina success.

Scholarship on mentoring outside of rhetoric and composition offers tangible solutions to encourage Latina retention and success in higher education. For example, González (2006) calls on policy makers to facilitate change and address institutional climate concerns. He proposes that academic leaders and institutional-change agents need to realize that in order to sustain higher education for an increasingly diverse student population, they must address the difficulties Latinas and other BIPOC women face in succeeding in institutions of higher learning (362). Similarly, Ek and her colleagues (2010) argue that universities need to focus on retaining faculty of color and offer specific approaches, such as prioritizing cluster hires and increasing the number of Latina recruiters. They also suggest providing financial support, institutional legitimacy, and space to mentoring groups that focus on faculty of color. Last, they suggest engaging in formal and informal dialogues with Latinas about their experiences in academia (550). Each one of these scholars argues that mentorship and institutional change are crucial for the success of marginalized and minoritized populations in higher education. In the next section, we provide some context to the concept of comadrismo on which we base our mentoring model for Latinas in rhetoric and composition.

Comadrismo: A Brief Framing

> [Comadrismo] encompasses some of the most complex and
> important relationships that exist between women. *Comadres*
> are best friends, confidants, coworkers, advisors, neighbors,
> godmothers to one's children.
>   —Nora de Hoyos Comstock, introduction to
>   *Count on Me*

The term *comadre* comes from the Latin *commater*, which means "female sponsor" or "godmother." Traditionally, children baptized in the Catholic Church are given a "comadre," a godmother who is supposed to guide them through their young spiritual life. Outside of the religious context, Paul Allatson defines comadrismo more broadly as "the complex set of relationships, reciprocal duties and dependencies, and mutual support networks and friendships between women that are not necessarily determined by the obligations of traditional godmother status or familial ties, but which nonetheless confirm a place in a constructed community of women" (2007, 76). Whether the term is used within a religious or secular context, *comadre* clearly refers to women whose relationships have strong kinship.

Additionally, the term *comadre* can imply a relationship based on political awareness and attention to social change. Melissa Camacho explains that in Puerto Rico the term refers to a "feminist icon" and "empowered leader" who advocates for her community through her activism (2012, 124), while Cristina Herrera describes "comadrazgo" as an "adopted sisterhood" and more importantly as "a strong female alliance used to combat the cultural and familial strains placed on [Latina[5]] women" (2011, 52). Both Herrera (2011) and Camacho (2012) acknowledge the key role comadres serve for one another and their communities in surviving colonial and patriarchal challenges.

Building on this general understanding of the term *comadre*, we draw from Teresa Maria Linda Scholz's notion of comadrismo, an intersectional feminist framework that attends to asymmetrical power relations and challenges hegemonic forces to consider the agency of BIPOC women. Scholz proposes that comadrismo functions "as a way to highlight the complex relationships between discursive and material counterhegemonic practices, and between victimhood, voice, and agency, within transnational communities" (2016, 83–84). Comadrismo is an intersectional approach to social justice that complicates the binaries of "agency and victimhood" and "discourse and

---

5. Here Herrera says "Chicana" because she is discussing a Chicana fictional character. However, her work includes the larger Latina community. For the purposes of this article, we inserted "Latina."

materiality" in order to account for the diverse lived experiences of BIPOC women.

In our work, we build on three main points of Scholz's (2016) comadrismo framework: comadrismo embraces the complex, collective actions of Latinas, values the political potential of counternarratives, and challenges feminist work that universalizes women's experiences. The key here is that the comadre paradigm moves beyond the "maternal and Western neoliberal individual" to focus on those who are "communally connected" (Scholz 2016, 88). In our experiences as Latina academics, community is key to sustainable and effective mentorship practices as we always see ourselves working collectively for Latinas and BIPOC women and not just for ourselves.

Additionally, Scholz claims that counternarratives from comadres "can provide the richest theoretical insight into women's discursive and material resistance and self-representation" (2016, 89). According to Aja Y. Martinez, counternarratives and more specifically counterstories highlight "that the experiential and embodied knowledge of people of color is legitimate and critical to understanding racism that is often well disguised in the rhetoric of normalized structural values and practices" (2020, 69). In an academic context, counternarratives can highlight university practices that are unjust and harmful for Latinas. Moreover, the power in sharing stories of injustice can create "a space of support and nurturing" because as "stories are recounted, women's experiences with repression are understood within a broad relational system" (Scholtz 2016, 92).[6] In other words, when we share our stories, we understand how systems of oppression operate, and we are then in a position to challenge those systems and advocate for political change.

Perhaps most importantly for the field of rhetoric and composition with its substantial tradition of feminist scholarship, using a framework

---

6. In Scholz's (2016) work, women share their stories with other comadres in prison to understand the sexual and physical violence they experience. We are not comparing experiences but focusing on the importance of the sharing of stories.

of comadrismo can help feminist scholars to challenge models of feminism that reproduce universalized ideas of women's experience. As Latinas, we are often made to feel too sensitive or too angry when we experience microaggressions, and often our peers do not believe or address the grievances we bring to superiors. Comadrismo challenges hegemonic feminism by creating a framework that reveals how Latinas "respond to overlapping systems of oppression" (Scholz 2016, 96). Comadres call out feminists who are not intersectional or who are not actively working toward justice for all women. Here the concept of comadrismo disrupts individualistic actions and promotes collective work among Latinas.

Comadrismo as Model for Mentoring Latinas in Rhetoric and Composition

In the remainder of this article, we present comadrismo as a framework with which to create mentoring relationships in rhetoric and composition that challenge hegemonic models of feminism while supporting the success and development of Latina academics. Harris and González emphasize that in order to survive and thrive in white-dominant academic environments, BIPOC women must "recognize and honor the connections among body, mind, culture, and spirit—connections that are denied by the rationalist and masculine-dominated culture of the academy" (2012, 7). Accordingly, we draw on our experiences with mentoring as connected to body, mind, culture, and spirit to propose seven themes that facilitate the practice of comadrismo mentoring.

In this section, we use a dialogue format to discuss comadrismo as a mentoring model in order to illustrate that even though both of us are Latinas in rhetoric and composition working in R1 public universities, our backgrounds, experiences, and beliefs differ, so it would be inappropriate for us to speak in a single voice. Therefore, we use a first-person dialogue format to structure this section in order to work against singular narratives of identity and experience and to avoid essentializing one Latina experience through academia.

The format of a dialogue framed by seven key themes emerged organically in our collaborative process. In order to effectively convey our dialogical and dynamic relationships to one another and with other mentors and mentees, we knew the format of this article must be different from a typical article. We initially wrote about our individual experiences as mentors and mentees. Then we exchanged those writings and discussed the salient points and experiences, some having to do with one another and some having to do with common mentors and mentees. We identified the most prominent themes that emerged and named them according to their contributions to comadrismo. We decided to present these themes in a dialogue format in order to emphasize the relational characteristic of comadrismo as well as each of our individually nuanced perspectives on our mentoring experiences. In the final part of this process, we revised and expanded those initial writings, taking time to respond to each other in writing in order to create a dialogue. Each part of this collaborative process was incredibly organic; the themes came from the experiences we had in common, and the dialogue seemed to be the best way to show how each of us experienced the mentoring that was happening. Our experiences shaped the themes and dialogue of the article so that we could highlight our individual experiences together.

Theme 1: Kinship

Comadre 1. For me, kinship is an essential part of what demarcates comadrismo from other mentoring approaches. Here, I would define kinship as chosen family whose connectedness is founded in social relationships. For Latinas, academia can be isolating in two ways: we are geographically separated from our families who raised us—and we are often, but not always, very close to these families—and we are in a predominantly white environment that at times contradicts some of our cultural values. Therefore, we often attempt to build relationships with other Latinas seeking cultural commonalities, and sometimes those relationships grow into a new chosen family.

The chosen families that we nurture grow from a genuine desire to see other Latinas be successful. To paraphrase Afro-Latina rapper Cardi B ("Cardi B" 2017), instead of the adoption of a competitive "Why her and not me?" mentality, kinship advocates a "How can I get next to her?" mentality that is genuinely invested and personally involved in the success of other Latinas. Just as my successes belong to my family as much as they belong to me, my successes also belong to comadres who have provided not just mentorship but kinship. Additionally, in my experiences, the chosen families we build in academia overlap with our families who raised us, which makes the kinship rhizomatic. I've attended weddings, visited newborn babies, cared for children overnight, and even gone on family trips with comadres. My interactions with other Latinas in academia almost always necessarily mean interactions with their partners, children, parents, siblings, and so on. This deep and intimate level of involvement with one another demonstrates how kinship addresses the whole person.

Of course, here I want to reference our relationship because it epitomizes kinship to me. Very early in our friendship you demonstrated a personal commitment to me as a person. You were one of the first people I told about my mom's diagnosis, and your continued support through the most difficult experience of my life, losing my mom, made me feel less alone in this already isolating journey as a Latina in a PhD program. You understood my familial obligations as a Latina that are specific to our cultural expectations. For me, this experience established the practice of confiding in you, a mutually respected person whom I've built a long-term, trusting relationship with, a relationship that enables me to sustain myself and continually facilitates my successes. I also attempted to provide this same personal support when you were navigating the job market and were pregnant. I went shopping with you for job-market clothes because I knew how much you didn't want to go. And when your child was born and I was gone for the summer, I offered up my house for your visiting relatives in hopes of supporting you in any way I could, even though I couldn't physically be there.

Because academia does not often offer enough support to graduate students (and even faculty) who are experiencing family changes, academics often have to depend on networks of friends to provide help during such times. In fact, academia continues to operate in a manner that challenges women who are caregivers and mothers by having meetings, classes, and other mandatory service or informal yet important socializing outside of 9-to-5 work hours. Both of our life-altering experiences—a death in my family and a birth in yours—demonstrate that when academia falls short of understanding the particular responsibilities that fall on Latinas in such instances, we must rely on one another, nuestras comadres, para ayudar.

Comadre 2. I remember the night you told me about your mom. We cried together outside of our critical race theory classroom. I also remember the kindness with which your mom and dad always treated me and my husband. Getting to know your family has made our friendship stronger, and I believe it has contributed to our ability to be honest and trusting with one another—qualities that academic collaborations depend on.

Kinship and care do not mean that comadre relationships are always without conflict. Disagreements and disappointments are often part of the important relationships of our lives, and with comadres it is just the same. You and I have had some difficult conversations, yet we trust each other enough to be able to see that our conflict comes from a place of care. The kinship that we've built over the years has allowed us to become more than colleagues and more than friends. We are comadres.

This kind of kinship can be built through an effort to get to know and to mentor the whole person. Comadres should create space for conversations about issues outside of academia. What is going on in your comadre's life? What are the external factors contributing to or hindering professional success? How can we help comadres to reach the ever-elusive work–life balance? What are the emotional obstacles in the way of completing a dissertation, an article, or a book man-uscript? These are important questions to explore in mentoring the whole person. Now, I'm not insinuating that comadres pretend to act as mental health professionals or life coaches. However, without space being made to address personal issues that might be going on, any other sort of advice, feedback, or mentorship can falter. Making space for personal conversations that may make comadres vulnerable may require that the senior comadre open up first about her personal life.

A few words about family, hobbies, or even weekend plans can change the dynamic of the conversation so that the junior comadre feels safe in sharing some of her own experiences.

Theme 2: Fuerza

Comadre 2. To be a Latina in academia—to be a Latina in general—you need a lot of fuerza. When you are trying to navigate an institution that was not created with you in mind, it is easy to feel weighed down by the intersectionality of oppression. This is an obstacle that many of us continue to face when we are one of the handful of people of color in our departments. We can either be marginalized or most often tokenized—used to provide the "much needed" diversity to an otherwise white faculty. Both of these result in the disempowerment of BIPOC women in academia.

Latina academics need fuerza not only to persist and survive but also to be able to turn the negative into positive. What I mean here is that in order not just to survive but actually to thrive, we need the skills to be able to take the anger and discouragement that comes from being a Latina in academia and make it the driving force of our antiracist practice. For example, if I am angry that my department's history of rhetoric curriculum does not incorporate any minoritized voices in a significant way, instead of swallowing the anger, I must have the fuerza to speak up about it and fight for its change.

A good comadre to me is an example of fuerza. They have turned the racism of the academy into the motivation for their antiracist scholarship. They are a model of how to fight back and avoid complacency, despite the risks that we take as graduate students or junior faculty of color when we confront the academic status quo. A comadre is an example of how to turn obstacles into opportunities for critical work. She can teach me how to have the fuerza to push past the pain, to be productive through the tears.

Comadre 1. Being confidently outspoken in spaces that make me feel unwelcome (such as academia) does not come easily for me. I have found that it's necessary to have this behavior modeled for me and in turn to model it for others. The way that I learned not to accept the inequities I experience was by listening to other comadres and watching their actions. I have seen many fearless comadres fight against injustices—sometimes for themselves and other times on behalf of those in more precarious positions—and stand up to powerful people and institutions. This is an important aspect of fuerza because I have also been told to keep my mouth closed and my head down in order to survive the tenure track. However, seeing that such actions benefit only the individual and not the community, I've taken the advice of and modeled myself after comadres who have demonstrated fuerza to thrive despite relentless challenges of the university.

Additionally, fuerza provides an impetus to continue to be vocal and visible when challenging negative forces in academia and to work on scholarship that reflects my political commitment to antiracist work. I know that younger or more junior Latinas are watching and listening to learn from me as well. I want to be the comadre who demonstrates we will not stand for mistreatment and the comadre whose work overtly states my commitments to social justice.

Theme 3: Networks of Care

Comadre 1. When you are a first-generation college graduate, like myself, graduate school can be a complicated maze. Networks of other Latinas can help facilitate success for those of us who are new to navigating what can be a very traditional institution. Or when Latinas face hardship, they can provide advice for other Latinas so that they do not experience similar hardships. Such networks are rhizomatic: they function multidirectionally.

For example, a group of Latina professors at my current institution maintains a nonuniversity email group not only to share good news, events, and everyday life experiences but also to ask where to turn and how to deal with troublesome situations. Within the past week, members of this group, which has only eight people, have asked for resources concerning a hiring-discrimination incident in a Latina's department, discussed how to deal with a white colleague who expressed frustration about a Latina professor's medical leave taken to receive cancer treatment, and strategized approaches to a meeting called by a Latina's chair with all-white colleagues (asking if she should attend with a union representative). Because the faculty in this group span various departments across the university, varied titles and positions of power, and many previous experiences at other universities, the group is a hive mind of knowledge to help others navigate difficulties. These networks help comadres navigate academia to survive and address the material conditions we face, often at predominantly white institutions.

Comadre 2. Networking among Latinas can be difficult, particularly when a graduate student or junior faculty is the only Latina in her entire department. Structured networking possibilities, such as an email group, make it easier for Latinas to connect with other comadres and share knowledge. There are also less-structured networks of support that more advanced comadres should help build for their junior comadres. For example, one of my graduate school mentors connected me with the woman who helped me negotiate my job offer, and this connection not only has opened up opportunities to engage with communities of color in my current institution but has also introduced me to supportive people in my town who have become dear friends. A comadre is a nexus, creating a network of BIPOC women who look out for each other.

Theme 4: Empathy

Comadre 2. When graduate students come to my office hours, they are often looking for someone who will understand how they feel as young women and young BIPOC women in a white-male-dominated institution. (It is interesting yet not entirely surprising that male students don't often seek me as a mentor.) These women want to talk about experiences of exclusion and marginalization. They share with me the crushing weight they feel, especially as new graduate students with heavy course and teaching loads. They fear the university will force them to assimilate into the normative academic culture that mimics capitalist, heteropatriarchal, Euroamerican cultural norms.

What I have to offer these students, at least initially, is empathy. I nod my head. I tell them that I understand how they feel. I assure them that I have been in a similar position and that I made it through. As a comadre, I try to put myself in their shoes. I think this can be very valuable and encouraging for female graduate students of color. In my empathy, I become an example not of bootstrapping my way through academia but of shared vulnerability and strategic perseverance. By sharing my own experiences with, for example, the incessant microaggressions of the institution, I show them that I am also vulnerable, that academic life also gets me down. A comadre commiserates with her fellow comadres, not as a way to show pity but as a way to show understanding. But the empathy of a comadre should not be understood as passive inaction. Empathy comes with the urgency to persevere, not through assimilation but through strategies that sustain the soul.

I remember one of my graduate school comadres telling me, when I feared that a conference presentation on immigration and neoliberalism would not be received positively, that as a Latina academic standing in front of a room of fellow scholars and speaking my piece, I was already bound to upset some folks who are not accustomed to BIPOC women taking the lead. My comadre helped me to reflect about my place in academia. She helped me to realize that I was probably always going to feel like an outsider; but instead of being discouraging, this thought reaffirmed my purpose. I, like the BIPOC women that I now mentor, need to persevere in academia because academia is in dire need of dissenting voices. I see my place in academia as the perpetual outsider, not the tokenized minority who will bring unthreatening diversity to higher education but the one who will ruffle some feathers. I still must remind myself of that when I am feeling doubtful about my place in academia or when I think how much easier it would be just to keep my head down.

I echo the words of my comadre and remind the young BIPOC women I mentor that their presence in academia is already a radical move since academic spaces are not often designed with them in mind. By helping them see the important role of dissent and difference in academia, I hope to encourage them to persevere while holding on to their critical values and beliefs.

Comadre 1. Empathy really gets at what makes comadres special in our lives. A common understanding of the challenges we face is a necessary foundation for the urgency we feel to persevere. Just as I talk with senior colleagues about the challenges I face, I also listen carefully when other women come to me with their stories that need to be heard. Your comment about graduate students coming to you resonates as I look back at my graduate student experience. This interaction was common between my mentor and me; simply listening and acknowledging that she understood my frustrations and struggles were significant.

As there are few Latina PhDs, it's quite difficult to find Latina professors (and even BIPOC women professors) in our field at primarily white institutions. I constantly recognize that simply encountering me is important for students. As you mention, just being in this space is a radical move. I was in my PhD before I encountered a Latina professor, so I know that I may be the only or one of few BIPOC women professors students encounter. With this in mind, I consider how my empathy can be expressed when I interact with students. One way I do this is by normalizing conversations about race and racism in the classroom. Not only do I assign readings that address issues of race and other intersections, but I also take the lead in talking openly about race and racism, usually in a gendered way. In doing this, I attempt to open the door between myself and BIPOC women in my classes so that they feel comfortable coming to talk with me.

Theme 5: Collaboration

Comadre 2. I think you and I have been strong comadres who not only support each other emotionally but are also invested in each other's success in academia. Collaboration has been key to our comadrismo. I think I have presented in more panels with you than with any other person, starting with that first panel presentation that we did together at the Two-Year College Association West conference in Mesa, Arizona.

A comadre looks for ways to collaborate with her comadres. While collaboration makes sense between comadres at different points in the academic track (for example, between graduate student and faculty mentor or between junior faculty and senior faculty), collaboration is also valuable when done horizontally between peer comadres. In today's hurried academic environment, many faculty members are not willing and/or able to collaborate with students. In my seven years of graduate school, I never had a real opportunity to write with a faculty member, not even with some of my most dear and influential comadres. Women in academia often take a disproportionate portion of the service and administrative work. This leaves very little time for them to work on and publish their own research, let alone to mentor and collaborate with graduate students. Horizontal collaboration (VanHaitsma and Ceraso 2017) fills the gap when collaboration between junior and senior comadres is not possible.

Of course, the senior comadre may have connections that the junior will not have, and that's one of the benefits of this sort of collaboration. While this may not necessarily be the case in horizontal collaboration, fellow comadres can still draw on each other's strengths when collaborating, even if they have equal amounts of political capital.

Comadre 1. I would say you and I have engaged in a mutually beneficial professional relationship. Very early in our friendship we gained trust in providing thoughtful, thorough, and critical feedback to one another's work and writing. We've rehearsed countless conference presentations for one another in hotel rooms. We've provided rounds of feedback on seminar papers, grant applications, conference proposals, job materials, and publications. We've collaborated on conference presentations, as conference organizers, and on publications. I trust that your feedback will ask tough questions with the intention of improving my argument, not to needlessly poke holes in it.

Because the academy is a place with a white middle-class model of mentorship, it's important to receive feedback not only from other comadres who understand where you are coming from and the premises upon which you build your arguments but also from comadres who value the type of knowledge production you are engaging in. Mentorship from white peers on writing can steer Latinas to use concepts from only white scholars or to delegitimize nontraditional epistemologies. Importantly, the intersectionality of our various subjectivities has been crucial in this process. For example, your feedback from the perspective of a Colombian immigrant continually decenters my nonimmigrant, Mexican-centric viewpoints and challenges me to be more inclusive in my scope. To feel comfortable giving and receiving that type of feedback, comadres must trust one another and know that we have our professional well-being in mind.

Theme 6: Paying It Forward

Comadre 2. An imperative for me as I think of how I mentor other BIPOC women and woman-identified graduate students is the idea of paying it forward. Drawing on the National Association of Colored Women's (NACW) motto "lifting as we climb," paying it forward denotes the importance of helping other women as we learn to successfully navigate academia. Paying it forward also implies the debt that we as Latina academics owe to other women, Latinas and others, who have helped us along the way. Like you, I was fortunate enough that I had a really strong network of comadres during graduate school. Of course, I consider you to be one of these comadres. These women were a support network for me emotionally, academically, intellectually, and professionally. The fact that I was lucky enough to have comadres makes me want to pay it forward. I have not climbed these walls of academia by myself. Other women lifted me, and now it is my turn to lift those who come after me.

Comadre 1. I love the NACW's concept of "lifting as we climb" because I feel so lucky to have had others do that for me throughout the years. I try to do this in any way I can, whether it be by providing feedback on job materials for my peers or helping with childcare when single-mom comadres need help or advocating for other graduate students who were in more vulnerable positions than I was. I particularly remember mentoring a first-generation Latina undergraduate student when I was in my PhD program. We were paired through a program, and we met once a month for lunch to chat about her classes and life in general. Although I didn't feel like I was doing much, I reminded myself that I would have loved to have someone—anyone—help me navigate the university as an undergraduate student because I had no idea what I was doing as a first-generation college student. She worked a lot and had trouble in her writing classes, but by the time I graduated, she was talking about going to graduate school. I tried in all the ways to pay it forward so that she would know that she belonged at the university just as much as the next student.

Additionally, I pay it forward with other women and BIPOC women colleagues who are graduate students. I've advised friends on searching for an academic job, collaborated with others on writing projects and conference panels, and helped with applications for grants that I've previously won. I am always eager to share my successes to facilitate the successes of others. I've heard stories of other academics being protective of their materials and not wanting to share their work. However, you provided me with a perfect example of how a comadre pays it forward. As you were a year ahead of me, you shared your dissertation proposal and your job-search materials with me. You were successful, so I followed your model, and I was successful as well. For this, I am grateful.

Theme 7: Tangible Support

Comadre 1. As academics, we often like to think of what we do in abstract terms: contributing to knowledge production, effecting change through teaching and scholarship, and engaging with the community. However, we often fail to address the fact that this is a job, just like many others, where we have to meet certain criteria to ensure job security, where we are often paid unequally based on our race and/or our gender, and where we have to consider our health insurance and retirement benefits. In other words, we do not talk often enough about the material conditions of academia. For me, comadrismo not only supports the scholarly self but also considers, recognizes, and facilitates the material self in the world. Comadres have helped me significantly in tangible ways, and such tangible support is worth consideration when focusing on mentoring the whole person.

One concrete way to support comadres is to help with the cost of conferences. Conferences are important professional-development opportunities, especially for graduate students and junior scholars (who also tend to be the least financially able to attend multiple conferences a year for various reasons). Sharing hotel rooms with graduate students or covering the cost of a meal can do a great deal to lower the costs for other comadres.

Many times during graduate school, a tenure-track comadre invited me to share her hotel room that was paid for with her annual travel funds so that I didn't have to pay for lodging. This particular comadre even rotated the various graduate students she offered to share a room with so that she could help as many people as possible. She made me understand that this was an important part of mentoring: easing the financial burden for those who are in more precarious financial positions than yourself. While there are many discussions in the field about how senior faculty can help junior faculty and graduate students, there is not much discussion about how Latinas and other BIPOC women especially benefit from tangible support.

Comadre 2. You are right in saying that we don't talk about the financial and material conditions of labor in academia. The first time that I read Villanueva's *Bootstraps: From an American Academic of Color* (1993), I was surprised at how candid he was about the financial difficulties that junior faculty of color can face. I had never heard academics talk about money in this way. The unstable job market in academia is such that when a recently minted PhD gets a job, she is supposed to be grateful, no matter the labor conditions. Not to mention, we are so accustomed to being underpaid and overworked as graduate students that any income above what we were making as GTAs seems like a winning lottery ticket. But the conditions of labor—whether they be teaching load, service expectations, pay, benefits, cost of living—can help or hinder success in academia.

A comadre is aware of these aspects of the job, does what she can to help ease the strain on graduate students and junior faculty, and works to make these labor conditions visible. When I was on the job market, I was told by the department head that salary for my position was not negotiable. One of my comadres helped me to figure out what *was* negotiable, to outline what conditions of labor would help me to succeed (e.g., summer pay, research funds, pretenure course release), and to negotiate for those conditions. Without that mentoring, I would never have known that I should be negotiating. In fact, I've spoken to many female junior faculty who have told me they did not negotiate at all.

Conclusion: Living Comadrismo

Within the context of academia, Sara Ahmed refers to diversity work in two ways: "the work we do when we are attempting to transform an institution" and "the work we do when we do not quite inhabit the norms of an institution" (2017, 91). We see comadrismo as embodying both types of diversity work. By employing comadrismo in our interactions with others, we are attempting to transform the institution so that it is a space that welcomes, serves, and retains BIPOC women. By employing comadrismo in our mentoring practices, we are not only recognizing that we don't always inhabit the norms of the institution but also trying to help others who don't inhabit these norms. This difficult work takes dedication, passion, and vulnerability but has the potential of transforming our institutions, our disciplines, and ourselves.

By committing to comadrismo as a feminist mentoring practice—through kinship, fuerza, networks of care, empathy, collaboration, paying it forward, and tangible support—Latinas can provide holistic support to one another as humans, teachers, and scholars who are committed to antiracist, feminist work. Together, the seven characteristics of comadrismo create a mentoring approach that is culturally specific, that values the ways of knowing and being of BIPOC women, and that recognizes the importance of community for academic survival. Advocating for such culturally specific mentoring models will help rhetoric and composition to support and retain BIPOC women, thereby diversifying the field, the students we attract, and the research we do. Comadrismo can also influence the discipline's hierarchies of knowledge by making salient the ways of knowing and being of BIPOC women and other underrepresented communities in academia. Insofar as we care about valuing diverse contributions and supporting diverse people in our field, we must consider mentoring models that reject a white middle-class status quo.

Finally, practicing comadrismo injects a much-needed feminist ethos into academic life. The ability to be vulnerable and to recognize the connections between our personal and emotional lives and the academic work we do can be deeply fulfilling. As we reflect on our diverse paths in academia, we feel fortunate to have had comadres who have helped us along the way. We also acknowledge the spiritual satisfaction that comes from mentoring a comadre in ways that do not attempt to silence her truth. Practices of comadrismo seek to feed the soul as well as the CV. Ultimately, it is our belief that academia at large would benefit from discouraging assimilation to white middle-class norms and would benefit immensely from encouraging, highlighting, and valuing the ways of being and ways of knowing that Latinas bring to academia.

References

Ahmed, Sara. 2017. *Living a Feminist Life*. Durham, NC: Duke Univ. Press.

Alaoui, Fatima Chrifi, and Bernadette M. Calafell. 2016. "A Story of Mentoring: From Praxis to Theory." In *Women of Color Navigating Mentoring Relationships: Critical Examinations*, edited by Keisha Edwards Tassie and Sonja M. Brown Givens, 61–81. Lanham, MD: Lexington Books.

Allatson, Paul. 2007. *Key Terms in Latino/a Cultural and Literary Studies*. Malden, MA: Blackwell.

Ballif, Michele, Diane Davis, and Roxanne Mountford. 2008. *Women's Ways of Making It in Rhetoric and Composition*. New York: Routledge.

Burciaga, Rebeca, and Ana Tavares. 2006. "Our Pedagogy of Sisterhood: A Testimonio." In *Chicana/Latina Education in Everyday Life: Feminista*

Perspectives on Pedagogy and Epistemology, edited by Dolores Delgado Bernal, C. Alejandra Elenes, Francisca E. Godinez, and Sofia Villenas, 133–42. New York: State Univ. of New York Press.

Camacho, Melissa. 2012. "La Comay: An Examination of the Puerto Rican Comadre as a Feminist Icon, Patriarchal Stereotype, and Television Tabloid Host." *Studies in Latin American Popular Culture* 30:124–37.

Cardi b Goes Off on Haters. 2017. YouTube, uploaded by Anti social, Nov. 24. At https://www.youtube.com/watch?v=mXDEZ6t3rC8.

Cavazos, Alyssa Guadalupe. 2012. "Latina/os in Rhetoric and Composition." PhD diss., Texas Christian Univ.

Comstock, Nora de Hoyos. 2012. Introduction to *Count on Me: Tales of Sisterhoods and Fierce Friendships*, edited by Adriana V. Lopez, ix–xiii. New York: Simon and Shuster.

Ek, Lucila D., Patricia Quijada, Iliana Alanís, and Mariela A. Rodríguez. 2010. "'I Don't Belong Here': Chicanas/Latinas at a Hispanic Serving Institution Creating Community through Muxerista Mentoring." *Equity & Excellence in Education* 43, no. 4: 539–53.

Fishman, Jenn, and Andrea Lunsford. 2008. "Educating Jane." In *Stories of Mentoring: Theory and Practice*, edited by Michelle Eble and Lynèe Lewis Gaillet, 18–32. New York: Parlor Press.

Gindlesparger, Kathryn, and Holly Ryan. 2016. "Feminist Fissures: Navigating Conflict in Mentoring Relationships." *Peitho* 19, no. 1: 54–70.

González, Juan Carlos. 2006. "Academic Socialization Experiences of Latina Doctoral Students: A Qualitative Understanding of Support Systems That Aid and Challenges That Hinder the Process." *Journal of Hispanic Higher Education* 5, no. 4: 347–65.

Harris, Angela P., and Carmen G. González. 2012. Introduction to *Presumed Incompetent: The Intersections of Race and Class for Women in Academia*, edited by Gabriella Gutiérrez y Muhs, Yolanda Flores Niemann, Carmen G. González, and Angela P. Harris, 1–14. Logan: Utah State Univ. Press.

Herrera, Cristina. 2011. "Comadres: Female Friendship in Denise Chávez's *Loving Pedro Infante*." *Confluencia* 27, no. 1: 51–62.

Kynard, Carmen, and Robert Eddy. 2009. "Toward a New Critical Framework: Color-Conscious Political Morality and Pedagogy at Historically Black and Historically White Colleges and Universities." *College Composition and Communication* 61, no. 1: W24–W44.

Martinez, Aja Y. 2020. *Counterstory: The Rhetoric and Writing of Critical Race Theory.* Urbana, IL: National Council of Teachers of English.

Okawa, Gail Y. 2002. "Diving for Pearls: Mentoring as Cultural and Activist Practice among Academics of Color." *College Composition and Communication* 53, no. 3: 507–32.

Ore, Ersula. 2016. "Pushback: A Pedagogy of Care." *Pedagogy* 17, no. 1: 9–33.

Scholz, Teresa Maria Linda. 2016. "Beyond 'Roaring Like Lions': Comadrismo, Counternarratives, and the Construction of a Latin American Transnational Subjectivity of Feminism." *Communication Theory* 26:82–101.

VanHaitsma, Pamela, and Steph Ceraso. 2017. "'Making It' in the Academy through Horizontal Mentoring." *Peitho* 19, no. 2: 210–33.

Villanueva, Victor. 1993. *Bootstraps: From an American Academic of Color.* Urbana, IL: National Council of Teachers of English.

———. 1999. "On the Rhetoric and Precedents of Racism." *College Composition and Communication* 50, no. 4: 645–61.

2

Beyond Skin Deep

Confessions of a Transnational Indígena/Latina Scholar
Recovering Her Trenzas in Three Acts

Blanca Gabriela Caldas Chumbes

Abstract

Contextualizing positionality not only embraces vulnerability but also responds to the need for transparency (Madison 2011) and accountability by not allowing researchers to dodge the bullet of "being proven wrong" (Madison 2011, 6). This reflexivity is required for scholars to critically understand our selves "as knower, redeemer, colonizer, and transformational healer" (Chilisa 2012, 174). Accepting Madison's (2011) invitation to answer a simple question—Who am I?—I write this autoethnographic piece, which takes me back to three key moments of my life in searching for my place in academia after moving to the United States to become a scholar. Moving into different immigration status, brownscales, and linguistic landscapes, I—a transnational indigenous Latina scholar—reflect on my ongoing process of unlearning and relearning that shapes me as a researcher and a pedagogue.

> Hay que sacarlo todo afuera, como la primavera
> Nadie quiere que adentro algo se muera
> Hablar mirándose a los ojos
> Sacar lo que se puede afuera
> Para que adentro nazcan cosas nuevas
> —Mercedes Sosa, *Mercedes Sosa en Argentina*

Key moments or emotional bookmarks—be they journal entries about discovering my brownness, utterances for racially "coming out," or pronouncements in ceremony—become a springboard for an examination of my upbringing as a cultural white in working-class South America, the hits and misses as I grapple with my new positionalities in the United States, and the challenges of existing within the walls of the ivory tower while struggling to reclaim my roots with 4,060 miles of distance between my homeland (Peru) and my new land (the United States). I find the process of self-examination necessary for understanding my own disconnections and fragmentations in relation to the communities I serve through my scholarship—Latinx/ Mexican American bilingual/bicultural teachers. Engaging in self-reflexivity pushes me to question, examine, and attune my epistemological and axiological stance to keep the coherence of my research agenda, holds me accountable to do critical research, and reminds me of my own commitments and my oppositional stance to dominant and colonial approaches to research.

Part of being self-reflective is being willing to face one's subjectivities and disclose one's positionality as vital parts of research, principally to understand how those subjectivities shape research (e.g., site choice, data analysis, methodology, tools, presentation, etc.) (Jones 2002). Contextualizing positionality not only embraces vulnerability but also responds to the need for transparency (Madison 2011) and accountability by not allowing researchers to dodge the bullet of "being proven wrong" (Madison 2011, 6). Accepting Madison's (2011) invitation to answer a simple question—Who am I?—I write this autohistoria-teoría (Anzaldúa 2015), which takes me back to three key moments of my life that forced me to confront my own desconocimientos (see Gonzales and Garcia, chapters 3 and 6, in this volume). Confronting these desconocimientos, or shadows, is a process of confronting personal and collective wounds, one that is crucial to arriving at a "pearl of great insight, a theory" (Anzaldúa 2015, 2) in my search for my place in academia after moving to the United States to become a scholar. Autohistoria-teoría is self-writing that fuses "personal narratives with theoretical discourse, autobiographical vignettes and theoretical prose" (Anzaldúa 2015, 6) in order to engage in self-knowledge and, especially, to confront self-ignorance (Pitts 2016) as a way to re-member (Dillard 2016) what I was encouraged to forget.

Act I: "I'm 'white,' that's what I discovered yesterday" (September 15, 2007)

The first subhead of this chapter comes from a journal entry I wrote after a month of living in the United States during my first semester as a master's student of bilingual education. I sat down in disbelief at the stories told in class by my Mexican American classmates, who, in tears, described the racism they had experienced, which permeated their lives: being spat at on the streets, enduring mistreatment in school, and feeling impotent when schools forced them to mainstream, thus depriving them of linguistic and cultural support to achieve quick assimilation. I had read plenty about culture shock before moving to the United States, but nothing prepared me for the discovery of my privilege and whiteness.

> I'm "white," that's what I discovered yesterday. I have never thought of that before in my whole life. It dawned on me that I lived a great life back in my hometown: I could buy an apartment downtown, I had access to what the majority didn't, a great job in the largest binational language school in my country, and so on. Then, I arrived here, new culture, back to school after many years; adjusting to my new job and classes. Here I am trying to figure out what's on my mind, a war is being fought here, a war against the people in power whose wish is to deprive people of their own culture and language. And here is my last issue: "us." Who are "us"? Should I take part in this fight too? Am I brown like the people I'm aiming to teach and support? This issue concerns me as well, and it's time to take sides. I have the power to change things, to change myself too as I have never fought for anything like that, for a minority, where I belong here in the USA, far from my little luxuries and the comfort I was used to. I have to figure it out somehow. Solo soy *Blanca* ahora. (personal journal, September 15, 2007)

Holland and her colleagues (2003) describe the importance of using both culturalist and social constructivist theories in a dialogical position to better understand identity, which was challenged when the social and geographical context changed for 2007's Blanca. My hometown is what Harvey (1990) calls a simulacrum of what Western metropolises are and signify in terms of lifestyles, consumption, and a sense of instantaneity and disposability. Even when we hold on to certain cultural artifacts (food and sites), it is tacitly understood—and seldom contested—that we are to rid ourselves of indigenous or ethnic links to comply with the taken-for-granted rules of what is "normal." The adoption of the habitus of the dominant culture decides which practices are "correct" and which are to be excluded to maintain homogeneity and normalcy (Bourdieu 1990). Although I did not grow up in a Western country, I was a white cultural citizen in Lima, Peru.

My position as a professional in Lima gave me certain privileges to advance in my career and create a social network and even the opportunity to immigrate to a country I thought I would assimilate into quickly. As I described in the journal entry, I enjoyed social, economic, and cultural privileges throughout my career as an English teacher; a booming career in the aughts in Perú gave me privilege, and even though I knew I would lose some of my privileges when I became an international student, I did not expect to be in the social position where I later found myself. I understood poverty because I was born into it, and I believed that I had somehow "made it," in spite of my disadvantages, owing to my belief in meritocracy. After my arrival in the United States, my social position changed from that of a young professional to simply being "brown," a term I had never heard before until my professor (who identified as a Chicano) brought it up in class.

Everyday practices and behaviors that shape identity can be adopted with awareness and reflection or be adopted unconsciously. Kondo (2009) describes how while doing research she became aware of her unconscious acquisition of certain behaviors by looking at her reflection in a display. When I wrote that journal entry in the fall of 2007, I believe I had what I call a "Kondo moment," in which I had the chance to see my reflection, too. Those nepantla (Anzaldúa and Keating 2002) moments are fascinating instances of the constructive chaos I faced when confronted with seeing my cultural whiteness paired with the contradictions of being an educated woman and being stereotyped and marginalized due solely to my skin color and "accent." I understood that time in September was a moment to reassess my identity to avoid fossilization. The last line, "Solo soy *Blanca* ahora" (I am just *Blanca* now), communicates the rejection of my white cultural identity, even though the process of shifting from one salient identity to another is not automatic. Chubbuck argues that the process is achieved neither by following certain steps like the ones taken in Alcoholics Anonymous groups nor by an accumulation of knowledge. It is rather "an ongoing process that requires significant rewriting of the narratives used to interpret lives and maintain congruence of self, done in the context of a community of support and accountability" (2004, 329). This trajectory is not free of cultural disequilibrium (Brown 2002), guilt, disbelief, resistance, and struggle with a coalition of people from different ethnic backgrounds since it is usually taken for granted—both ways—that owing to one's skin color, one "gets it" (Quijada Cerecer 2010). Identity formation is actually a messy process.

I tried to examine my own whiteness as a social and cultural construct since "whiteness as an ideological construction cannot be simply conflated with white people" (Kincheloe and Steinberg 1998, 17). After all, it is not just skin color that might make a person "white" (Aveling 2006). The examination of my own cultural whiteness in my identification as a Latin American woman with brown skin is "the process[] whereby . . . individuals often move themselves—led by hope, desperation, or even playfulness, but certainly by no rational plan—from one set of socially and culturally formed subjectivities to another" (Holland et al. 2003, 7).

Whiteness has less to do with skin color and more to do with ideological practices spread worldwide by colonialism and neocolonialism. It is a social construction based on negation related to the other. This negation can also be applied to people who are marginalized because of their skin color and refuse to be categorized as the other, which might result in their embrace of the dominant Eurocentric culture or the whiteness postculture (Perry 2004) as a sign of a higher level of development that is exempt from ties with the past (living in the now, planning for the future) and deemed to be "better" than any ethnic culture.

These social constructions are created to mask privileges, colonialism, exploitation, victim blaming, and segregation (Giroux 1999; Shome 1999; Brown 2002; Lipsitz 2006). It was hard to admit that my position as a culturally white professional made me complicit in the further marginalization of my own kin, who, I believed at the time, needed to be more "like us" to stop their victimization and to succeed—all the while acknowledging that a culturally white education does not automatically lead to equal access. The deconstruction of my white cultural identity did not end after writing that journal entry in 2007. Questioning my previous privileges and how I lost them when coming to the United States was just the beginning.

Act II: "I am Chicana" (April 27, 2011)

The subhead of this section comes from a conversation I had as an instructor in an undergraduate class discussing an article on Spanish for Chicanos and what the word *Chicano* embodies (Urrieta 2009). It became clear to me then that my permanency in this country in terms of residence (I had married a US citizen the previous year) and my growing professional and personal roots in this land had forced me to reformulate my role in this society. That discussion in class was the springboard to name the world (Freire 1993) of my own version of Chicanismo hybridized with my other salient selves. Chicanisma was born out of the need to contest the male-centric focus of the Chicano movement and centers the intersectional lives of Mexican/Mexican American mestizas in terms of race, class, ethnicity, gender, sexuality, and spirituality at personal and political levels (Anzaldúa 1990; Castillo 1994). I said "my own version" because even though Chicana feminism resonates strongly with my experience, I did not (and do not) come from that specific and contextualized experience.

That class was the first time I called myself a Chicana, even though I had exercised agency as an activist educator that reaffirmed my affinity with a Chicana identity without naming it. Like Della Porta and Diani (2006), I felt that even a person who does not belong to a certain group might create a new synthesis from a blend of different references paired with acceptance in certain affinity groups. For me, these references included the use of cultural artifacts such as language, critical texts, and writings focusing on the intersections among class, race, language, and gender as well as my being surrounded by people who educated, supported, and sustained me in my resistance to the embeddedness of whiteness in the multiplicity of my identities. That group of people—my friends—identify as Latinx, Chicanx, Tejanxs, and what Ignatiev and Garvey (1996) call "race traitors." My identification as a Chicana was delayed probably from fear of being accused of lacking authenticity but also of falling into the paradox of appropriation and identification (Goodman 2000). Appropriating and erasing the differences between Chicanas' experiences and mine and thinking, "I know just how you feel . . . we are all alike," are a danger (Goodman 2000, 1064). There are undeniable differences between my trajectory and that of a Chicana, no matter how strongly I identified with my friends and colleagues who were actually Chicanxs. This is the reason why, even though calling myself that felt right at that moment, I was still hesitant to do that, and it did not take too long for me to stop identifying as such. Gloria Anzaldúa's (1987) words, however, showed me the mestiza way as a resting place to connect to my private borderlines and gave a new meaning to an identity confined to official Peruvian documents that already labeled me as "mestiza" (see Ramírez, chapter 10, in this volume). The label *mestiza* connected me with Chicanx and Tejanx friends as a collective identity in my personal and professional circles in the United States. It felt like home.

This renaming, however, forced me to look hard at my past selves since it helped me make sense of myself only "from an Anglo point of view" (Anzaldúa 1987, 79). In other words, I had done this self-reflection only as a response to the (co)construction of my positionalities in the United States (Cahnmann, Rymes, and Souto-Manning 2005).

The examination of my roots remained dormant and unexplored yet important. Through painful but necessary digging, which Sealey-Ruiz (2017) calls the "archaeology of self," I excavated my history more in depth as a springboard for a deeper conscientization (Freire 1993). This meant remembering that I come from a working-class family where neither of my parents finished high school and my mom barely finished elementary school. This also meant confronting the anger I had felt as a schoolgirl during the 1980s and 1990s amid economic turbulence, state violence, dictatorship, terrorism, and scarcity. This anger stemmed from my perceptions of having been shortchanged: furious at my parents for not being able to afford a better education for me; at my school, where I was one of the fifty students—all of whom expected to become homemakers in the near future—in dilapidated classrooms; and at my teachers for not being able to hide their apathy. This anger helped me find the cracks in the system that afforded me opportunities to take advantage of it. In retrospect, I realize that for a long time my rage was a way to avoid—to feel the pain of the learned self-hate—the erasure of my family origins, my original language, my indigeneity and thus to embrace the myth of meritocracy to pretend I was a self-made woman.

Flashes of my fragmented memory are also fueled by the voice of my ninety-plus-year-old aunt Filomena as I read an interview I conducted with her years ago. She mentioned that because of her indigenous features and clothes and the fact that she is "illiterate," she was always treated with disdain, regarded as ignorant or as one of "those people" (Freire 1993). She shared an account of how my father left for the city, disgusted by his family's appearance, manners, accent, and beliefs: "Mi hermano dejó el pueblo cuando era adolescente para buscar una mejor vida y aunque viene a visitarme con regalos yo sé que no le gusta estar aquí, le recuerda a su pasado."[1] She told me this,

---

1. Translation: My brother left town when he was a teenager to look for a better life, and although he comes to visit me with gifts, I know he doesn't like being here. It reminds him of his past.

mixing Spanish and Quechua, while asking me to read the Bible for her. From my tía Filomena, I learned my first feminist lesson as she told my sisters and me how she beat my uncle the first time he tried to hit her; little did she know that story remained imprinted in my mind and guided me as I started navigating the world.

I also recall my abuela María's voice as she tried to teach me to braid my hair while I gave her a hard time by not sitting still. "Supaypawawa!,"[2] I remember her calling me as she chased me down in my family's small apartment whenever I slipped away; her Quechuan voice was foreign and familiar at the same time. With her nickname for me—the child of the devil—she foresaw who I was to become: a disobedient and defiant contestona[3] who transgresses what was/is expected from her as a girl/woman, traits I struggle to channel strategically as I play the game of academia (Urrieta 2009). However, other voices—this time from the ivory tower—pushed me back through the scholarly mill in survivance mode (Brayboy 2005). Dissertation, job hunt, and fellowship and grant applications were my main focus during those years, so I dedicated my time to pushing through, giving little attention to my mental well-being, my body, and my family. Nevertheless, those female voices never left me, so I did not end up losing myself while gaining a PhD.

Act III: "I take this obligation freely, without any mental reservation or purpose of evasion. So help me God" (September 11, 2018)

Almost eight hundred people from different parts of the world were there: tears, hugs, and hope. Sitting alone in that auditorium, I could not bring myself to finish the last sentence of the naturalization oath, "so help me God." Among flowers and balloons, there was no celebration for me, nor did I expect one. "This won't change anything; they're just words," I repeated to myself like a mantra. But words do

---

2. Translation: child of the devil.
3. Translation: a female who talks back.

conjure up and change things because oaths are performative utterances (Austin 1962). Just like my grandma had christened me supaypawawa, now I was American.[4] What other borders had I just created by uttering those words? "I'm doing this for my mom," I consoled myself, holding back the tears now, coming to terms with the fact that the privileges and knowledge I had acquired since I left home did not belong solely to me but for the benefit of the family I had left behind (Brayboy 2005). I was stretched across continents, grasping at both the roots I was trying to strengthen at home and the roots I was creating here, also home. I have not processed yet the ripples of this new identity I voluntarily took upon myself. When showing my brand-new passport, I felt judged by the Peruvian customs officer or the supermarket attendant who used the passport to verify my identity when I used my debit card. They saw "el nopal en mi frente,"[5] as mexicanos[6] would say. I cannot tell them that I have that blue booklet because I want to transplant my mother to Minnesota to take care of her during her last years on earth, to walk with her around Como Lake, as I have been dreaming since I first moved here. That booklet does not save me from scrutiny at the US airport in Fort Lauderdale, and I do not expect otherwise. I will always comprise all the stereotypes people might see whenever they see my brownness and hear my voice full of el Sur: an illiterate, "illegal," brown, and very fertile woman, eager to give birth to anchor babies. If they only knew! No energy to explain to all of them: I do not need to ask for permission to exist.

So, who am I supposed to be now? Torres helped me find some clues as she explained to me (and others like me) that "women of Latin American descent born in the United States or those who have immigrated to the U.S." are called "Latinas" (1991, 141). Despite the growing use of the term *Latina* in the field of bilingual education, I have always felt ambivalent about that term. Granted, I have used it to

4. A citizen of los Estados Unidos.

5. A Mexican expression used to describe someone who has obvious Indigenous facial features but pretends to be of European white descent.

6. People from the United Mexican States.

avoid the daunting task of explaining myself to people for whom that information may not have mattered: my skin color and my accent were an easy giveaway for the assumption of that pan-ethnic and Anglo-centric label. The proximal geographic connections of the women in Torres's work (from Puerto Rico and México) with the United States make the use of *Latina* more understandable, although I wonder if Gloria Anzaldúa would call herself "Latina" or if the Chilean writer Isabel Allende would call herself "Latina" after settling down in California and obtaining US citizenship. I agree with Urrieta that labels such as *Latina/o* and *mestiza* can be problematic because they can eclipse other salient identities and hide uncontested racial hierarchies that have persisted since colonial times in Latinoamérica: "The indigenous people of Latin America are left unnamed, engulfed within a sea of 'Hispanos' or 'Latinos.' The indígena population is therefore left silent and either learns to be Hispanic or Latino. . . . In terms of the Mexican mestizo, for example, everyone has an equal claim to Indianness and Europeanness, while reaping unequal benefits since mestizaje is more of a historical claim to whiteness (Spanish) and an explicit, or at best implicit, rejection or escape out of Indianness" (2003, 152).

I feel interpellated when Urrieta asks, "What does it mean to be an indigenous person from Latin America or of Latina/o heritage within the current politics of U.S. categories?" (2003, 153). He goes on to name the pain of the erasure of his indigeneity del Sur. "Do I have the right to call myself indigenous?," I wonder as I examine my face, remembering the time a gringo[7] complimented me for my beauty as he thanked the Spaniard for mestizaje, as though if it had not been for the rape of my female ancestors, I would not have been able to have certain Western features that make me desirable. What I can see on my face are the features of my awila,[8] along with the character she predicted I would inherit from her but without her lived experience as

7. Kutipanakuy: el pishtaco.
8. Translation: grandmother.

a mujer campesina.[9] As I nurture this emergent indigenous identity, I wonder what this work might look like when living in another part of the world, navigating the whitest and westernmost institution of academia, where people like me are considered subjects to be researched, observed, labeled, and archived. My quest is not exempt from difficulties. The connection to my family history on my father's side disappeared with my aunt's passing eight years ago. My father's few memories of his childhood living in la chacra[10] were all I could record of the past I was longing to collect, and he would not say anything else before his death a couple of years ago. Nevertheless, not all is lost; I still have relatives who can help me piece together our past and grapple with issues that affect us now. I have also found opportunities to engage in spiritual and quotidian practices, despite the distance of 4,060 miles, that serve as powerful reminders of who I am, both personally and professionally. I still have to explore my mother's side of my family; her wounds are finally healing, and her voice is getting stronger as she ages—maybe she will be ready to speak as her time for moving to Minnesota approaches.

My emergent indígena identity has made me reflect on doing research that is more attuned to my developing and ever-evolving understanding of myself as a transnational indígena Latina scholar and my role in academia. After long reflection, I decided on the inclusion of "Latina" in my identification, not despite its anglocentricity but on purpose to signal my place as a naturalized estadounidense.[11] I also decided to include my emergent indígena identity as a Quechua woman as I unearth those saberes[12] passed down to me that consciously and unconsciously have informed my life and work and are inscribed in my body. The unchecked and unmarked privileges, prejudices, and questions of power and positionality are issues that I as a scholar need to (re)examine every step of the way while doing

9. Translation: peasant women
10. Translation: rural land.
11. Translation: people from the United States of America.
12. Translation: knowledges.

research and responding to calls for self-exploration to uncover motivations, fears, and knowledge. Chilisa brings to the forefront the following questions on the quest for self-awareness: "Where do I stand with regard to the researched? Am I still the colonizer? Who are the researched? Are the researched still colonial subjects distinct from the colonizer because of their incapabilities, or are the researched active agents capable of generating solutions to their social challenges?" (2012, 236). I think this examination can become a process of "scarification" (Wilson 2008) since I need to examine my own disconnections and fragmentations to make sense of how I relate to others and how they relate to me. Engaging in self-reflexivity pushes me to question and examine the coherence of my research with the way I live and relate to others.

I adhere to the notion of relational accountability (Wilson 2008): what a researcher chooses to study should reflect the needs of the community she belongs to. This aspect of accountability is intimately related to who the participants are, how that influences the collaboration of all involved in the research, and what is behind the representation of my partners in research (Jones 2002) to avoid researcher-centric research projects (Chilisa 2012, 294). Relational accountability influences the modes of gathering and interpreting information that showcase a community's ways of knowing and being. This approach is attuned to a Chicana epistemology of cultural intuition (Solórzano and Yosso 2002) founded in personal experiences—in the shape of testimonios (Beverley 2000; Cervantes-Soon 2012), life histories (Geiger 1986), counterstorytelling (Delgado 1989; Solórzano and Yosso 2002), existing literature, and professional experience in the field. In other words, my work as a scholar is based on my own life trajectory, knowledges, understandings, and political commitments.

My work with Latinx/Mexican American bilingual teachers has strengthened my membership in this community in the United States, the links to my country, and my most salient identities. Being part of this community holds me accountable for the way I portray it to avoid misrepresentation as I put my research at the community's service, while I welcome the complexities and challenges of the experience

(Madison 2011). This accountability also pushes me to do critical work and reminds me of my commitment to an oppositional stance to dominant and colonial approaches to research: selfishness, misrepresentation, the researcher as objective observer, the neocolonized participants as objects.

Supaypawawa and Her Trenzas

Madison (2011) invited me to answer a simple question for starters: Who am I? This has taken me back to my discovery of both my unmarked "whiteness" as a Peruvian professional educator in my country, my "brownness" a month after having arrived in the United States as an international student, and my struggles in attempting to reconfigure myself in the US context as a Chicana, Latina, mestiza, and indígena with new salient selves more attuned to my self-identification as a human and as a professional at this moment of my life as an emergent scholar.

The seemingly personal quest to find my footing as a transnational individual in the United States has professional dimensions as well because this search is deeply intertwined with my own conscientization process as I examine my conocimientos and desconocimientos. As a teacher-educator and researcher interested in the formation of Latinx/Mexican American bilingual teachers, I am involved in a collective engagement and shared repertoire. Issues such as racism, xenophobia, linguicism, and discrimination are part of the everyday reality of brown bilingual teachers across the United States. Therefore, it is an ethical responsibility for me not only to denounce these issues in my field as a researcher but also to use my own research as a tool—not as an end in itself—that allows me to serve as a critical secretary (Apple 2011) for the community I belong to (see Gutierrez, chapter 4, in this volume). My quest to obtain a more politically clear educational philosophy (Bartolome 1994) encourages me to look for ways to do research "against the grain" (Cochran-Smith 2009) but not "from the balcony" (Bakhtin, quoted in Apple 2011, 230) and to try to disrupt traditional societal discourses that inform what teachers and researchers should or should not be (Marsh 2003), look like, and sound like.

The privileges I have obtained also come with ethical responsibilities. As García, Corona, and Alvarez illustrate in their chapters in this collection, it is my responsibility to guide my hermanas who are following the same path and to provide them with the tools for success while keeping their integrity within the toxic walls of academia. I still hold this responsibility, even when, as Martinez shows us in her chapter, other people of color have not yet discovered how academic spaces were not designed for brown and black bodies. This responsibility also means helping my sisters look within themselves and uncover their herstories to inform their work as educators and researchers for the benefit of our families/communities—in other words, for our own futures.

References

Anzaldúa, Gloria. 1987. *Borderlands / La Frontera: The New Mestiza*. San Francisco: Aunt Lute Books.

———, ed. 1990. *Haciendo Caras / Making Face, Making Soul: Creative and Critical Perspectives by Women of Color*. San Francisco: Aunt Lute Books.

———. 2015. "Preface: Gestures of the Body—Escribiendo para idear." In Gloria Anzaldúa, *Light in the Dark / Luz en lo oscuro: Rewriting Identity, Spirituality, Reality*, edited by AnaLouise Keating, 1–8. Durham, NC: Duke Univ. Press.

Anzaldúa, Gloria, and AnaLouise Keating, eds. 2002. *This Bridge We Call Home: Radical Visions for Transformation*. New York: Routledge.

Apple, Michael. 2011. "Global Crises, Social Justice, and Teacher Education." *Journal of Teacher Education* 62, no. 2: 222–34.

Austin, J. L. 1962. *How to Do Things with Words: The William James Lectures, Delivered at Harvard University in 1955*. Oxford: Clarendon Press.

Aveling, Nado. 2006. "'Hacking at Our Very Roots': Rearticulating White Racial Identity within the Context of Teacher Education." *Race Ethnicity and Education* 9, no. 3: 261–74.

Bartolome, Lilia. 1994. "Beyond the Methods Fetish: Toward a Humanizing Pedagogy." *Harvard Educational Review* 64, no. 2: 173–94.

Beverley, John. 2000. "Testimonio, Subalternity, and Narrative Authority." In *Handbook of Qualitative Research*, 2nd ed., edited by Norman K. Denzin and Yvonna S. Lincoln, 555–65. Thousand Oaks, CA: Sage.

Bourdieu, Pierre. 1990. *The Logic of Practice.* Stanford, CA: Stanford Univ. Press.

Brayboy, Bryan McKinley Jones. 2005. "Transformational Resistance and Social Justice: American Indians in Ivy League Universities." *Anthropology and Education Quarterly* 36, no. 3: 193–211.

Brown, Cynthia Stokes. 2002. *Refusing Racism: White Allies and the Struggle for Civil Rights.* New York: Teachers College Press.

Cahnmann, Melisa, Betsy Rymes, and Mariana Souto-Manning. 2005. "Using Critical Discourse Analysis to Understand and Facilitate Identification Processes of Bilingual Adults Becoming Teachers." *Critical Inquiry in Language Studies* 2, no. 4: 195–213.

Castillo, Ana. 1994. *Massacre of the Dreamers: Essays in Xicanisma.* New York: Plume/Penguin Books.

Cervantes-Soon, Claudia G. 2012. "Testimonios of Life and Learning in the Borderlands: Subaltern Juarez Girls Speak." *Equity & Excellence in Education* 45, no. 3: 373–91.

Chilisa, Bagele. 2012. *Indigenous Research Methodologies.* Thousand Oaks, CA: Sage.

Chubbuck, Sharon M. 2004. "Whiteness Enacted, Whiteness Disrupted: The Complexity of Personal Congruence." *American Educational Research Journal* 41, no. 2: 301–33.

Cochran-Smith, Marilyn. 2009. "Toward a Theory of Teacher Education for Social Justice." In *Second International Handbook of Educational Change*, 2nd ed., edited by Michael Fullan, Andy Hargreaves, David Hopkins, and Ann Lieberman, 445–67. New York: Springer.

Delgado, Richard. 1989. "Storytelling for Oppositionists and Others: A Plea for Narrative." *Michigan Law Review* 87, no. 8: 2411–41.

Della Porta, Donatella, and Mario Diani. 2006. *Social Movements: An Introduction.* Malden, MA: Blackwell.

Dillard, Cynthia B. 2016. "Towards an Education That (Re)members: Centering Identity, Race, and Spirituality in Education." *Tikkun* 31, no. 4: 50–54.

Freire, Paulo. 1993. *Pedagogy of the Oppressed.* Translated by Myra Bergman Ramos. New York: Continuum.

Geiger, Susan N. G. 1986. "Women's Life Histories: Method and Content." *Signs* 11, no. 2: 334–51.

Giroux, Henry. 1999. "Rewriting the Discourse of Racial Identity: Towards a Pedagogy and Politics of Whiteness." *Harvard Educational Review* 67, no. 2: 285–320.

Goodman, Diane J. 2000. "Motivating People from Privileged Groups to Support Social Justice." *Teachers College Record* 102, no. 6: 1061–85.

Harvey, David. 1990. *The Condition of Postmodernity: An Enquiry into the Origins of Cultural Change.* Oxford: Blackwell.

Holland, Dorothy, William Lachicotte, Debra Skinner, and Caroline Cain. 2003. *Identity and Agency in Cultural Worlds.* Cambridge, MA: Harvard Univ. Press.

Ignatiev, Noel, and John Garvey. 1996. *Race Traitor.* New York: Routledge.

Jones, Joni L. 2002. "Performance Ethnography: The Role of Embodiment in Cultural Authenticity." *Theatre Topics* 12, no. 1: 1–15.

Kincheloe, Joe L., and Shirley R. Steinberg. 1998. "Addressing the Crisis of Whiteness: Reconfiguring White Identity in a Pedagogy of Whiteness." In *White Reign: Deploying Whiteness in America,* edited by Joe L. Kincheloe, Shirley R. Steinberg, Nelson M. Rodriguez, and Ronald E. Chennault, 3–30. New York: St. Martin's, Griffin.

Kondo, Dorinne K. 2009. *Crafting Selves: Power, Gender, and Discourses of Identity in a Japanese Workplace.* Chicago: Univ. of Chicago Press.

Lipsitz, George. 2006. *The Possessive Investment in Whiteness: How White People Profit from Identity Politics.* Philadelphia: Temple Univ. Press.

Madison, D. Soyini. 2011. *Critical Ethnography: Method, Ethics, and Performance.* Thousand Oaks, CA: Sage.

Marsh, Monica Miller. 2003. *The Social Fashioning of Teacher Identities: Rethinking Childhood.* New York: Peter Lang.

Perry, Pamela. 2004. "White Means Never Having to Say You're Ethnic." In *Life in America: Identity and Everyday Experience,* edited by Lee Baker, 339–58. Malden, MA: Blackwell.

Pitts, Andrea. 2016. "Gloria E. Anzaldúa's Autohistoria-Teoría as an Epistemology of Self-Knowledge/Ignorance." *Hypatia* 31, no. 2: 352–69.

Quijada Cerecer, David Alberto. 2010. "A White Guy Who Doesn't Get It? A Multilayered Analysis of One Activist's Effort to Build Coalitions across Race." *Race Ethnicity and Education* 13, no. 2: 173–90.

Sealey-Ruiz, Yolanda. 2017. "When Celebrating Diversity Isn't Enough: The Need for Racial Literacy in Our Schools." Lecture, Univ. of Michigan Teaching Works Seminar Series, Ann Arbor, Nov. 13.

Shome, Raka. 1999. "Whiteness and the Politics of Location." In *Whiteness: The Communication of Social Identity*, edited by Thomas K. Nakayama and Judith N. Martin, 107–28. Thousand Oaks, CA: Sage.

Solórzano, Daniel, and Tara J. Yosso. 2002. "Critical Race Methodology: Counter-Storytelling as an Analytical Framework for Education Research." *Qualitative Inquiry* 8, no. 1: 23–44.

Sosa, Mercedes. 1982. *Mercedes Sosa en Argentina*. [Buenos Aires, Argentina]: Universal.

Torres, Lourdes. 1991. "The Construction of the Self in US Latina Autobiographies." In *Third World Women and the Politics of Feminism*, edited by Chandra Mohanty, Ann Russo, and Lourdes Torres, 127–43. Bloomington: Indiana Univ. Press.

Urrieta, Luis. 2003. "Las identidades también lloran, Identities Also Cry: Exploring the Human Side of Indigenous Latina/o Identities." *Educational Studies* 32, no. 2: 147–68.

———. 2009. *Working from Within: Chicana and Chicano Activist Educators in Whitestream Schools*. Tucson: Univ. of Arizona Press.

Wilson, Shawn. 2008. *Research Is Ceremony: Indigenous Research Methods*. Black Point, Nova Scotia: Fernwood.

3

Beyond and within My Skin

Testimonios of a Latina Immigrant

Laura Gonzales

Abstract

This chapter illustrates how a bilingual Latina immigrant from Bolivia comes to understand her identity in US academia. Stories of migration, mentorship, and (re)identification shape the author's understanding of her identity and her role as a Latina who has the privilege to build sustainable coalitions with women of color both within and beyond academic spaces.

Introduction

This chapter is about my ongoing journey to understand and grapple with what it means to be a Latina, a Bolivian, an immigrant, a professor, and a cis-gendered woman with white skin who works to remain accountable to her multiple communities. At this moment in my career, in the summer of 2020, I'm in my second tenure-track position at a research-intensive university, where we just finished our spring semester in the midst of a global pandemic. I believe it's too early to share stories or make predictions about what this current moment means for us as scholars, teachers, community members, caretakers, partners, and hermanas Latinas in the academy, but I do know that things won't ever be the same. And for many who continue experiencing racism and oppression in all aspects of life on colonized lands grounded in slavery and anti-Blackness, things were never that different, anyway (Black Latinas Know Collective 2019).

What I want to talk about is my journey to continue negotiating what it means for me and my body, my languages, and my presence both to take up space and to invest in complex and constantly evolving communities and coalitions (Walton, Moore, and Jones 2019). My goal in sharing these stories is to push our academic disciplines to continue to try to understand the nuanced complexities that exist within communities such as Latinx and particularly within a fictional label that is imposed on various groups of people who have vastly different histories, experiences, and stories. As Terese Guinsatao Monberg explains, when we are analyzing cultural-rhetorical work in context, it is important to acknowledge how individuals experience and navigate the world "*within* their own borders or communities," noting how people who may be institutionally or systematically defined under one label navigate their own "recursive spatial movement" (2009, 22, emphasis in original).

Through grounded testimonios[1] of my experiences as a Latina immigrant, I thus illustrate my "recursive spatial movement" in coming to better understand and (re)imagine my own identity and my role as a Latina in academia. I argue that this recursive effort toward self-understanding is for Latinas critical not only to seeing our own roles as Latinas within and outside academic institutions but also to helping us build coalitions of mentorship and friendship among and through identity markers. As Ana Milena Ribero and Sonia C. Arellano explain, "Cooperation among Latinas ensures that our experiences and knowledges are valued and that our successes also benefit our communities" (2019, 340; see chapter 1). And as the Two-Spirit Cherokee scholar Qwo-Li Driskill (2016) reminds us, the weaving of stories in relationship to community can help researchers and activists develop coalitional methodologies for approaching and sustaining

---

1. Chicana feminist educator J. Estrella Torrez explains that "as both a methodology and a pedagogy, testimonios emerge from within Chicana and Latina feminist scholarship as knowledges that challenge the hegemonic methodologies which may systematically subordinate Chicanas and Latinas" (2015, 106).

community work. Through testimonios, I share stories of embodied knowledge and expertise that illustrate cultural histories and lived experiences in/and community (Cobos 2012). I thread together testimonios to illustrate my journey in recursive movement, specifically through and to the recognition of the connections among my experiences, the histories of my family and my mentors, and my role within and beyond academia.

Looking in the Mirror

I remember sitting on the bathroom sink, mouthing words into the mirror at my lala's house in Orlando, Florida. Six weeks had passed since Mami and I had joined my dad, brother, and grandparents in Orlando, leaving behind our home and friends in Santa Cruz, Bolivia.

"We're moving to Disney World!," Mami had told me back in Santa Cruz. "We're moving to Disney World with Mickey Mouse, to a place where Daddy will find a job and where we will be happy. Papi and Robertito are going first. You and I will finish out the school year here so that you can start third grade in Orlando. We'll live with your lala for a little bit, just while we find a house that we like. Aren't you excited?"

I knew mi mami wasn't excited, but she was trying. Giving it another go to keep our family together. I pretended I was excited, too.

We were scared.

Six weeks had passed since coming to Orlando, and I was looking into the mirror, trying to figure out how I could feel so different when I looked so similar to my classmates. Blond hair and light skin let me blend in with the crowds on the playground, with the long lines in the lunchroom, with everyone else who lived in the land of Disney World and Mickey Mouse.

But I knew I was different, and everything about this place seemed different. I looked into the mirror, moving my mouth to sound out new consonants in this new language I was learning. Trying to make my words blend in as much as my perceivably inoffensive skin. Trying to be who they are and sound like they sound and like what they like and do what they do. It's interesting that the desire to assimilate, and the acknowledgment that I could assimilate, had already seeped into my third-grade bones.

In describing her experiences as a white Chicana, Cherríe Moraga explains, "I must reckon with the fact that for most of my life, by virtue of the very fact that I am white-looking, I identified with, and aspired toward, white values, and that I rode the wave of that Southern Californian privilege as far as conscience would let me" ([1981] 2015, 29). Coupling my whiteness with an immigrant mentality, I too embraced and strove for what Moraga describes as "white values," seeking to mask my differences and, in particular, my language in order to fit within what I perceived to be the standard practices and values of the "American way." I moved my mouth to make new words while striving to hide my accent, flattening my intonation to match the voices I heard around me in my new home. To fit in, I thought, I should look, sound, and feel like my classmates, leaving behind the language, the flavors, and the sounds that raised me. Yet masking our histories only imposes violence on ourselves and our communities, for there will always come a time when assimilation will not be enough.

I Want to Be a Teacher When I Grow Up

I slammed the door and sat in my papi's Mitsubishi Galant. He wasn't "papi" anymore, though; he was my "daddy buddy," a new nickname to represent my new favorite language. The language that allowed me to blend in and no longer be the "special new classmate from Bolivia who doesn't speak English." The new language that would help me hide my secrets about being different and being from a different place. The language of the Spice Girls and Nickelodeon and the language of my friends. The language I (thought I) had fully learned by fifth grade.

"What's wrong, baby? What happened? Why are you slamming the door like that?"

"I don't wanna go to middle school. Sixth grade is gonna suck."

"School always sucks. But for some reason you like it. So why will sixth grade be any different? You don't wanna go to a new school?"

"Well, I DID wanna go, but then Ms. Weiss wouldn't sign my paper so I can be in the same classes next year with Michelle and Melissa, so now I'm gonna be all by myself."

"Why? What form?"

"They passed out a form where your teacher has to sign to recommend you for advanced classes in middle school. Ms. Weiss signed the form for Michelle and Melissa, so they're going to be in the advanced classes next year. Ms. Weiss wouldn't sign the form for me because she said advanced classes were not for special people who speak two languages. She said I was special because I spoke Spanish first and then learned English, and so I can't be in the advanced class."

"It's okay, baby. I bet you they will move you into the advanced classes later, once you get to middle school. That teacher is just a gringa."

"Are all teachers gringas, Daddy?"

"Yep, at least most of them."

"Well, then I wanna be a teacher when I grow up. I can pretend to be a gringa but then let kids who speak Spanish go to the advanced classes."

The products of my fifth-grade logic demonstrate early realizations of who I am, how I am perceived, and the privilege that I carry. At such an early age, I already realized that I could not and cannot escape my history, no matter how hard I tried and continue to try. Moraga explains that white Latinas "must acknowledge the fact that, physically, [we] have had a *choice*" about marking our ethnicity ([1981] 2015, 28). We can decide to hide in crowds on the playground, in the classroom, or in a faculty meeting, and we can decide when to speak up. This choice is rooted in white privilege, a privilege that contrasts with the experiences of "women who have not had such a choice, and have been abused for their color" (28). In her discussion of "a pedagogy of care," Ersula Ore explains, "From the moment I step into the building I am marked an outsider. Regardless of external signifiers of a teacherly ethos . . . I am still assumed to be a student. My black body in these clothes, in this space, denies me any other identity" (2016,

9). Thus, it is white Latinas' responsibility to recognize and, I argue, leverage our privilege to enact justice and to build coalitions with others who both share and don't share our experiences. As Blanca Caldas explains in chapter 2 in this volume, we as immigrant Latinas have to configure our identities in new contexts while also avoiding generalizations and fetishizations of histories and groundings that do not belong to us (see also Ríos 2016).

Special

Many of Mami's fears came true as the years passed in our new life in Florida. It wasn't all Mickey Mouse and fun. In fact, by the time I was in high school, my dad had gotten fired from his job at Disney World. We were several months behind on our mortgage and had lost faith in the "American Dream." We also almost lost our house. I graduated from college with a bachelor's degree in English (to prove that I could finally speak it!) in three years, in part because I had earned the credits but mostly because I wanted to walk across the graduation stage before both of my parents left Florida and moved back to Bolivia. My brother and I stayed in Orlando, siempre juntos en la lucha y en la vida.

In the years following my parents' move back to Bolivia, I took pride in having a "stable" home for my brother as I juggled my work as a teaching assistant in my master's program and as a manager responsible for all the cashiers and grocery-bagging people in a local supermarket. I'll never forget the first Christmas after my parents left when I was finally able to buy my brother the new Xbox 360. It was the first time in several years that my brother had a house with a Christmas tree that actually had presents underneath it, and for that I was so proud. We had everything because we had each other, but this year we had a little extra, too.

In my master's program, I became interested in researching and teaching writing, and I was grateful to have mentors who helped me join a discipline that they said "needed my voice." I didn't have a clue what they meant by that statement, perhaps because I also didn't read scholarship written by people like me. Instead, I spent several years trying to make my voice fit within this new (to me) academic discourse, and I enjoyed doing so because, after all, fitting in was still my specialty. From mouthing foreign words in front of my grandma's mirror as I tried to hide my accent to figuring out the "proper register" my professors sought in my academic writing, I knew this was a formula that I could decipher. And I did.

Years later, after graduating with my MA in writing and rhetoric and, much more importantly, after watching my baby brother walk across his own graduation stage as he earned his BA, I began to consider applying to PhD programs. I wanted to be a "doctor." And I also wanted to make enough money to potentially quit my grocery store job.

As I began asking for recommendation letters in my department, one of my mentors, a white, cis-gendered, queer-identified male full professor and department chair, asked me to have coffee to "discuss my future." Intimidated, I agreed. I had never had coffee with this mentor before, so I remember walking into the coffee shop nervous and worried after spending a few minutes googling "what academics order at a coffee shop." I hadn't been to a Starbucks before.

As my mentor and I sat down, he looked me in the eyes and said, "Laura, I read your statement of purpose for your PhD program, and I wanted to talk to you about it." I nodded and said, "Okay. Well, thank you for making time to read it, and thank you for the coffee."

"I like what you say in the statement, but I'm not sure it communicates how special you really are."

"Special? How do you communicate 'special'?"

"Well, um, your last name is Gonzales, right? Do you speak Spanish?"

"Yes," I said as my mind imploded. (*Oh crap, how did he notice? Did I not use the right register in my statement? I thought I'd proofread everything—shoot! How embarrassing.*)

"When did you learn to speak Spanish?"

"My mom said I started talking pretty early in life. That's when I learned Spanish." (*Whoops, was that too direct? I don't know what he means.*)

"Oh, so you learned English after Spanish?"

"Yes, that's right. I learned English when we moved to the US."

"Oh! Well, that's wonderful!"

"Huh?" (*No, it wasn't so wonderful*).

"I think you should put that on your application. Tell them that English is not your first language. You should show them how special you are."

"I'm sorry, but what exactly do you mean by 'special'? I don't even have any publications yet. I tried to send out a couple of things, but they never got accepted."

"What I mean is that you're not like other people applying to PhD programs. There are many people applying who are from the US and who didn't have to learn English as a second language. People who didn't have to try as hard to get where you are. And even among the people who learned English as a second language, there are very few people from South America who are in the position that you are and who want to get a PhD. You're special."

I suddenly had flashbacks to the "special red chair for our special classmate from Bolivia who doesn't speak English," which my third-grade teacher had made me sit in during class upon my arrival to the United States. I hated the word *special*, and, to be honest, I still do. Yet I have to admit that this meeting with my mentor (along with it being the very first time I had a caramel macchiato at Starbucks) taught me a lesson that I would continue learning, unlearning, and relearning in academia: the struggles and experiences of marginalization that you worked so hard to mask or forget could often be the stories you want to or need to tell in order to be understood in academic spaces. The key, at least for me, is to understand how to tell these stories and to whom and, perhaps more importantly, to understand how to honor the stories of others as you decide whether and when it might be appropriate to share your own.

I did decide to mention my language-learning experiences in my applications to PhD programs, writing about the moment that I decided to major in English after my teacher didn't let me be in "advanced language arts" in middle school. I wrote about how my mom helped me with my homework and how we had to look up words in the English–Spanish dictionary in order to write my essays together. I explained how writing mattered to me because it was a time I got to spend with my mom—time that I now deeply long for.

And I got in! I got into a PhD program that would allow me to continue pursuing questions related to language, identity, and writing in my program and throughout my career. The interactions with my mentor in the coffee shop had been neither comfortable nor entirely helpful. I had left more confused than when I had arrived, and I had continued to worry about how or why I should talk about my previous experiences in an application to a PhD program. Yet in conversation with my previous experiences, with the teachings of my mentors, friends, and family, I began to put together my own story and my own entrance into academia, not always feeling as if I needed to hide who I was in order to be acknowledged. In a few months, I moved to Lansing, Michigan, leaving my sunny Florida home away from home.

Diversity on Paper

I firmly believe that many scholars and students from marginalized backgrounds don't really get to "go away to school," even when they're going away for a PhD program and when their family lives on another continent. I was in Michigan, going to new student orientation, no longer working at a grocery store, no longer teaching four classes per semester. Yet I was still what my dad continues to call me: "Laura, the mountain of the family," he says, "because everyone clings on to you."

My first year as a PhD student was the first time in my life when school was my only job—at least the only job I got paid to do. The rest of my life involved long family phone calls to figure out how to make my parents feel better about being so far away from their children, trips to Florida to see my brother and friends, and a constant juggling of stress, excitement, snow, and guilt. With the opportunity to focus on school more than ever, I began seeking opportunities to learn about new fields, new areas, and new places. With encouragement from my mentors, I began applying for awards and fellowships that sought to increase "diversity and inclusion" in areas such as technical communication, digital writing, computers and writing, and others. Indeed, within the first couple of years of being in my PhD program, I had been awarded several "diversity" grants that put me at the table with conference organizers and association leaders. The notion of being "special" continued to follow me, even as I admittedly applied to programs that I had no previous background or experience in. What made me "special" in a place I had never been to? And, again, what does the word mean in these contexts?

Soon I began to realize something that I continue both to struggle with and to leverage in my role in academia. With growing attention paid to diversity and inclusion, many academic spaces (e.g., conferences, professional organizations, publication venues) are feeling important and valuable pressure to include, welcome, and sustain (I hope) diverse participants (i.e., nonwhite/Western/male/cis/able-bodied). Important initiatives across my own fields and disciplines—rhetoric and composition, technical communication, computers, and composition—focus on supporting and sustaining diversity and inclusion after many years in which those fields remained largely homogenous. As I began learning about these fields and opportunities in my PhD program, I was incredibly grateful to be welcomed, encouraged, and supported in new areas (though, of course, all of my experiences weren't positive). Simultaneously, though, I realized that within these spaces I was still perceived as "special" on many levels. My presence and inclusion made (and continues to make) people simultaneously comfortable and uncomfortable. I am the "diversity" that helps organizations meet quotas, but I also remain largely inoffensive because of my whiteness. My practice in assimilation, linking back to those afternoons spent mouthing words in front of the bathroom mirror to mask my now nonexistent accent, has made me the perfect "diversity" candidate: I am diversity on paper, the diverse voice that is welcomed to the table so long as I continue to align with whiteness.

Acting Out the Vision

In her illustration of "the blow up" on the path to conocimiento, Gloria Anzaldúa tells the story of a conference on feminism that she attended where white women did not support and felt threatened by the voices of women of color who protested racist policies enacted by the sponsoring organization. As Anzaldúa explains, "Though most white feminists acknowledge racism, they distance themselves from personal responsibility, often acting as though their reality and ways of knowing are universal, not culturally determined. They assume that feminist racialized 'others' share their same values and goals. Some view gender and race oppression as interchangeable. As members of a colonized gender, they believe they're experts on oppression and can define all its forms; thus they don't have to listen/learn from others" ([2002] 2013, 564).

Although Anzaldúa appears to be discussing non-Latinx white women, I do think that white Latinas (myself included) can also fall into this pattern of claiming to understand oppression in all its forms, particularly if we don't take the time to listen to and build coalitions with others who do not share in our privilege. In my own journey, in realizing the comfort that my presence brings to white people in white spaces, I also recognize the fact that I will never fully "fit" in these spaces. My skin does not erase my history, my roots, and the ties to my communities that I continue to foster through love and relationality. As a white Latina, I benefit from privilege in many capacities, being perceived as a "safe" or comforting version of diversity to be welcomed in academia and other spaces of power. At the same time, bringing comfort to whiteness often yields microaggressions or hostility from people who can look at me and claim that I'm not a "real" Latina, that perhaps I am a "good" immigrant, or, worse, that if I am Latina, so are they, despite the fact that they have no roots in Latinx communities outside their own exploitive research. Bringing comfort to whiteness also does not take away from the fact that whereas in many academic spaces I am still "welcomed" and "invited," Black Latinas in the academy continue to be excluded, exploited, and erased.[2]

As I write this chapter, I'm thinking about a webinar I attended last night hosted by the Instituto de Liderazgo Simone de Beauvoir, a feminist-rights organization in Mexico City, Mexico.[3] The webinar was titled "Mujeres que resisten: Indígenas y Afromexicanas frente a la pandemia" (Women Who Resist: Indigenous and Afro-Mexican Women Facing the Pandemic). During this webinar, several Indigenous and Afro-Mexican women identified the coalition-building initiatives that their organizations and communities are undertaking to foster support for Indigenous and Afro-Mexican women during the COVID-19 pandemic. Several participants pointed to the fact that supporting Indigenous and Afro-Mexican women requires collaboration across boundary lines—across communities, racial and ethnic affiliations, gender identifications, government, businesses, nonprofit organizations, and more. At the same time, women leaders noted that these types of collaborations can take place only if the needs of the most marginalized are privileged. "We need to consider Indigenous and Afro-Mexican women with disabilities and our Indigenous and Afro-Mexican transgender hermanxs," the leading webinar participants exclaimed. This approach to collaboration has deep roots in Indigenous, Black, and Latinx/Chicanx epistemologies. And yet practicing collaboration and coalition building is often a process rife with mistakes. As we continue working toward these goals in and beyond academia, I believe that we as Latinas—and I'm talking here to my white Latina hermanas specifically—have to continue working toward centering the perspectives of the most marginalized in our communities, noting that this process of power redistribution does not mean that our own struggles and flaws are not valid or important. Rather than pushing to claim and reclaim mestizaje in a way that

2. See, for example, the case of the prolific Dr. Lorgia García Peña at Harvard University (Taylor 2020)

3. See the institute's website at https://ilsb.org.mx/quienes-somos/.

appeases whiteness, we should, as the Indigenous rhetorics scholar Gabriela Raquel Ríos (2016) continuously shows us, demonstrate where our values lie as Latinas, where we are willing to put up our privilege to combat anti-indigeneity and anti-Blackness. This, for me, is a constant and recursive process, one through which I continue to learn and grow.

References

Anzaldúa, Gloria. [2002] 2013. "Now Let Us Shift . . . the Path of Conocimiento . . . Inner Work, Public Acts." In *This Bridge We Call Home: Radical Visions for Transformation*, edited by Gloria Anzaldúa and AnaLouise Keating, 540–79. New York: Routledge.

Black Latinas Know Collective. 2019. "The Statement." Last modified Apr. 30. At https://www.blacklatinasknow.org.

Cobos, Casie C. 2012. "'An Other Chican@ Rhetoric from Scratch': (Re)Making Stories, (Un)Mapping the Lines, and Re-membering Bodies." PhD diss., Texas A&M Univ.

Driskill, Qwo-Li. 2016. *Asegi Stories: Cherokee Queer and Two-Spirit Memory*. Tucson: Univ. of Arizona Press.

Monberg, Terese Guinsatao. 2009. "Writing Home or Writing as Community: Toward a Theory of Recursive Spatial Movement for Students of Color in Service-Learning Courses." *Reflections* 8, no. 3: 21–51.

Moraga, Cherríe. [1981] 2015. "La Güera." In *This Bridge Called My Back: Writings by Radical Women of Color*, edited by Cherríe Moraga and Gloria Anzaldúa, 22–29. Albany: State Univ. of New York Press.

Ore, Ersula. 2016. "Pushback: A Pedagogy of Care." *Pedagogy* 17, no. 1: 9–33.

Ribero, Ana Milena, and Sonia C. Arellano. 2019. "Advocating *Comadrismo*: A Feminist Mentoring Approach for Latinas in Rhetoric and Composition." *Peitho* 21, no. 2: 334–56.

Ríos, Gabriela Raquel. 2016. "Mestizaje." In *Decolonizing Rhetoric and Composition Studies: New Latinx Keywords for Theory and Pedagogy*, edited by Iris D. Ruiz and Raúl Sànchez, 109–24. New York: Palgrave Macmillan.

Taylor, Kate. 2020. "Denying a Professor Tenure, Harvard Sparks a Debate over Ethnic Studies." *New York Times*, Jan. 2. At https://www.nytimes.com/2020/01/02/us/harvard-latinos-diversity-debate.html.

Torrez, J. Estrella. 2015. "Translating Chicana Testimonios into Pedagogy for a White Midwestern Classroom." *Chicana/Latina Studies* 14, no. 2: 101–30.

Walton, Rebecca, Kristen Moore, and Natasha Jones. 2019. *Technical Communication after the Social Justice Turn: Building Coalitions for Action.* New York: Routledge.

4

Research and Raices

Understanding Intersections of Self and Scholarship

Lorena Gutierrez

Abstract

In her book *Teaching to Transgress* (1994), bell hooks describes how her theorizing about Black feminism began when as a young child she questioned particular incidents in her life. I too began questioning and theorizing at a young age. I grew up in Colton, California, as the daughter of Mexican immigrant parents, Maria Elena and Gregorio Gutierrez, and the sister of Luselena, Eriberto, Leticia, and Veronica. It was here that my curiosity and desire to understand issues about language, identity, and the schooling experiences of culturally and linguistically diverse communities emerged. In this chapter, I share how my scholarly pursuits in language and literacy with migrant and seasonal farmworkers are grounded in my raices (roots)—a heritage of farmwork that extends across borders, time, and place—and in my experiences as an emerging bilingual.

Introduction

Mi madrecita querida has always loved to garden. Anything and everything she plants flourishes strongly and beautifully. Friends, family, and neighbors often come over and ask her for cuts of particular plants or ask her what she feeds them. Daily watering, trimming, cultivation of the soil, and love—lots of love—are secrets to her success. Droughts do not exist in her garden. Mother nature cannot tame this jardinera. After all, are there even seasons in Southern California?

77

As a young child in El Agostadero, Mascota, Jalisco, Mexico, my mother grew up in a family of sembradores, farmworkers. My abuelito Eduardo, her father, was a humble sembrador. Meanwhile, my abuelita Lucia, her mother, was a housewife. My abuelito had tilled the lands of a wealthy family of hacendados since the age of eight. Like many Mexican boys of his time, my abuelito was expected to contribute to the family when he became old enough to work. This was particularly true for him as the only male in a single-parent household. He faithfully cultivated land that was never his for more than sixty-five years. As the eldest of thirteen siblings, my mother helped her father till that land. She still recalls the backbreaking labor in the fields, and her voice fills with nostalgia, laughter, and tears as she recounts how she and her brother Chuy would pray to las ranitas (frogs) to bring rain and therefore send them home and away from the backbreaking work of la labor.

Only two hours south of El Agostadero was my father's hometown of Acatlán de Juárez. Like my mother, he too was deeply connected to land. As a young child, my father was sent to live with an uncle who owned a mango orchard. My father harvested sweet and fragrant manila mangoes. Although he transitioned to the heavens many years ago, I still remember him biting through the peel of mangoes while we kids would grimace at the thought of eating the peel. "La cascara también se come," he quickly reminded us. The smell and taste of mangoes were more than food. They were vehicles to memories of the past. La pisca y los recuerdos en la huerta.

Given the history of agriculture in my family, I have always wondered how the skills of la siembra, sowing and cultivating, skipped a generation with me. On various occasions, my mother has given me plants and instructed me on how to care for them. Many plants have passed on under my care if she has not rescued them beforehand. In the process of rescuing my plants, my mother has often replanted them in new and fertile soil. Replanting them can be a tough process, though. As you draw out the plant and expose its raices, you never know if it will thrive in new soil.

Flourishing in New Soil

As with plants, it was hard to say how my parents would grow in new soil when transplanted to the United States. Both migrated to the United States in the mid-1970s and met there through my mother's brother Chuy, who worked at a local diner with my father. They eventually settled in Colton, California, where they raised five children.

In this chapter, I use the metaphor of la siembra to critically reflect on the ways my voice, research, and scholarship are grounded in my raices as the daughter of Mexican immigrants, Maria Elena and Gregorio Gutierrez. I question what it means to grow up bilingual from Mexican immigrant parents and how that experience informs my scholarship and teaching. I invoke the legacies and intuition of the mujeres in my life, in particular my mother, Maria Elena, mi abuelita Lucia Peña, and my tía Lucia Torrez, who was the first to acknowledge my passion for literacy as an emerging bilingual. I write in hopes that my daughter, Camila, and other Latinx youth can look at their roots—histories, intergenerational knowledge, language, and culture—and know that excellence lives in them even when the sociopolitical times we live in say otherwise.

On My Block

I began theorizing about language, literacy, and identity at a young age in my humble home on Virginia Drive in Southern California. Spanish was the norm on Virginia Drive. Spanish was the language spoken in my home, the language of Marco Antonio "El Buki" Solis and Vicente Fernandez, whose music blared through my mother's kitchen radio; it was my first language and the language I identified with.

I was first exposed to English through my older sister, Luselena, and brother, Eriberto. Like many children of immigrants, they were exposed to English in school. I used to sit next to my sister while she spoke on the phone with friends, and I repeated everything she said. *Everything.* Thus, my first classroom of language learning was in the center of my home: the living room.

While Spanish was the norm in my home and neighborhood, public education quickly taught me another norm. Like many children of immigrants who spoke a language other than English in their home, I was placed in a Transitional Bilingual Education program in kindergarten. However, my twin sister was not. We grew up in the same home and spoke the same languages. Although I was too young to name what I was experiencing, my journey into public education reflected the ways of "emerging bilinguals": students who are learning English in school while functioning in their home language and who are, ultimately, in the process of becoming bilingual (García and Kleifgen 2010). As happened to me, emerging bilinguals face tracking and curricular differentiation in their educational journeys (Oakes 1986). Marcelo Suárez-Orozco and Carola Suárez-Orozco assert that "while on the surface language is about communication, it is also a marker of identity and an instrument of power" (2001, 135). Thus, language became a marker of difference for me at a young age. This difference was further demarcated as I began transitioning to mainstream classes in the third grade. The transition began slowly; I first visited a mainstream class for an hour a day, then two hours, and in the fourth grade I moved officially into the mainstream. During this transition, my friends still in the Transitional Bilingual Education program grew distant from me. "She's going to the smart classes!," my friend Olivia would comment. Although only eight years old at the time, Olivia had a sense of the ways that student intelligence and education were associated with particular groups of students and the English language. I was keenly aware that she was wrong because everyone in the bilingual education program was smart, too.

My experience is not an isolated one. Unfortunately, many emerging bilinguals and immigrant newcomers face segregation and isolation in their bilingual education programs, which are, more often than not, on the margins of their schools (Olsen 1997). Everything—from what language you speak to what accent you speak it with and what you wear—are perceived as indicators of how "American" you are (Olsen 1997).

In fourth grade, I lost contact with most of my friends and had to make new ones. The latter was tougher than learning a new language. No matter how much I tried, I could never fit in with my peers and new friends in the mainstream classes. I always had the sense that I wasn't one of them. Although as a child I blamed myself for not fitting in, over the years I have learned that the prejudice and stigma suffered by emerging bilinguals is systematically perpetuated and sustained in policy and practice (García, Wiese, and Cuéllar 2011). In 1998, Proposition 227 in California changed the way emerging bilinguals were taught, specifically students who were at the time identified as having limited English proficiency. Rather than seeing students' home languages as an asset, Prop 227 worked to suppress students' home languages as rapidly as possible and to teach them English within a year until it was repealed by Prop 58 in 2016. It is no coincidence that once students are identified as emerging bilinguals, it becomes very difficult for them to grow out of that designation and move beyond the bilingual track.

Language Brokering

Although forming peer relationships in school was challenging for me, in my home and neighborhood I was on high demand. My mother, our vecinas, and my tías had me translating anything from utility bills to homework and mail, to name only a few things. I drew on Spanish and English not only to translate but also to read between the lines as I read the world around me. Even though I had older siblings who could translate, my brother was not expected to contribute to household duties inside the home. Meanwhile, my older sister had become a mother and moved out of the house. Therefore, I was left responsible for helping my mother run the house. Of the many times I was a language and cultural broker for my mother, I cannot forget about one particular experience.

As a construction worker, my father often endured seasons of unemployment. Spring, summer, and fall tended to be filled with job opportunities. Winter could be a hit or an overwhelming miss. This particular year had been rough, and my parents were forced to consider applying for federal assistance, including food stamps and Medi-Cal. For them, *this was a last resort.* My mother put her pride aside and went to the county offices to apply, with my twin sister and me in tow. It took us more than an hour to get to the offices by bus even though they were in our city. "Take a number," a security guard told us as we walked in. We took a number and sat down in the midst of families waiting their turn. Once our number was called, we were faced with a white social worker who handed my mother a thick stack of paperwork to fill out on a clipboard and instructed her to return it to her when completed. My mother nodded to affirm that she understood the social worker, but when we turned away from her, my mother leaned into me and asked, "¿Que dijo?" I quickly translated as we sat down to fill out the many pages of paperwork. Of course, it was in English—another difficult and time-intensive challenge to get through.

When we gave the social worker our completed paperwork, we were greeted with unwelcoming glances as she flipped through the stack to see if all was complete. Upon finding an incomplete section, the social worker looked at my mother and asked, "Why didn't you fill this out?" My mother turned to me, not understanding what was being asked of her. As I translated, the social worker's body language and condemning smirks became evident. "We don't have the information with us to fill out that section. We can bring it tomorrow," I replied. The social worker didn't pay attention to the words coming out of my mouth. She was too busy boiling over to say, "Speak English. We're in America!" She looked straight at my mother with this statement. The body language, the tone, and the stares were universal. No translation required. My mother understood exactly what was being said, as many immigrants have faced this same violence. The lack of recognition and dehumanization that occurs through this type of violence reflects the racist nativist discourses that affect the daily lives of Latinx immigrants. Lindsay Pérez Huber defines racist nativist discourses as "the institutionalized ways people perceive, understand, and make sense of contemporary U.S. immigration, which assigns values to real or imagined differences, that justifies the perceived superiority and dominance of the native (whites) and reinforces hegemonic power" (2011, 382). The perception of Latinxs as criminals, foreigners, or threats to "American" identity is just one example of what racist nativist discourses look like. When theorizing how violence is enacted on the oppressed by the oppressor, Paulo Freire argues that "violence is initiated by those who oppress, who exploit, who fail to recognize others as persons—not by those who are oppressed, exploited, and unrecognized" (2000, 55). Everything about our interaction with the social worker was violence grounded in racist nativism. The gestures, the commentary, the tone, her incessant need to remind us what language she believed we needed to speak, and her burgeoning desire to insist on teaching us what country we were in, as though we were not citizens of this country—all reflected violent racist nativism. While my mother had swallowed her pride to apply for government assistance, her dignity was snatched away without a moment's notice.

What I didn't know then is that these acts of racist nativism against Latinxs happen everywhere, especially in institutions of authority such as health-care facilities and social service offices as well as with public officials such as police officers (Urciuoli 1996). Experiences like this one marked my life and cemented my commitment to fighting for people's right to their own language and to educating folks about the connections among language, power, culture, and identity.

With my mother, I lived the day-to-day trials and triumphs of living and learning across language and culture. For an immigrant Spanish speaker, navigating a country where English is the language of power is anything but easy (Macedo 2000). I witnessed condescending smirks and comments toward my mother when she could not speak English. These types of interactions are not new; language has historically been a source of stigma for Latinxs in the United States (García Bedolla 2003). As I grew older, I became very good at navigating these situations for her, yet I also desired to do something about the injustices I saw her face. For my father, speaking Spanish was a means to preserve culture and instill a sense of pride in our Mexican raices. For many Latinxs in the United States, Spanish can be a source of pride in one's Latinx identity (García Bedolla 2003).

"Aquí se habla Español"

My father was always intentional about ensuring that his children spoke Spanish. When English made its way into our home, he never failed to remind us, "Aquí se habla Español." He said it was important for us to speak Spanish "porque somos Mexicanos." One of my most vivid memories of the ways that my father taught us about the importance of culture was when he took my brother, twin sister, and me to a powwow in Southern California. It was rare when we had a family car that we all could fit in, but the tight squeeze did not stop him from taking us on a family outing. He loaded three of us up in the cab of his construction dump truck (which fit only three passengers at a time when seat belt safety regulations were rarely enforced) with a few blankets to spend the night at the powwow. Upon arriving, we saw many ceremonial dances performed by Indigenous tribal community leaders. As we observed the ceremonies, my father told us about the ways that Indigenous communities had survived colonization and attempts to erase their culture. However, they preserved their language, ceremonies, oral traditions, and cultural ways of being. My father connected their histories and survivance (Vizenor 1994) to his belief in the importance of speaking Spanish. However, he was not supportive of language practices such as speaking Spanglish and weaving in and out of English and Spanish.

If I was overheard weaving in and out of English and Spanish, he would ask point-blank, "¿Vas hablar Español o Inglés?" His questioning made me feel forced to choose one language over the other. In our home, we were to speak Spanish only and avoid any language mixing, at least when he was around to hear us. Choosing between languages made me feel the weight and complexity of belonging to two different cultures. Ni soy de aquí, ni soy de allá. I didn't feel the "aquí" when people such as the social worker made my mother and I feel like foreigners in this country. But weaving in and out of Spanish and English and creating new words in Spanglish defied what my father defined to be "de allá." To be "de allá" meant speaking Spanish. To be "de aquí" meant speaking English. This experience at the crux of cultural borderlands is beautifully depicted in Gloria Anzaldúa's book *Borderlands / La Frontera* (1987).

Through the difficult experiences I lived with my mother and my father's insistence that we speak Spanish as a means of preserving culture, I developed an interest in understanding the relationship among language, identity, and culture. I pursued these interests in graduate school, and they continue to be part of the reason why I entered the professoriate.

Cultivating Scholarship in Graduate School

As a graduate student, I volunteered with Michigan State University's High School Equivalency Program (HEP). HEP serves migrant and seasonal farmworkers in attaining their General Educational Development, or GED, degree. Although I initially volunteered with the intent of finding a Latinx community on campus, the students quickly became more than community. They sustained me and motivated me to persist in my doctoral program. However, I often wondered how I could relate to their experience when I had never engaged in farmwork and had never been highly mobile. I often felt like an imposter to their experience.

One of the many students I met was Andrés, an eighteen-year-old Mexican American who was employed in seasonal farm work. Andrés was originally from San Diego, California, but due to the violence in the neighborhood where his family lived, his mother decided to move their family to Michigan. Andres was a participant in my study about the educational experiences and language practices of youth migrant and seasonal farmworkers in the Midwest. I had the good fortune of meeting Andrés during a community service event at a homeless shelter. Although both of us had been in program spaces together, we had never talked in depth until we were serving salad and biscuits at a soup kitchen with other HEP students and staff. In between serving warm meals to the hungry on a wintery evening, Andrés reintroduced himself and explained that he had enrolled in the program after being disciplined for speaking Spanish in high school and then getting kicked out. At school, he had often attempted to translate for newly arrived Latinx classmates who spoke little to no English, but his teachers had disapproved of his language brokering (Alvarez 2014), and this upset Andrés. When asked why he would get upset when teachers demanded that he speak only English in class, he said, "I get really mad when they [teachers] tell me I can't speak Spanish. . . . When they would yell at students who didn't speak English, I would stick up for them because they didn't understand what they were telling them, and I would tell them. They [the students] would tell me that it's okay, to just be quiet . . . and it would get me mad how they [the students] didn't understand, but they were still being yelled at."

"Why would you get mad?," I asked.

"Just 'cause my mom doesn't speak English, and she's gotten yelled [at] before," he answered. "When we're out and about, we've been told to go back to Mexico, and stuff like that gets me mad, and putting my mom in that position gets me mad."

My heart sank. I knew this experience too well. He had explained how he felt when his high school teachers in rural southern Michigan would not allow him to speak Spanish and the way he would defend the emerging bilinguals in his class. Prior to the program, Andrés had been kicked out of public school multiple times. He credited the negative consequences (i.e., multiple detentions and suspensions) of resisting the de facto English-only policy in his high school as the reason why he was disciplined out of school. Andrés eventually grew tired of his teachers enforcing an English-only rule and disengaged from school. He refused to participate in class and relied on his peers to answer questions about class content and assignments. He ultimately transitioned to HEP during his senior year of high school after learning about it through one of his teachers in a rural Michigan farming town.

I could see myself reflected in him as he shared the source of his frustration and anger. Although the contexts of our situations were different, we shared the experience of being linguistic brokers and witnessing violent remarks directed toward our mothers. I could not fathom continuing the interview because Andrés's experience hit too

1. Sembrando la tierra, circa 1967. Jose Martin Salcedo (*left*), Lorena Gutierrez's uncle, and Eduardo Salcedo (*right*), her abuelito, in the fields of El Agostadero, Mascota, Jalisco, Mexico.

close to home. For some researchers, this conversation would be just another interview. Researchers are expected to remain objective, after all. For me, though, interviews reveal people's lives, and culturally, racially, and linguistically diverse people experience these uncalled-for situations too often. The interview ended soon after that. I thanked Andrés for his time and for having the confianza to share his life experiences with me. I packed my things and drove away on Michigan's slippery and frosty roads. That day and every time I have listened to the recording of his interview, I am transported to the twelve-year-old Lorena Gutierrez, who grew up helping her mother navigate spaces and people that were not prepared to serve Spanish-speaking communities, such as schools, welfare offices, and banks, by translating for her. And those situations never cease to occur. Language brokering is a part of me. It's what I do.

Although I felt like an outsider to the experiences of migrant and seasonal farmworkers, talking with them and studying their language, literacy, and educational experiences taught me how similar we truly are. While writing my dissertation, I developed a strong desire to visit my abuelito Eduardo in El Agostadero. I felt stuck in the writing process, and El Agostadero kept calling me. I even shared this desire with my adviser and mentor and was advised to listen to my gut. I didn't listen, though. Unfortunately, it wasn't until my abuelito broke his hip during the summer of 2014 that I went to see him. I spent two weeks caring for him in June 2014 after hip surgery kept him in bed for weeks. Coincidentally, he was recovering from surgery as the men in town who worked as sembradores awaited las lluvias. The first lluvia in June was commonly known as Mother Nature's signal that it was time to sembrar. My grandpa knew this because he had spent sixty-five years of his life working in the fields. One morning we were awoken by rain. The sembradores rode past on their horses to work in the fields, while my abuelito somberly stared out the window of his room and watched his close friends and fellow sembradores ride off to plant the season's harvest. Although I knew that the fields were important to the lives of the migrant and seasonal workers that I worked with, witnessing my abuelito miss las lluvias y la siembra crystallized the meaning of farmwork and the fields in the lives of those who participated in my research. Working in the fields is a source of knowledge, experience, and connection to la Madre Tierra. It is what my abuelito knew best. Mother Earth was his teacher, his lifetime companion. The fields had made it possible to feed his children, including my mother, the oldest of thirteen. The fields had embraced him with open arms when his children had grown up and migrated to the United States and when his life partner, my abuelita Lucia, had departed to the heavens. Being with the land was his daily ceremony.

Unbeknownst to me earlier, I needed to experience this to remind me that I, too, have a heritage of farmwork in my family. I witnessed it in my grandfather's eyes as he yearned for the fields, and I experience it in every bite of the sweet guayaba that my mother has so passionately grown every year since I can remember. After all, the fields that my abuelito tilled are named "El Guayabo." I smell it in every plumería my mother prides herself in growing. I remember it in the mangoes my dad would eat, in the stories he would share, and in my visit to la huerta de mangos after my father passed away. I am no imposter to the fields. It runs in my blood, in my history. Robin Wall Kimmerer states that "a people's story moves along like a canoe caught in the current, being carried closer and closer to where we had begun" (2013, 36). And so throughout my own journey as a Latina scholar and leader, I have been the canoe being carried closer and closer to the heritage of farmwork in fields that my family and ancestors have gifted me with. However, as generations have passed, the fields have changed for us. For my abuelito, the fields were in Mexico; for my parents, the fields became the United States; and for me, the fields are the classroom.

La Siembra in the Classroom

My fields have ranged from a surround-sound, dimly lit university movie theater to traditional classrooms and, most recently, digital online spaces for learning. I never planned to teach online, but COVID-19 forced most K–12 schools and institutions of higher education into emergency online learning. China started experiencing COVID-19 in December 2019, and the virus rapidly made its way to Europe and the United States. It was not until March 10, 2020, that I realized the gravity of COVID-19: campus events were canceled or postponed, and my students were coming to class worried about the pandemic. It was the last week of classes for the winter quarter, and everyone was ready for spring break. However, the pandemic did away with our plans. *Everyone's plans.* In-person finals, canceled. Spring break trips, canceled. Life plans, canceled. People swarmed the stores for essential items to get through the quarantine. Face masks became an essential and required thing to wear in public. Employees were laid off everywhere you turned. In April 2020, unemployment rates skyrocketed to 14 percent nationally, and more than twenty-one million people were unemployed because of the COVID-19 pandemic (US Bureau of Labor Statistics 2020). Businesses closed until further notice. Learning and working moved into our sacred spaces at home with little to no time for us to prepare. Everyone knew someone who had COVID-19, or they themselves had the virus. People lost loved ones to the pandemic. A global pandemic is in full effect (the pandemic is still ongoing as I write). And yet many K–12 schools and institutions of higher education chose to continue business "as usual" by moving learning to online platforms. Within the University of California system, students, staff, and faculty faced the challenge of ending the winter quarter and beginning the spring quarter at the onset of the pandemic.

Teaching at this time was both a heart-wrenching challenge and a calling home. Initially, I thought it would be difficult to connect with students through distance learning. However, the trauma experienced with the pandemic and the deaths of George Floyd, Breonna Taylor, and others at the hands of police brought us closer than ever before. At the University of California, Riverside, 56.3 percent of students are first-generation college students in their families, 42.8 percent are low income, and more than 70 percent are Hispanic, Asian, Black, or Indigenous (University of California 2019). The demographics of students at Riverside are among those most affected by COVID-19. Thus, teaching this quarter required empathy, strong networks of care, and a grounding of myself in who I am and the values instilled in me. Ana Milena Ribero and Sonia C. Arellano (2019) capture these elements as they advocate for comadrismo as a feminist framework for Latina mentorship (see chapter 1 in this volume). I draw from Ribero and Arellano's elements of comadrismo to give my testimonio and to make sense of how I was able to teach in humanizing ways during the pandemic.

Empathy in the Pandemic: "We Will Get through This Together"

Leading up to the first day of class of the spring quarter in 2020, I struggled to work on course syllabi and to figure out how to start my courses knowing that *everyone*—my students, my teaching assistants, me, and rest of the world—were literally on survival mode because of COVID-19. On the first day of class, I chose to be transparent about the impact of the pandemic on my own life. During our first synchronous class meeting on Zoom, I told my students: "I am not okay, we are not okay. We will get through this together." I explained how the pandemic was bringing me to tears on a daily basis, how I was not sleeping well, how worried I was about family members getting COVID-19, and how uncomfortable I felt pursuing "business as usual" within the university when the lives of my students, their families, and my own were at stake. Although I was concerned about sharing too much about myself with my students, I had to be vulnerable and transparent about my own experience living in the time of COVID-19 if I expected them to share their experiences as well.

Many of my undergraduate students lost their jobs, or immediate family members were laid off until further notice. Others were concerned about catching COVID-19 and that their loved ones would get the virus. Some students had a difficult time focusing on schoolwork because they were also tasked with teaching their children at home (because public schools were closed) on top of being full-time students and caregivers. Others were adjusting to learning from home with family members always around and with limited space to complete schoolwork. And most painfully, a pair of twin sisters lost their father to COVID-19. I learned about these situations only because I opened the door for students to share these experiences with me when I shared my own. Knowing the challenges my students were facing allowed me to put myself in their shoes and to teach from a place of empathy. Ribero and Arellano characterize empathy like this: "Empathy comes with the urgency to persevere, not through assimilation but through strategies that sustain the soul" (2019, 348). For me, sustaining the soul meant grounding myself in the organic way of teaching and caring for others that is deeply entrenched in the fields that my family sowed. Each and every time my abuelito, mother, or father planted a seed in their fields, they tilled the soil to make sure it was the correct environment for their harvest to grow in; they consistently nourished the land with water and abono (fertilizer); they trimmed what was no longer needed; and they patiently awaited the harvest. Teaching with empathy meant extending myself beyond what is expected of me as a professor and working from the root of my core as the daughter of Elena and Gregorio Gutierrez, the granddaughter of Eduardo Salcedo, and the mother of Camila. In order to sustain my own soul and those of my students during a time of global crisis,

I too had to figure out what environment my students would thrive in, find ways to nourish them, and await the harvest of their efforts. *La siembra is in my blood.* Teaching during COVID-19 required that I work from the heart to help my students persevere in humanizing ways. It meant drawing upon the teachings, values, and legacy of my ancestors, despite knowing that they are not valued in the institution of academia. *This was a calling home.*

Teaching during a pandemic became a calling home literally and metaphorically. Teaching from home with a toddler always present became a challenge that required my mother's help. I would go over to her house, the home in which I grew up, with my daughter in hand to work in any space I could find while my mother watched her. My sister's room, the kitchen table, the couch, and my mother's backyard became my work spaces. Office hours, live lectures, and faculty meetings were held there. Some of the most difficult moments in teaching were held there, including phone calls with grieving students and their family members. This crisis was literally a calling home. Working in my childhood home, surrounded by family.

Metaphorically, I was called home to ground myself in my raices. *My history, my family, and my values are my raices.* Although empathizing with my students comes easily to me, empathizing with myself does not. Teaching during the pandemic meant that I often found myself wanting to do what I would normally do as a professor: meeting my learning objectives, assessing student learning, and meeting the expectations the university has for me as a professor, among many other things. Doing all of this, however, is continuing business as usual. I was torn between honoring my students' lives during a pandemic and doing business as usual. The mujeres in my life held me accountable, though. My mother, sisters, teaching assistants—Tanisha Johnson, Margarita Vizcarra, and Amy Scott Williams—and my hermana del alma, Amal Ibourk, kept me grounded. The weekly meetings with my teaching assistants were more like sister circles, where at the beginning of every meeting we shared a rose, a positive experience or moment of joy, and a thorn, a difficulty or struggle, in our lives. Some of us struggled to work from home as mother-scholars of color, others worried about loved ones who were essential workers, and we all attempted to cope with the pandemic and the social outrage that erupted after the murder of George Floyd and Breonna Taylor at the hands of police. My students and I were experiencing similar roses and thorns, and anytime I swerved toward business as usual, my teaching assistants would remind me, "We're in a pandemic!"

No matter how many years of teaching experience I had, nothing prepared me to deal with the level of grief my students faced this quarter. Grief is the pain of loss. Although many associate grief with the personal loss of a loved one, grief during the pandemic was felt not only for the loss of loved ones but for graduation ceremonies that were called off, plans postponed, expectations lowered, and employment desired or dreaded (depending on your perspective). I witnessed students grieving time and time again and attempted to support them as best I could. Although I wanted students to master course content, attending to their grief and needs was my top priority. Abraham Harold Maslow (1943) argues that people's physiological, safety, and security needs, love and belonging needs, and need for esteem must be met in order for them to reach a level of self-actualization where their full potential can be reached. Knowing Maslow's hierarchy of needs, I could not teach without acknowledging my students' needs.

Witnessing their grief became a secondhand trauma for me that was difficult to bear. Amal Ibourk heard me and supported me during our daily Zoom work meetings when the weight of this secondhand trauma was overwhelming me to tears. She gave me advice on how to teach online and kept me accountable to getting work done when the roller coaster of emotions that accompanied the pandemic plunged down a hill. My mother prayed for my students and their families when I shared news that the father of three of my students had COVID-19 and, unfortunately, had passed away. She listened to me when I shared that I was at a loss for words for my students. As someone who lost her father at a young age, I knew there were no words to alleviate the pain my students felt. She saw in me how their loss triggered my own grief.

The examples of the women who supported me as I taught during the pandemic reflect the importance of kinship and networks of care in times of crisis. Ribero and Arellano (2019) affirm the importance of empathy, kinship, and networks of care in the mentoring of Latina scholars. My networks of care and the kinship that were fostered throughout the pandemic sustained me as a Latina scholar in ways I did not even know I needed. These women and my ancestors called me home to center myself on who I am, what matters most, and what my purpose is. Being true to who you are, knowing your gifts have been with you all along, receiving support and reciprocating it, and acting with love and courage to be of service to others are what make a Latina leader.

The Harvest

Those who work in the fields may or may not see the harvest they have so carefully cultivated with love, patience, and backbreaking labor. The person who plants the seed is oftentimes not around long enough to see it flourish. As an educator, I face this situation every time I teach. I plant the seeds of knowledge, love, and care, but not all seeds flourish in their time with me. Kimmerer captures my sentiments with her words: "Knowing her grandchildren would inherit the world she left behind, she did not work for flourishing in her time only. It was through her actions of reciprocity, the give and take with the land, that the original immigrant became indigenous. For all of us, becoming indigenous to a place means living as if your children's future mattered, to take care of the land as if our lives, both material and spiritual, depended on it" (2013, 9).

As I reflect on the legacy of farmwork that was left to me by my abuelo, my father, and my mother and that is now my own, I am reminded that the siembra is not just about the harvest, as Kimmerer suggests. Rather, it is about the process: the tilling, the planting, the watering, the pruning, and the harvesting. It involves reciprocity, intentions for growth, and a commitment to take care of the land. Although the grief and pain of secondhand trauma are still raw and present, I taught knowing that no amount of assignments, reading, or intellectualizing would preserve my students' humanity during a global pandemic. I taught knowing that their lives mattered: physically, mentally, spiritually, and emotionally. I modeled what it looked like to teach with love, care, and empathy so that they can do so for the children who will inherit a life after COVID-19. I taught knowing that our whole beings mattered, not just the academic parts of ourselves. Our physical, mental, emotional, spiritual, and material lives depended on our ability to see each other for who we are at this time of crisis. I taught as if their lives depended on me, and at times I depended on them. I taught knowing I had more tears in my eyes than answers. I hope that my tears in such trying times will foster compassionate, present, and loving educators who will pay it forward to their own students, families, and communities. My teaching, research, and scholarship are the fruit of my abuelito's wildest dreams and my parents' cosecha.

References

Alvarez, Steven. 2014. "Translanguaging Tareas: Emergent Bilingual Youth as Language Brokers for Homework in Immigrant Families." *Language Arts* 91, no. 5: 326–39.

Anzaldúa, Gloria. 1987. *Borderlands / La Frontera: The New Mestiza*. San Francisco: Aunt Lute Books.

Freire, Paulo. 2000. *Pedagogy of the Oppressed*. Translated by Myra Bergman Ramos. New York: Continuum.

García, Eugene E., Ann-Marie Wiese, and Delis Cuéllar. 2011. "Language, Public Policy, and Schooling: A Focus on Chicano English Language Learners." In *Chicano School Failure and Success: Past, Present, and Future*, 3rd ed., edited by Richard R. Valencia, 143–59. New York: Routledge

García, Ofelia, and Jo Anne Kleifgen. 2010. *Educating Emergent Bilinguals: Policies, Programs, and Practices for English Language Learners*. New York: Teachers College Press.

García Bedolla, Lisa. 2003. "The Identity Paradox: Latino Language, Politics, and Selective Dissociation." *Latino Studies* 1, no. 2: 264–83.

hooks, bell. 1994. *Teaching to Transgress: Education as the Practice of Freedom*. New York: Routledge.

Huber, Lindsay Pérez. 2011. "Discourses of Racist Nativism in California Public Education: English Dominance as Racist Nativist Microaggressions." *Educational Studies* 47, no. 4: 379–401.

Kimmerer, Robin Wall. 2013. *Braiding Sweetgrass: Indigenous Wisdom, Scientific Knowledge, and the Teachings of Plants.* Minneapolis: Milkweed Press.

Macedo, Donaldo. 2000. "The Colonialism of the English Only Movement." *Educational Researcher* 29, no. 3: 15–24.

Maslow, Abraham Harold. 1943. "A Theory of Human Motivation." *Psychological Review* 50, no. 4: 370–96.

Oakes, Jeannie. 1986. "Keeping Track, Part 1: The Policy and Practice of Curriculum Inequality." *Phi Delta Kappan* 68, no. 1: 12–17.

Olsen, Laurie. 1997. *Made in America: Immigrant Students in Our Public School.* New York: New Press.

Ribero, Ana Milena, and Sonia C. Arellano. 2019. "Advocating *Comadrismo*: A Feminist Mentoring Approach for Latinas in Rhetoric and Composition." *Peitho* 21, no. 2: 334–56.

Suárez-Orozco, Marcelo, and Carola Suárez-Orozco. 2001. *Children of Immigration.* Cambridge, MA: Harvard Univ. Press.

University of California, Riverside. 2019. "Enrollments: Demographics." At https://ir.ucr.edu/stats/enroll/demographic.

Urciuoli, Bonnie. 1996. *Exposing Prejudice: Puerto Rican Experiences of Language, Race, and Class.* Boulder, CO: Westview Press.

US Bureau of Labor Statistics, Department of Labor. 2020. "The Employment Situation: May 2020." At https://www.bls.gov/news.release/pdf/empsit.pdf.

Vizenor, Gerald Robert. 1994. *Manifest Manners: Postindian Warriors of Survivance.* Hanover, CT: Wesleyan Univ. Press.

Part Two

Research, Recovery, and Learning from Our Histories

5

Building Stories and Changing Spaces

Mentoring in the Archives

Stefani Baldivia and Kendall Leon

Abstract

This chapter articulates a Latinx mentoring approach that takes the form of institutional change making through creating counterstories in university archives. More specifically, this form of mentoring centers on three things: (1) recognizing that stories make change, (2) changing institutions by changing the stories of those institutions, (3) and empowering students by sharing tools and approaches to building stories that connect students with their home communities. The authors encourage sharing counterstories of mentoring that empower women of color in leadership roles to self-define meaningful work to celebrate a diversity of experiences and a breadth of interests.

Introduction: Mentoring beyond the Individual

Institutions are rhetorical entities made up of people, practices, and stories. As women of color who practice Latinx mentoring on a college campus,[1] we know that the stories making up the work and

---

1. As archivists and rhetors, we understand the importance of naming and labeling. As Christina Cedillo powerfully states in the interview of her in chapter 6, at times she also identifies as "a Latina when I want to show solidarity with women whose roots are also in Latin America . . . [and also as] Indigenous, though not Native, because it's important for me to honor the experiences and struggles of the peoples who still speak the original languages and live the original ways and who,

learning spaces we inhabit are often told from the top down. Mentoring likewise often takes a vertical approach, with a more experienced mentor guiding the development of, as in our cases, a student (Lechuga-Peña and Lechuga 2018). As Ana Milena Ribero and Sonia C. Arellano (2019) argue, the normalized academic mentoring model is one based on white middle-class norms, which presumably disavow mentoring practices that are more attuned to the needs and experiences of women of color. Fortunately, in our own lives we have had women-of-color mentors who have shared their expertise in navigating what feels like the unwelcoming landscape of education. These mentoring relationships typically enact what Ribero and Arellano describe as practices of comadrismo, which "is built upon a trusting kinship relationship and functions among women with deep commitments to anti-racist work" (2019, 336; see also chapter 1 in this volume). We can attest to the positive impact of this kind of mentoring that aligns with our whole experiences as women of color on white-dominant campuses and with our pedagogical and activist commitments. At the same time, the data show that there are not enough of us in higher education to fill these roles, with only 2 percent of Latinos successfully obtaining a doctoral degree in 2016–17, a statistic that does not account for gender (Excelencia in Education 2019, 28). In fact, we all are likely aware of the fact that "Latinas have the lowest percentage of graduate degrees compared to all women of other non-Hispanic racial groups combined" (Gándara 2015, 10). Furthermore, as other contributors to this collection demonstrate, this form of mentoring may perpetuate the invisible burden of the labor of one-on-one mentoring that educators of color find themselves taking on, mostly out of the kindness of our hearts

---

therefore, are especially culturally, linguistically, and racially marginalized in the US and Mexico." We are grateful for her articulation of what we have struggled to clearly explain. We extend her language to claim Latinx mentoring as mentoring that moves outside the individual and is inherently relational.

but equally often because institutions "fix" the problem of racism through exceptionalizing a few.[2]

In response, our mentoring approach, as we outline in this chapter, takes the form of institutional change making through creating counterstories. More specifically, our mentoring centers on (1) recognizing that stories make change, (2) changing institutions by changing the stories of those institutions, (3) and empowering students by sharing tools and approaches to building stories that connect students with their home communities. A *counterstory*, as Aja Martinez writes, "functions as a method for marginalized people to intervene in research methods that would form 'master narratives' based on ignorance and on assumptions about minoritized peoples like Chican@s" (2014, 53). As this ignorance shapes our experiences in academic spaces, it results in misunderstanding how best to teach and mentor marginalized students (and academic professionals) as well as in erasing their experiences in how we define and identify our institutions. One such research method that perpetuates the master narrative involves the approach taken to building an institution's archival collection.

Creating and maintaining an archival collection are not neutral activities because "those with the most power and wealth in society will dominate the field of knowledge, so that it serves their interests," and collections are frequently built to "maintain the existing social order by perpetuating its values, by legitimizing its priorities, by justifying its wars, perpetuating its prejudices, contributing to its xenophobia, and apologizing for its class order" (Zinn 1977, 18). Archives, then, can be considered both a record and a mechanism of power and control. Collections reflect *and* produce dominant ideologies. Conversely, historiographic stories can also be an educational space to learn about collective resistant practices.[3] Latinx students respond

2. See chapter 3 in this collection on Laura Gonzales's experience of being identified as "special" because of her cultural and linguistic background.

3. See chapter 7 by Michelle Hall Kells in this collection for further discussion about the transformative impact of archives.

positively to relationship-based affirmations that "foster a learning environment that is welcoming, familiar, and safe for students who have been historically underserved in education" (Covarrubias, Herrmann, and Fryberg 2016, 55). Research illustrates a positive correlation between academic achievement and mentoring for Latinx and Indigenous students that emphasizes their interdependent relationships (Fryberg, Covarrubias, and Burack 2013). As Latinx mentors, our work has sought to affirm the strengths of our students as members of larger communities—relating their classwork to their home environment or campus community. When we are faced with institutions full of folks not like us, with few mentors available, within systems that seem impenetrable, these historiographic stories function as "testimonios." As Laura Gonzales explains in chapter 3 of this volume, "Testimonios . . . are stories of embodied knowledge and expertise that illustrate cultural histories and lived experiences in/and community." The collecting of these testimonios may function transgressively in two ways: as an instructive narrative and as a resistant methodology.

In our own scholarly and personal journeys as women-of-color academics, testimonios we gleaned from the archives taught us resistant tactics and the power of identification. We first share with you our stories of developing our critical and resistant identities, which we learned through archival stories, before we adopted this stance methodologically to build such collections as resistant practice.

Our Stories: Personal and Institutional

Kendall's Story

I grew up surrounded by demoralizing stories of failure, falsehoods, and violence. In our family narrative, women and an internalized cultural hatred were to blame for all of our family problems with drug abuse and poverty. Shame and avoidance of agency were the threads in our family tapestry. Shame also demarcated my geographic community. I was raised in low-income housing in the "bad" neighborhood that had been banished from the rest of the city. Surrounded on all parts by the city, our neighborhood was considered county land, which meant that city services such as sidewalks stopped at the boundary of our neighborhood. It took only about twenty minutes to walk to the university campus from my house, yet our neighborhood and the campus felt worlds apart. Growing up, I was always good in school, but I found myself making the choices that I felt I was destined to make. After running away from home at sixteen to escape the sexist violence, I lived with numerous friends and started working all sorts of jobs to support myself so that I could at least graduate from high school. By some sheer luck, the mother of my boyfriend at the time took him and me to the local college to apply during open-admissions day. It still astounds me twenty-plus years later that I am now a faculty member at that same college.

My entire college career felt like a series of chance moments that forever altered my trajectory. Like Laura Gonzales in this collection, I never thought of who I was or my background as anything "special" or as an asset. I focused on surviving, which often meant that I hid this part of me, as I still do today. I felt disconnected from my own heritage communities and from my new university community. Because I chose to leave home and gain an education, I was ostracized; because I was a first-generation college student of color, I felt alienated on campus.

Again, through what at the time felt like sheer luck, I was later accepted to a PhD program that allowed for cross-disciplinary work. It was because of this program that I was encouraged to engage in an archival research project on the mundane professional writing of a Chicana feminist organization, the Comisión Femenil Mexicana Nacional, which built Chicana activism. It was through my reading of these stories at one of the University of California's (UC) special collections, the California Ethnic Minority Archives at UC Santa Barbara, that I came to build my own Chicana identity.

As I read the testimonios of the comisión's leaders who made Chicanidad through their organization, I learned what it meant to be an agent and to make change as a person who is treated as nonagential and in spaces where people of color typically inhabit the margins. These mujeres became my mentors in the way they made their identity and not just wore it as a label; rather, they intentionally made and remade and negotiated what it meant to embody that identity in practice. It was through their testimonios, captured in this special collection, that I came to claim Chicana identity—as a resistant, active subject.

Stefani's Story

I am a first-generation scholar who identifies as Chicana and serves as an archivist for the Meriam Library Special Collections and University Archives Department at California State University, Chico. My undergraduate degree is in Native American studies, so I was mentored by both Indigenous (Yurok, Lakota, Tolowa) and Chicano faculty who helped me formulate a decolonial critical pedagogy. One professor in particular introduced me to the Ejército Zapatista de Liberación Nacional, or the EZLN, an Indigenous uprising in response to the implementation of the North American Free Trade Agreement in 1994. The EZLN made known to the world its ideology of anti-imperialist, libertarian socialism, guided by Indigenous Mayan beliefs, with an armed paramilitary uprising, which has since evolved into an autonomous political infrastructure. The Zapatista critique of neoliberal capitalism and Zapatista women's analysis of patriarchy within the Mexican state's "mal gobierno" in particular appealed to me as a Chicana from a low-income, food- and housing-insecure Southern Californian home who was recently thrust into a predominantly white northern California state school.

I grew up in San Bernardino, in the heart of the Inland Empire in Southern California. My family was working class but struggled with housing and food insecurity. Both of my parents were third-generation immigrants, and although they understood Spanish, my mother experienced harsh discipline for speaking anything but English in the classroom. She actively discouraged me from learning Spanish and spoke it only when she wanted to have private conversations with family in my presence. Because of this, English is my first language, and to this day I struggle to wrap my tongue around Spanish vowels. This was always confusing because I was raised culturally Mexican. She and my nana attended mass, regularly invoking the patriarchal heteronormative values of the Catholic Church: boys could be rough and crass; girls had to be presentable and demure. We ate corn tortillas with most meals, made tamales during the holidays, and celebrated nuptials and baptisms with mariachis. However, my family insisted that they were "of Mexican descent" or "Hispanic," seeking to emphasize their European Spanish ancestry and drawing a distinction between more recent immigrants down the block: *they* are Mexican; *we* are different.

It was within this baffling climate that I was raised. I understood injustice as the differential treatment of Black and brown people by *individuals*. My classes in ethnic studies and Native American studies allowed me to see how *institutions* facilitate inequality. I didn't begin to actualize the power of my own Latina identity until I was confronted with the homogenous environment of higher education. I chose to attend the farthest northern California state institution in order to exert my independence from family but was totally unprepared for the stark contrast of my new conditions to my multicultural Southern California home. I had so many feelings, but when I was introduced to ethnic and Native American studies courses, I was provided a language with which to describe my emotions and a framework through which to organize.

One professor encouraged students to critically challenge and disrupt institutions, especially those posing as neutral or apolitical. Formally trained as a historian, he taught us to interrogate historical objects and their presentation by analyzing primary sources (diaries, letters, speeches, photographs, interviews, maps) as well as by archiving (collecting, appraising, describing, and accessing); we learned to frame both modes as susceptible to ideological contamination by elites and powerful institutions. My mentors encouraged me to interrupt the dominant narrative of white supremacy; I learned that praxis should be driven by theory and theory informed by praxis. An undergraduate Chicana working as a federal work-study student assistant in special collections at a predominantly white institution, I was regularly confronted both by the lack of representation of student voices in the university's archives and by the overwhelming abundance of white settlers' perspectives in special collections. Shelving the works in special collections, I became especially attuned to the role that "stock stories" play in reinforcing power relationships and institutions.

My approach to librarianship—information literacy, information creation, and information curation—is guided entirely by the values I honed during this formative time. I am especially compelled by the Zapatista concepts of "caminando preguntamos" and "mandar obedeciendo": the former translates loosely to mean "as we walk, we ask questions," and the latter means "lead by following." "Caminando preguntamos" is the Zapatistas' traditional manner of achieving consensus (Ramirez Sanchez 2012, 191). Similarly, "mandar obedeciendo" is a critique of traditional electoral politics: the leadership of many by an individual. In Zapatista autonomous communities, self-determination and self-governance are exercised through "bien gobierno," or "good government councils" (Ramirez Sanchez 2012, 189). Leaders are volunteers who take direction from the communities they represent, rotating in and out of service. When these concepts work together, they provide a framework for participatory leadership. For me, when framed in concert with the theoretical structures of information literacy, they decentralize the individual and emphasize the collective. They encourage critical reflection and allow for decisions to be made without knowledge of a final destination, but they emphasize that we are collectively creating a learning community, which is in itself a resource we can draw on by asking reflective questions of each other and ourselves (Nava 2018, 122).

Our (Kendall's and Stefani's) histories of coming to be attest to the fact that the counterstories told through archives can become a form of mentoring, not just in the way we identify with people but also in the way we learn about the practices that they enact. These stories can be especially impactful for folks like us when we find ourselves in spaces where we are identified as marginalized and disempowered and in spaces where mentors who similarly identify are few and far between. In standing next to the leaders of the past, we actively reinvent their narratives.

Composing Institutional Counterstories

It is imperative that we take seriously the task of changing institutions through the stories they tell, specifically through historiography. As a rhetoric-and-writing teacher and as an archivist, we recognize that our mentoring fosters practices to compose institutional counterstories.

Methodologically, the approach we take to archival building works to reclaim control of the mechanism through which our campus's stories are told. We also consider the fact that control over archival building relies on the "capacity to find documents, preserve them, and decide what is or is not available to the public" (Zinn 1977, 20). University archives frequently present a limited view of a campus experience, told from the perspective of those with the resources—time, money, and awareness—to devote to compiling such records, namely administrators and departments. Archival collections, especially ones that tell the story of institutional making, are designed from what Richard Delgado describes as "stock stories": "Stock stories feign neutrality and at all costs avoid any blame or responsibility for societal inequality. Powerful because they are often repeated until canonized or normalized, . . . stock stories [are described as a] version of events [that] is indeed reality, and any stories that counter these standardized tellings are deemed biased, self-interested, and ultimately not credible" (quoted in Martinez 2014, 70). Through the development and presentation of a university archive that feigns neutrality by ignoring the contributions of large groups of people and events that have shaped the institution, some of our underrepresented students feel disconnected from our campuses. To be transgressive, then, our professional practice needs to change the stories and collective memories of our institutional spaces. In so doing, universities need to make apparent the way that the producing and maintaining of these stories are never neutral (Schwartz and Cook 2002, 9).

University archives have historically been keepers of administrative records and institutional documents, but "the history of any institution of higher education is incomplete without the history of the student body" (Christian 2002, 111). In her enchiridion for university archives, *Varsity Letters* (1992), Helen Samuels challenges the profession with the question of the archivists' role at the university level. Samuels presses that archivists "must become active participants in the creation, analysis, and selection of the documentary record. This places archivists, librarians, and other curators in the role of documenters of their institutions, rather than simply keepers of their records" (265). When archivists take an active role in documenting their institution, creating records that document student perspectives on campus life is an obvious next step (Samuels 1992, 265). This is especially true for campuses with large minoritized student populations, such as the ones where we work.

To be transgressive in our mentoring, we propose actively guiding students on our campus not only to learn survival skills for navigating institutions but to create opportunities for them to change the institutions themselves. We extend counterstory from the personal to the institutional, from the text to the material artifact, as we share our experiences in rewriting our university's story to include students. Applying the Zapatista concept of "caminando preguntamos," we asked students to see each other as leaders, thus establishing a learning community within the classroom. This approach also utilizes Rebecca Covarrubias, Sarah Herrmann, and Stephanie Fryberg's (2016) research affirming students' interdependent relationships with each other in the classroom environment and the larger campus community. Because we believe that the stories our institutions tell matter, we begin our project narrative by outlining our campus context.

Background: Our Campus and the Students

California State University, Chico (Chico State), is a teaching-intensive campus and the second-oldest institution of the twenty-three colleges in the California State University system. The campus is recognized by the California State University system as located on "sacred traditional lands" of the Mechoopda tribe (California State University, Chico n.d.c), and the tribe itself identifies tribal communities historically residing successively at Little Butte Creek, three and a half miles from downtown Chico, and at several camps in Chico's present-day downtown (Mechoopda Indian Tribe of Chico Rancheria n.d.). However, the online history of the university and its cultural traditions focuses predominantly on the initial donation of land for the school by City of Chico founder John Bidwell. The history discusses celebrations to "memorialize John Bidwell and distinguished deceased members of the faculty and trustees" and discusses school identifiers, such as a live wildcat mascot, without recognizing other potential or actual influences on the school's cultural history (California State University, Chico n.d.a, n.d.d.).

This commitment to a metanarrative extolling the virtues of economic leadership, dominion over the land, and white settler colonialism extends to the campus's history of record keeping. The University Archives at Chico State consist mostly of administrative records. Materials that document the school's history have been captured only opportunistically, and there is no commitment to an institutional records retention schedule. In sum, the bulk of historical materials representing the university's history stem from a male, cis-gendered, heteronormative perspective.

The current outlook for Chico State is significantly more encompassing now, though. The school is led by the first woman president in its history and the first openly gay president of the California State University system (Storm 2016). The student population is 54 percent female and 31.7 percent Hispanic/Latinx. (The largest racial group in the student population is white, at 43 percent). In the fall of 2018, 60 percent of Chico State's undergraduate student population identified as first-generation college students, and many of those students are low income, which is 150 percent below the federal poverty level (California State University, Chico n.d.b). The university is a recently designated Hispanic-serving institution, and more than 30 percent of its students self-identify as Latinx. Despite the statistics about the school's changing student demographics, a narrative persists in which these students are considered "underprepared" and "underrepresented." We believe that the label *underprepared* is misapplied, but we agree that our students are underrepresented with regard to their experiences and lives, which are minimally reflected in the campus narratives that ultimately shape campus policies and practices. In response, we participate in formal and informal mentoring of first-generation and Latinx students on campus by being involved in on-campus organizations designed to promote the success of students from underrepresented populations.

Rebuilding Campus Stories in Our Archives: The CAT Project

The narrative and cultural divide between archived history and the current student makeup of Chico State is increasingly recognized by staff and faculty within the university's Meriam Library and campus academic departments, particularly when these personnel have worked with similar deficits at other academic institutions. Library personnel in the Special Collections and University Archives Department have found that student perspectives are significantly underrepresented in the historic and contemporary archives of Chico State. Faculty in the Department of English have similarly worked to build a student-driven chronicle of the academic programs and social and cultural institutions of the campus and surrounding area—institutions that are underrepresented in the university's archival history.

Toward this end, in the fall of 2017 the Special Collections and University Archives Department launched the Chico Archives Toolkit (CAT) project. The CAT project was conceived as a guide to help elevate undergraduate students' "awareness of their role as records creators, cultural workers, and historical participants on the Chico State campus" (Meriam Library 2018). This project served both as a promotional tool for the University Archives and as an opportunity to increase student representation and to diversify our current collections. Special Collections and University Archives staff coordinated workshops in the fall and spring of the 2017–18 academic year, inviting student organizations and clubs to participate. They also collaborated with Chico State's Student Life and Leadership Office to incentivize student-club participation. Each student club that registered two representatives for the workshop received $25 in credit from Student Life and Leadership for its financial account if those representatives attended.

In the workshop, Special Collections and University Archives personnel provided an overview of the role of university archives, presenting the problem of underdocumented communities and the power of student organizations as cultural workers. Then, they provided introductory instruction on records-management best practices. A major component of the instruction is that born-digital materials require intentionality in their creation, access, and preservation. However, the backbone of the CAT project is to empower students to recognize their presence on the Chico State campus as inherently valuable and to show that the documentary evidence of their nonacademic experiences has a place in the campus's historical record. For participating in the workshop, students also received a physical toolkit consisting of an eight-gigabyte flash drive for storing electronic records as well as a lignin-free box and acid-free folders for long-term storage of print materials. CAT offers students an opportunity to document their perspectives of Chico, California, and the United States during this complex time.

In the spring of 2018, the CAT workshop was facilitated as part of a First-Generation Staff and Faculty Association second-annual community-building event called "1st GEN Symposium: We Are Here." Kendall attended the 1st GEN Symposium and was able to join the CAT workshop, which was modified slightly to illustrate to campus staff and faculty that the Special Collections and University Archives Department was building the school's collections while encouraging the campus's active student clubs and organizations to take control of the records-creation process for the purposes of adding the records they found to the archival collections.

After the symposium, we worked together to plan an assignment for first-generation college students enrolled in "English (ENG) 130: Academic Writing," a course cross-listed with the Educational Opportunity First Year Experience program, to gather primary sources and create oral histories. The ENG 130 course was designed to help build students' rhetorical analysis abilities while also helping them recognize rhetoric in the world around them. The first half of the course helped students engage with and analyze responses to racial injustice, focusing on issues such as language rights, police brutality, and Confederate monument removal. The monument topic asked students to consider perspectives on public memory making, which served as a segue to the University Archives project. The second project, Digital Stories, invited students to draw on their knowledge of rhetoric and writing strategies to compose their own rhetorically effective stories about students on the Chico State campus, which would then become part of the Meriam Library Special Collections. To do this second project, ENG 130 groups selected a student organization or movement on campus to document and collected a variety of multimedia artifacts connected to it. Organizations that the students selected to document included the Dream Center, Upward Bound, the Educational Opportunity Program, Students for Quality Education, and the Gender and Sexuality Equity Center. The students were required to collect a range of artifacts and to employ an effective style and structure to create stories usable for future generations.

Stefani attended two instructional sessions of Kendall's ENG 130 course. In the first session, she modified the CAT workshop to help students conceptualize how electronic records' creation-and-use processes can lead to e-records preservation. This initial instruction reinforced the value of the important cultural work done by student organizations' activism to the Chico State campus and the University Archives. In the second session, undergraduate students interacted with unprocessed historical materials from the University Archives: reading, understanding, summarizing, and interpreting those materials (Association of College and Research Libraries 2017). After the first instructional sessions, students began collecting primary-source materials and conducting interviews with student participants in the organizations. Some of the organizations that students researched and gathered materials on included a Latino service fraternity, the Dream Center, Students Upward Bound, and the Educational Opportunity Program—each of which provides resources and opportunities for underrepresented students to succeed in college. Many of the ENG 130 students were members of these organizations, and all of them participated in the Educational Opportunity Program.

The second instructional plan was necessary to help these students conceptualize how primary-source materials communicate information about the context in which they are created, specifically by interpreting unprocessed materials from the University Archives and applying only their own critical-thinking skills without the aid of archivists' interpretation. The second session proved to be productive as students (1) realized through examining the unprocessed materials the value in gathering a range of primary-source materials, including what otherwise may have seemed mundane, and (2) understood the rationale behind the need to strategically name and organize primary-source materials. Following the second session, students finalized their collections and designed and implemented a consistent approach to organizing and saving their materials.

In teaching this project, we discovered an institutionally internalized devaluation of students' experiences as being worthy of collecting. For example, although the students were active participants in the organizations on campus, they rarely considered including their own perspectives in the primary materials they gathered. This was especially troubling when one student in the group assigned to gather materials on the Educational Opportunity Program shared that he was having trouble getting interview participants. This is perhaps a typical problem for a primary-research project in a first-year class, but it was also unexpected because the class was a course cross-linked with the Educational Opportunity Program, and every single student enrolled in the class was in the program. When this was pointed out, the student earnestly asked, "Do our stories count?" By synthesizing the "caminando preguntamos" concept, students began to establish the necessary framework to see themselves and each other as a learning community and as a resource from which to draw. In response to this realization, Kendall invited the students to question how they valued their experiential knowledge and to question the accepted narratives of the college campus. Many of our students professed to feeling as if

our campus is a white space, despite the fact that the student population reflects otherwise. Part of this feeling, though, may stem from
the way our campus represents itself in the stories it tells.

Laura Rendon suggests that invalidation is built into the hierarchical models of teaching at most four-year institutions (1994, 45).
Indeed, most of the archival collections the students had been exposed
to amplified the voices of older white male administrators. Rendon's
validation theory can provide additional support for student success
and persistence in higher education. She suggests that offering students validation will foster academic and interpersonal development,
so "students feel capable of learning; they experience a feeling of self-
worth and feel that they, and everything they bring to the college
experience, are accepted and recognized as valuable" (44).

Challenging the belief that only certain stories "count" also
speaks to the potential of this type of project in a writing classroom to
expand students' sense of cultural capital. Tara Yosso (2005) expands
our notion of cultural capital to include various forms of capital that
we educators committed to building antiracist spaces can promote in
our students as a way to capture the talents, resources, and experiences
that students of color bring to our learning spaces. Included in this
expanded notion of capital is social capital, which includes networks of
peers and communities that help students navigate educational spaces.
In gathering the primary materials for the CAT project, students spoke
to organizational leaders and alumni. One student in the Latino fraternity contacted alumni brothers to interview them about their experiences in the fraternity and as Latinos on a white-dominated campus.
In so doing, the student learned from the experiences of these Latino
men while also expanding his own social network.

The second half of the writing project further promoted what
Yosso (2005) calls "navigational capital." Once the collections were
complete, the students approached the materials they collected as rhetorical responses to current issues that emerged from an exigence and
a context. Students wrote an essay in which they identified ways that
the documents demonstrated invention (how rhetors come up with

ideas), kairos (the time or era and the timeliness of a discourse), and the meaning- and change-making strategies employed by these student responses to our current rhetorical situation. In this way, the primary-source materials in these collections were treated as being as meaningful and effective as the published materials assigned to them to analyze in the first half of the class. Perhaps more importantly, the project represents an example of student-led research that encourages students to connect with affiliated communities, including the campus broadly. This relationality between students and their campus community allows them to recognize the value of their work beyond the individual class and beyond themselves and, more importantly, to learn from these groups the navigational strategies to maneuver within and ultimately change educational environments (Yosso 2005, 79–80).

Conclusion: Changing Spaces

Archival and other "officializing" narratives are not the only kinds of stories we can give space to or listen to. As academic women of color, we know how much everyday stories matter. The students coming to our offices ask about what our experiences of attaining higher education have been like, perhaps knowing that statistically not many folks look like us in these spaces. Students may share with us their everyday struggles in a predominately white rural area, or they may tell us about their struggles connecting their home space with the academic spaces they inhabit. Stephanie Lechuga-Peña and Chalene Lechuga (2018) assert that along with familism and a culturally relevant curriculum, mentorship and authentic caring are facilitators of educational success. We also lean on the Zapatista concepts of "leadership," "caminando preguntamos," and "mandar obedeciendo." We may not have the answers, but we understand that by asking questions and seeking answers together, we are building communities. In particular, caminando preguntamos encourages us to challenge ourselves as instructors so as to blur the boundaries that distinguish us from our students.

Of her Indigenous feminist scholarship, Kim TallBear writes, "I do not simply study indigenous communities, but I inhabit them, both local and virtual, within and without the academy. I am family, friend, and/or colleague to a stunningly diverse set of indigenous actors in many parts of the world" (2014, 3). This framework informs our approach to practicing relational Latinx mentoring as we affirm *our* interrelatedness as participants in both on-campus and off-campus communities. In so doing, we also encourage the sharing of counterstories of mentoring that empower women of color in leadership roles to self-define meaningful work in order to celebrate that we offer a diversity of experiences and a breadth of interests. Latinx mentoring is a stance and not a prescribed set of scholarly interests. In taking this stance, we must learn to practice mentoring in a way that does not further tax us with invisible work that contributes to the "leaky pipeline" of women of color in academia.[4]

Listening and giving space for our stories and affirming they matter can often be the most productive forms of mentoring. The testimonios that we share with the students and with each other about our lives being meaningful to our campus tapestry may ultimately be more impactful than officially archived stories. And this is what we believe is at the heart of our mentoring: changing institutions through the stories we tell and the stories we listen to. This is especially important when we consider that, like us, our students may turn to leaders and change makers from the past to build their own identities and trajectories. Such a tactic—the revisioning of the past to build a more equitable future—is a strategy of decolonization, Latinx methodology, and, by association, mentoring. In addition, it is not enough to help our students or each other to learn to navigate or dismantle institutions; we need also to teach and model using the tools necessary to radically remodel the whitestream spaces that we inhabit. This form of larger-scale mentoring, we believe, has the potential to lead to both empowered individuals and systemic change.

4. Read the Social Sciences Feminist Network Research Interest Group's recent article "The Burden of Invisible Work in Academia" (2017) for a concrete example of the cultural tax levied on women of color and its impact on retention.

References

Association of College and Research Libraries' Rare Books and Manuscript Section's Society of American Archivists Joint Task Force on the Development of Guidelines for Primary Source Literacy. 2017. "Guidelines for Primary Source Literacy." Society of American Archivists. Last modified July 24. At https://www2.archivists.org/groups/saa-acrlrbms-joint-task-force-on-primary-source-literacy/guidelines-for-primary-source-lite-0.

California State University, Chico. N.d.a. "Celebrating Our Traditions." At https://www.csuchico.edu/traditions/celebrating.shtml.

———. N.d.b. "Chico Facts." At https://www.csuchico.edu/about/chico-facts.shtml.

———. N.d.c. "CSU, Chico Traditions." At https://www.csuchico.edu/traditions/.

———. N.d.d. "The Wildcat." At https://www.csuchico.edu/traditions/wildcat.shtml.

Christian, Michelle. 2002. "Documenting Student Life: The Use of Oral Histories in University Archives." *Archival Issues* 27, no. 2: 111–24.

Covarrubias, Rebecca, Sarah D. Herrmann, and Stephanie A. Fryberg. 2016. "Affirming the Interdependent Self: Implications for Latino Student Performance." *Basic and Applied Social Psychology* 38, no. 1: 47–57.

Excelencia in Education. 2019. "Latinos in Higher Education: Compilation of Fast Facts." At https://fphpr.org/wp-content/uploads/2019/05/Latinos-in-higher-education.pdf.

Fryberg, Stephanie, Rebecca Covarrubias, and Jason A. Burack. 2013. "Cultural Models of Education and Academic Performance for Native American and European American Students." *School Psychology International* 34, no. 4: 439–52.

Gándara, Patricia. 2015. *Fulfilling America's Future: Latinas in the U.S., 2015*. White House Initiative on Educational Excellence for Hispanics. Washington, DC: US Government Publication Office.

Lechuga-Peña, Stephanie, and Chalene E. Lechuga. 2018. "Xicanisma/o and Education: Counter Storytelling and Narratives to Inform Latina/o Student Success." *Affilia* 33, no. 3: 300–316.

Martinez, Aja. 2014. "A Plea for Critical Race Theory Counterstory: Stock Story versus Counterstory Dialogues concerning Alejandra's 'Fit' in the Academy." *Composition Studies* 42, no. 2: 65–85.

Mechoopda Indian Tribe of Chico Rancheria. N.d. "History." At http://www.mechoopda-nsn.gov/history.

Meriam Library. 2018. "Chico State Student Organizations Archive Research Guide." California State Univ., Chico. Last modified Apr. 30. At https://libguides.csuchico.edu/CAT.

Nava, Lucrecia. 2018. "Caminando, preguntamos: Rotating Leadership as an Alternative for Sustainable and Effective Administrators." PhD diss., California State Univ., Los Angeles.

Ramirez Sanchez, Martha Areli. 2012. "We Are All Government: Zapatista Political Community. Contexts, Challenges, and Prospects." PhD diss., Univ. of Manchester. At https://www.research.manchester.ac.uk/portal/files/60987904/FULL_TEXT.PDF.

Rendon, Laura. 1994. "Validating Culturally Diverse Students: Toward a New Model of Learning and Student Development." *Innovative Higher Education* 19, no. 1: 33–51.

Ribero, Ana Milena, and Sonia C. Arellano. 2019. "Advocating *Comadrismo*: A Feminist Mentoring Approach for Latinas in Rhetoric and Composition." *Peitho* 21, no. 2: 334–56.

Samuels, Helen. 1992. *Varsity Letters: Documenting Modern Colleges and Universities.* Lanham, MD: Scarecrow Press.

Schwartz, Joan, and Terry Cook. 2002. "Archives, Records, and Power: The Making of Modern Memory." *Archival Science* 2:1–19.

Social Sciences Feminist Network Research Interest Group. 2017. "The Burden of Invisible Work in Academia: Social Inequalities and Time Use in Five University Departments." *Humboldt Journal of Social Relations* 39:228–45.

Storm, Amelia. 2016. "First Openly Gay CSU President 'a Step in the Right Direction.'" *Orion*, Mar. 30. At https://theorion.com/54901/news/first-openly-gay-csu-president-astep-in-the-right-direction/.

TallBear, Kim. 2014. "Standing with and Speaking as Faith: A Feminist-Indigenous Approach to Inquiry." *Journal of Research Practice* 10, no. 2: 1–7.

Yosso, Tara J. 2005. "Whose Culture Has Capital? A Critical Race Theory Discussion of Community Cultural Wealth." *Race Ethnicity and Education* 8, no. 1: 69–91.

Zinn, Howard. 1977. "Secrecy, Archives, and the Public Interest." *Midwestern Archivist* 2, no. 2: 14–26.

6

The Chingona Interviews

Christine Garcia

Abstract

"The Chingona Interviews" was written specifically for Latinx students seeking guidance on how to lead while navigating the academy and our communities. I interview two chicas fuertes and use Anzaldúan thought as a frame for each interview. I use the style of the interview, which Gloria Anzaldúa says is "part of communicating, which is part of writing, which is part of life" (quoted in Keating 2000, 3). This interview approach centers the leaders' voices and positions Anzaldúa as a modern-day Virgilian guide, allowing her insights, what she calls "conocimientos," to structure the interview questions and answers.

An Anzaldúan Exigence: The Introduction

Where were you the first time you read *Borderlands / La Frontera*? What about the first time you grappled with Anzaldúan thought in your writing? The first time you found someone else who knew Gloria, who had read and understood the importance of her work? I was in my second year in the master's of English program at Angelo State University, a mama with two kids and one on the way and a fire lit under me regarding all of the inequities and unfairness at work in my little West Texas town. I was enrolled in the course "Mexican American Literature" taught by Dr. Gloria Duarte, a professor of British literature but the only person of Mexican descent in the English Department and therefore by default professor of this course. Though she was not a Chicanx literature scholar by training, I do believe Dr. Duarte provided us with a wonderful curriculum. We read Graciela Limón's *The Memories of Ana Calderón* (1994), a shocking novel with a conclusion that I still struggle with. We vibed to the funkjazzpostmodern poetry of Juan Felipe Herrera.[1] And we explored artist and activist Luis Valdez both textually and visually, leaning in to the luxury of zoot suit fashion and the ancient rhythms of caló. Then, after Dr. Duarte had given us just enough literary exploration so that we had roots, we read *Borderlands*. I remember attending class that first evening after chapter 1, "The Homeland, Aztlán / El otro México," was assigned, sitting next to my fellow students, Brandy and Ruben, and talking in hushed, excited voices about what we had just experienced—the genre shifting, the language mixing. Was any of that history true?[2] We had just met our musa Tejana, a Texan who spoke *like* us and *to* us, to the pain and the hope in our hearts.

In the years following that revelation, I spent many hours with Gloria, sitting together in little diners in Albuquerque until all hours of the night, enjoying a warm sunrise and coffee on my parents' back porch in West Texas, and huddled tightly with her and my students in wintry New England, envisioning how to bring mestiza consciousness into being. Gloria's interviews were my Socratic dialogues during my

---

1. Juan Felipe Herrera, our twenty-first US poet laureate, is a poet, professor, and activist from California.

2. Gloria E. Anzaldúa says, "The writing is based on my experience, my life, that I then take that experience and reflect on it and that is where the *historia* comes from. *Historia* is a Spanish word for history, but it is also the Spanish word for story. And so, history is supposed to be the truth and story is supposed to be made up and I happen to think everything is made up, that history is just as fictitious as the novel" (from *Gloria Anzaldúa (b. 1942)*, video, in the Annenberg Learner series "Exploring Borderlands—American Passages: A Literary History," my transcription, at https://www.learner.org/series/american-passages-a-literary-survey/exploring -borderlands-video/).

doctoral studies in rhetoric,[3] when I really should have been studying Plato's actual Socratic dialogues. Her theories on writing, intri-
cately woven throughout her body of work, guided me as I formed my
own understanding of what it meant to be a professor of composition.
Anzaldúa explained, "The only thing I want to teach is what I want
to learn, which is writing. In the writing I incorporate visualizations,
meditation, concentration—all the magical things" (2000b, 68), and
I, her faithful student, listened.

But it isn't just you and I or just students in the classroom or
only people in North America who respond to Anzaldúa's writing and
theorizing on the borders that create and contain us. People across
Mother Earth who are engaged and invested in decolonial lifeways in
places such as Poland and Brazil—places with their own difficult histories of colonialism, racism, and sexism—read, teach, and celebrate
Anzaldúa's legacy. Anzaldúa's writings are powerful because they contain an epistemology of the life we all are striving to live, one of wholeness and fairness. Thinkers, scholars, and activists use her thought and
theory to map a praxis of liberation for women, queerfolx, the differently abled, our environment. Anzaldúa's writing teaches us how to
lead lives of authenticity and goodness, even in dark times. In fact,
her writing teaches us how to lead in general—no easy task for such a
rough-and-tumble bunch.

As a model, Anzaldúa gives us the concept of the "nepantleras,"
the "poetas, artistas, queer youth, and differently abled who have a
tolerance for ambiguity and difference, la facultad to maintain numerous conflicting positions and affinity with those unlike themselves"
(2005a, 94). What follows in this chapter are two interviews with
nepantleras who, much like Gloria, have shaped my own understanding
of what a leader is through their lived actions—womxn who defy and

---

3. The collection *Interviews/Entrevistas*, edited by AnaLouise Keating, contains
many interviews of Anzaldúa (see, for example, Anzaldúa 2000a, 2000b, 2000c) as
well as Anzaldúa's reflections on the interviews.

resist and love and teach in ways that calm fears, bridge gaps between conocimiento and desconocimiento,[4] and uplift their students.

First, I interviewed Dr. Christina V. Cedillo, a professor of rhetoric and composition at the University of Houston, Clear Lake. Dr. Cedillo grew up in the border city of Laredo, Texas, is an activist educator, and is one of the great contemporary thinkers in rhetoric-and-composition studies; I have witnessed her move deftly from recitation of rhetorical history to sound argumentation on the rights of the differently abled, with keen consideration for audience and the sharpest wit. In sum, she is the type of professor who will lead rhetoric-and-composition studies as a discipline into the feminine, queer, and diversely abled future. Next I interviewed Tanaya Winder. I met Tanaya when we were working in the Chicana and Chicano Studies Department at the University of New Mexico. Have you ever known someone who just makes you smile each time you are around them? A person who has a genuinely positive vibe? That is Tanaya. She is a member of the Duckwater Shoshone Tribe from the Southern Ute Reservation in Colorado, coordinator of the Upward Bound Program at the University of Colorado at Boulder, teaching faculty at the University of New Mexico, and one of the most soulful poets I have ever had the honor of watching perform. In each interview, we discuss leadership: the ways it manifests, the moments it is needed, and what it truly means to be a leader. We then frame the rest of our discussion around a few Anzaldúa quotes that I pulled specifically for each interview. Though my approach was fairly standard, what happens in each interview are moments of magic, moments where the interview dynamic is transcended and autohistoria-teoría occurs.[5]

4. Conocimientos are things we know and understand, whereas desconocimientos are those things we are ignorant about.

5. "I fuse personal narrative with theoretical discourse, autobiographical vignettes with theoretical prose. I create a hybrid genre, a new discursive mode, which I call 'autohistoria' and 'autohistoria-teoría.' Conectando experiencias personales con realidades sociales results in autohistoria, and theorizing about this activity

A Praxis of Proprioception: An Interview
with Dr. Christina V. Cedillo

CG: Gloria Anzaldúa tells us, "Conventional, traditional identity labels are stuck in binaries, trapped in *jaulas* (cages) that
limit the growth of our individual and collective lives. We
need fresh terms and open-ended tags that portray us in all
our complexities and potentialities" (2005a, 66). How do
you self-identify?

CVC: I identify as a Chicana, though also as a Latina when I
want to show solidarity with women whose roots are also in
Latin America. My family history includes white, Italian, and
Spanish (Jewish) roots through my two grandfathers, but my
two grandmothers were from Mexico, Coahuila and Nuevo
León, and they were Native. Since Mexican culture is what I
recognize as my home culture, I also identify as Indigenous,
though not Native, because it's important for me to honor
the experiences and struggles of the peoples who still speak
the original languages and live the original ways and who
therefore are especially culturally, linguistically, and racially
marginalized in the US and Mexico.

For the record, that's a distinction I make using those
terms, not necessarily one that other Indigenous or Native
scholars would use. However, I'm also trying to avoid the
use of words related to blood quantum, and that's difficult
because they are so historically habituated. This issue is a
big one for me as someone who engages decoloniality as a
researcher and as a person. As part of that work, I also identify as a teacher and also healer at times.

CG: Explain your work to me: What do you do? Who do you
work with? Why do you do this work?

---

results in autohistoria-teoría. It's a way of inventing and making knowledge, meaning, and identity through self-inscriptions" (Anzaldúa 2005b, 6).

CVC: As a researcher, I focus on the relationship between rhetorics of embodiment and embodied rhetorics, particularly at the intersections of race, gender, and disability. Rhetorics of embodiment are codes that say how you must exist or act to be considered a human being, a subject. I believe that when imposed by the dominant culture, these codes are harmful—for example, Aristotle saying women are failed men or contemporary politicians making statements that all people of Latinx descent are criminals. These arguments attempt to make the dominant culture's stereotypes indicative of our ontology. Embodied rhetorics are how we send messages and/or resist, from speaking out to just existing. Our lives are proof that our cultures have survived despite everything the dominant culture has done to us.

Decolonial theory drives a lot of my teaching and research as well because it speaks to my experiences; a lot of what we find in decolonial theory we already know from life, only maybe we didn't realize these ideas or practices had names. I'm constantly coming back to Gerald Vizenor, Malea Powell, Ramón Grosfoguel, Gloria Anzaldúa—writers who are talking about my world and that of many of my students from marginalized communities. But also scholars like Jacqueline Jones Royster and Remi Yergeau, who remind us that the norm is imposed circumscription bullshit.

More than anything, I think of myself as a teacher. This is why I do what I do in terms of research. For me, research for its own sake is useless; we have to share with our community, and we have to think of our students as part of that community. Before getting a PhD, I taught middle school. I always figured I'd be a teacher because I come from a line of teachers. The women in my family are either teachers or nurses, no joke, though I think those two vocations actually converge in the notion of healing. After all, we're "doctors," right? All of that is intertwined in my family. My maternal grandfather's mother was a midwife, and my maternal grandmother was who we went to when we had problems with ojo and susto or things like that. What I do, I learned from her. From her, I learned that Mexican culture is highly syncretic; the ancestors used the santos and rituals of the church to keep the old ways. A lot of what we do now is what we were doing five hundred years ago before the Europeans came, from the temazcal to "confession," though it was before Ōmeteōtl rather than "God." When people I know need help with these things, I work with them, teach them about these practices if I can. To me it's all connected: Irene Lara calls it "bodymindspirit."[6] These are the three things, which are one thing, that colonization has tried to break in us, so education that combats that violence must involve all three aspects of oneness.

Sometimes people wonder why I believe in those things when I'm "educated," but my cultural and spiritual education is what motivates me to use my privilege as best I can on behalf of my students and others to make room for them. To remind the whitestream that we are here. Hence, my spirituality is also a big deal to me, and it, too, is based in decolonization.

CG: This collection explores what it means to be a leader. What, in your opinion, is the most essential quality in a successful leader?

CVC: So, I'm a really big supporter of the idea that a person who wants to be a leader is at least a little suspect but that people who probably should be leaders don't want it! I think the reason it works out this way—or should, in my opinion—is because the most important quality in a leader is humility. This is not to be mistaken for weakness or the apologetic way that Latinxs are often taught to behave around others. Again, at least in Mexican culture, we get a lot of that: "Don't be too

6. For an explanation of Irene Lara's concept of "bodymindspirit," see her article "Bruja Positionalities" (2005).

loud. Don't be disrespectful. Try to shrink yourself and not take up too much room." But sometimes a situation calls for it. Are you really going to feel bad for talking back to someone who is racist? And yet I've known people who think that we owe people like that respect, even though their words or actions hurt. I think a leader has to balance being strong and authoritative when their gente need it with the humility to remember that it should never be about ego. My grandmother had an eighth-grade education, and what she knew I don't think my PhD can ever hold a candle to it.

There's a meme that says, "Your ancestors outnumber your fears. Feel your power." I think a good leader does feel that power but remembers that that power is a gift for them to use in service for their communities and the earth until they, too, are an ancestor.

CG: I think a major goal of an Anzaldúan approach to writing is finding a way to write about the tender spots inside of us in productive, transformative ways. It sounds like your research and teaching are a conduit for that to happen for your students. It brings me back to one of Gloria's later essays, "Geographies of Selves—Reimagining Identity" (2005a), where Gloria argues, "My struggle, like yours, is always to be fully who and what I am, to act out of that potential, to strive for wholeness, and to understand both the fragments and the whole of my being" (75). How does this resonate with you as a teacher?

CVC: People often think of literacy as knowing how to read and write, and it is, but I think of it more as learning to read situations and people and to compose responses in kind. That is rhetoric. This idea of literacy is, to me, closely related to Anzaldúa's concept of "la facultad."[7] It's not instinct; rather,

7. Anzaldua defines "la facultad" as having the capacity for an instant sense of knowing; she argues that oppressed peoples have a higher propensity for la facultad

it's a powerful praxis based in spatial and embodied rhetorics. I say this because, ultimately—and this is what I think we need students to realize—any notion of literacy that doesn't actually speak to our realities isn't useful. If literacy and education in general can't be put in service of understanding our place in the world and/or healing the generational trauma of -isms and phobias, then it's mimicry of the dominant culture's ways without the critical awareness necessary to resist. Why resistance? Because just knowing who you are when you're told who you're supposed to be is resistance. Without that, who are we? Our potential is limited by the vision imposed on us from the outside as writers, learners, individuals.

CG: What you are speaking on, the radical act of knowing ourselves, is an early theme foundational in *Borderlands / La Frontera*, which then morphs into the more extrinsically focused concept of "New Tribalism" in Anzaldúa's later works. In New Tribalism, we create new identity categories, new ways of describing ourselves, affiliating ourselves, and rooting ourselves.[8] In doing so, we compel ourselves to snap out of the haze of binaries and rote histories.

CVC: I often tell people that life on the border means an epistemology that is not based on either/or but [on] both/and. However, it can also lead to the problem of a fractured consciousness, of not knowing where you belong, until you learn to heal yourself by coming to a new consciousness, much like Anzaldúa describes. We can write ourselves into wholeness, but it's a model of writing that must incorporate all of

----

because of the myriad dangers they have to navigate in order to survive, thus heightening their "sixth sense," an awareness of their bodies in space and time and in relation to all other things.

8. See Blanca Gabriela Caldas Chumbes's contribution to this collection (chapter 2) for an exploration of rootedness through self-reflexivity.

the history and experiences and emotions that led us to that point. This is what the dominant culture might deem the phenomenological background but [what] those of us forced to inhabit the background would just recognize as life.

CG: This journey toward wholeness[9] is a trek to the center of the self, to loosely quote Gloria. I wonder if you could muse on this journey for me, this urge we have to figure out who we are. Gloria poses it as "an ongoing story, one that changes with each telling, one we revise at each waystation, each stop, in our *viaje de la vida* (life's journey)" (Anzaldúa 2005a, 75). What do you think?

CVC: Identity is intersubjective. We have many different identities because they're all contextual. In a way, I think of identity as a topos, not as an arrangement but an idea. When I was in my twenties, I moved to Los Angeles. I was just starting to figure out who I was, to learn about our history as a people, to unpack my own familial genealogy and what all this meant for me and my vision of a life. For me, that life journey was deeply connected to the physical journey; at the time, I thought the place one was in gave one an identity. It does to a certain degree, but now I think it is more about learning where and with whom we fit and don't fit as we get used to new locations, including those along the way. In other words, identity is a spatial and temporal construction.

Later on, during the PhD, I studied histories of rhetoric and focused on medieval women's religious texts because they

9. In Anzaldúan autohistoria-teoría, the urge toward wholeness is called the "Coyolxauhqui imperative," named after the aztecwarriormoongoddess Coyolxauhqui, who was decapitated and dismembered by her brother, the war god Huitzilopochtli, because of her plan to kill their mother, Coatlicue, the Serpent Skirt Woman, Goddess of Gods and Mortals. In "Gestures of the Body," Anzaldúa counsels, "The Coyolxauhqui imperative is the act of calling back those pieces of the self/soul that have been dispersed or lost, the act of mourning the losses that haunt us" (2005b, 1).

helped me to deal with some major trauma stemming from a superconservative religious upbringing. In this way, I learned about things like the humility topos and appeals to the body that women used to make it okay for them to write for public audiences. They reinvented themselves as mystics and saints who were definitely not submissive, and this taught me a lot about ethos, which shows how our identity is always an amalgam of how we present and how we are received.

I also learned a lot about how people try to circumscribe your interests or activities depending on your identity. I had several white male professors ask [me] why I would study medieval rhetoric, as if the whole idea was ludicrous because of who I am. As if I wouldn't want to look at women like Christine de Pizan, who was a single mother and defended women against misogyny in her professional writing, or Hildegard of Bingen,[10] a brilliant scholar and preacher who nonetheless used racism, anti-Semitism, to bolster her authority. These -isms haven't gone away but evolved, and it's by looking across time that we can understand how we got here, to a place where a lot of the stereotypes you see during this period are being deployed against Latinxs and other people of color. What my research across centuries shows is that such attacks on identity really haven't changed, and a big part of our everyday struggles is fighting for the right to say who we are.

CG: As a professor of rhetoric and composition, you hold a privileged place in the academy, yet sometimes academia can feel very much the opposite of privileged and even sometimes unsafe.[11] Gloria's experience in her PhD is telling; though *Borderlands / La Frontera* was an adopted text being taught

10. See Cedillo 2015.

11. In their contribution to this collection (chapter 9), Raquel Corona and Nancy Alvarez help us understand the trials of navigating the academy as Latinx.

in the PhD program at the University of California, Santa Cruz, where she was enrolled, she was consistently counseled by her "mentors" not to be so experimental in her writings, to respect genre, to commandeer her code meshing. In "Doing Gigs," Anzaldúa remarks that spaces like these, in academia and beyond, are "only secure and safe and comfortable for people complicit in the system. But if you're a resistor, challenger, if you're an activist, it's a very uncomfortable place, an alienating place" (2000a, 231). Do you agree?

CVC: One of the things I look at as a researcher and try to be careful of as a teacher is the issue of space. This semester in first-year comp, we're thinking through space and place and how they enable really influential spatial, bodily, and procedural rhetorics. In a forthcoming essay, I argue that instead of requiring that students change to fit academic spaces, we have to make spaces adapt to students' identities and needs. Until that happens, a lot of students are going to continue feeling out of place in school despite a lot of good intentions. In addition, I'm very interested in the way that proprioception[12] lets us know whether a space is friendly or hostile, meant for bodies other than ours. Again, kind of like Anzaldúa's facultad, proprioception is a source of bodily knowledge that tells us if we can feel safe or comfortable in a space or not. And we can use that in strategic ways.

But it means coming to terms with our discomfort and our willingness to be uncomfortable. Not everybody wants to, not everybody *feels* like they can—pun intended, I guess. So instead they try to assimilate or acculturate to the whitestream. But if you don't resist or fight for change once you're inside privileged spaces, then you're part of the problem, no matter how woke (you think) you are. You can't just know

12. Proprioception is our ability to sense our bodies in relation to the environment and to others.

things are colonial or racist or transphobic and write about it; you have to be anticolonial, antiracist, antitransphobia in all your praxes, in the everyday. You have to make room for others deliberately and thoughtfully, compassionately and carefully. That might look differently depending on the persons involved, but without some sort of resistance happening, you're complicit in a system that kills people's spirits and bodies because they don't fit the norm.

The Weight of Raindrops: An Interview with Tanaya Winder

CG: Anzaldúa writes, "Identity is relational. Who and what we are depends on those surrounding us, a mix of our interactions with our *alrededores*/environments, with new and old narratives. Identity is multilayered, stretching in all directions, from past to present, vertically and horizontally, chronologically and spatially" (2005a, 69). How do you self-identify?

TW: I identify as a *girl-on-fire*, as someone who carries light and warmth and flame. For Indigenous people, fire is so important; we use it to keep us warm, to cook food to nourish our bodies and our bellies, for ceremony, and to replenish if something needs to be burned down to return new growth. I believe each of us carries a fire in our hearts; that fire is our gift, our purpose, our spirit, the reason we were put on this earth. Whenever we come together in common causes or shared beliefs, I imagine each of us contributing our fire into one huge flame that reignites and nourishes each individual flame. We then can return to our work, replenished. I call myself *girl-on-fire* because I am unafraid of my own passion and gifts. I know I am meant to burn oh so beautifully.

CG: You are a girl-on-fire of many talents; we first met through the Chicana and Chicano Studies Department at the University of New Mexico, and I know you also direct the Upward Bound Program at the University of Colorado, Boulder. And you are also a touring poet and author! Can you talk to me about how your various creative and scholarly positions, both in the classroom and in the community, coalesce?

TW: I would say that I am a *heartworker*. I do heartwork. I try my best to use the gifts I have been given to uplift and empower others to find—and embrace—his/her/their gifts. I try to be a lighthouse for others in a storm. I do this by teaching both high school and college students. I do this by mentoring and guiding others through offering advice and a shoulder for support. I travel all across Turtle Island—North America—singing songs and poeming in hopes of healing, but always teaching others to believe in the power and strength of their voice and their ancestors' voices and the voice of the Creator speaking through each of us.

CG: In your opinion, what is that one specific quality that defines a good leader? And why that quality?

TW: Rootedness. Being rooted is the most important quality because you need to know where you come from before you can recognize the breadth and privilege of where you are and who you are, before you can understand where you need to go and why. Remaining grounded in my culture and community keep me responsible and accountable to everything I am doing. Rootedness reminds me of everything my ancestors, my grandmothers, my grandfathers, my father, my mother, and my sister did to get *here*—alive, resilient, strong, present, and connected—I never want to take *here* for granted because my ancestors sacrificed everything so that I could be *here*.

CG: Something I struggle with in my writing and in my day-to-day lived experience is authenticity—my desire to be truly authentic juxtaposed with the realities of norms, mores, gatekeepers, societal/familial/professional pressures. I view you as someone who balances authenticity, creative bravery, and the savvy of a businessperson. And, I think, it is in your writing that these come together to become something really transformative for your reader/listener.[13] Gloria remarks on this transformative act that happens with writing when she says, "In our common struggle and in our writing we reclaim our tongues" (Anzaldúa 1982, 163). What do you think?

TW: Whenever I am writing something that feels *real* in the utmost sense of realness—present, authentic, actually existing—I never feel that it is just *me* writing. I always feel as if my ancestors and Creator are speaking, writing, and singing *through me*. I am just a vessel for whatever message that needs to be birthed into this world, this realm, and this plane. I feel that each time I put pen to paper, finger to guitar string plucking notes, or open my mouth to release the tones that live in my throat that I am honoring my spirit. I am being love and loved and loving. In that way, I am reclaiming my place in this universe to help teach about the practice of radical love.

CG: One of your girl-on-fire talents is managing Native American artists under the Dream Warriors label, which you founded. Beyond helping other Native American artists rise in their creative endeavors, Dream Warriors also has a scholarship fund awarding money for Native youth to attend college. You really amaze me in your dedication to uplifting those around you. There is another Gloria quote that, in my opinion, could have been written about your heartwork and how you bring gifts of poem and song to your communities. Gloria wrote: "I call us 'divine warriors' because we have to fight. But it's not a physical fighting. It's fighting with the spirit. To be healthy you must awaken a sense of who you are and keep it strong and assert that you're OK, that you're

---

13. Winder's most recent poetry collections are *Words Like Love* (2015) and *Why Storms Are Named after People and Bullets Remain Nameless* (2017), and links to her many published poems are available on her website at https://tanayawinder.com/.

not sick, that society—religion, political, systems, morality, the movies, the media, the newspapers—that they're all
wrong and you're right" (2000c, 122). What do you think
about what Gloria is trying to teach us, this radical act of
self-acceptance?

TW: One of the elders in my community says you need to feed
your spirit. To me, this means that you need to nourish
yourself and the life force inside of you, but you also need to
be careful of what you feed your spirit. Are you surrounding
yourself with people who make you feel needed, important,
worthy, and loved? Are you putting yourself in spaces where
you feel empowered? This same elder also says to let your
spirit breathe. Growing up, I constantly put myself in cages,
in spaces, relationships, and situations too small to hold me.
I did this shrinking to try to make myself fit into that sick
society that wants us all to be the same cookie-cutter plastic
mold of anything other than different, anything other than
free. Each day is a spiritual battle to let go of the darkness and stand in the light. Each day is a spiritual battle to
breathe and love and let go of who or what threatens your
freedom.

As a writer and singer and heartworker, I am a "divine
warrior" because I believe in fighting for my spirit's wellbeing and freedom each and every day. I am a "divine warrior" because I believe in fighting for the well-being and
freedom of every other human being's spirit, too. Sometimes
I get tired, weary, and exhausted from fighting. There are
days I feel so drained that all I can do is breathe. And it takes
great courage to get up each morning to do it all again without succumbing to numbness from routine. It takes a strong
spirit to keep battling for good.

CMG: I wanted to get your response for one final Anzaldúa
quote, one of my all-time favorite Gloria quotes, to be honest. It makes me think of how students and writers respond

to you when you teach or perform, of this connection that happens within this shared moment of art. The quote reads, "I say *mujer magica*, empty yourself. Shock yourself into new ways of perceiving the world, shock your readers into the same. Stop the chatter inside their heads" (Anzaldúa 1982, 174). What do you think?

TW: My thoughts are always moving like raindrops scattered across my mind. How is it possible to hold so much hope and love and loss and longing and fear all at once? My hands cramp thinking of the weight they must carry in navigating me through the forest. I tried meditating one year to begin each morning emptying my mind and myself—each second focusing on breath, the rise and fall of my chest. Emptying is a painful practice. I heard once to think of each thought as a balloon: acknowledge its presence and let it go. I heard once that the point of meditation wasn't to think of nothingness, but to recognize your thoughts and how your mind maneuvers. My existence is a meditation. Some days I am in full triage mode, assessing traumas of my own and those I work with, those I serve through my heartwork. Some days I am balancing time and commitments with the hopes and wants of my art (which, too, is a daily practice, or at least I want it to be). Some days I can just breathe. Poeming is breathing, too. I want my words to be a breath of life and my songs to be a meditation that reminds each person to breathe because existing and resisting and loving and fighting are how we continue to remain present.

Remythologizing the Chingona: The Conclusion

I am grateful to both Tanaya and Christina for sharing their stories with us. I'd like to follow up these powerful interviews with a response to Gloria Anzaldúa's call to revision our narratives of Western tradition, including, specifically, our foremothers, the OG goddesses and creators, las mera meras, that we have always looked to for guidance in leadership situations.[14] In the Western tradition, Eve's bite of the apple from the tree of knowledge was humankind's first act of agency. This act of agency marked the fall of humankind, the moment that human beings learned of shame and evil. I disagree with this interpretation. I believe that Eve's original act of agency was righteous disobedience. In her decision to bite the apple, Eve cast aside the "status quo of Edenic conditions" (Anzaldúa 2005c, 120) and unconscious existence for carnal knowledge and self-actualization, neither of which is shameful or evil. Non-Western traditions support this interpretation. Gloria Anzaldúa advises us: "*Xochiquetzal*, a Mexican Indigenous deity, ascends to the upper world to seek knowledge from '*el árbol sagrado*,' the tree of life, *que florecía en Tamoanchan*. Eve snatches the fruit (the treasure of forbidden knowledge) from the serpent's mouth and invents 'consciousness'—the sense of self in the act of knowing. Serpent Woman, known as *Cihuacoatl*, the goddess of origins, whom you think of as La Llorona and sketch as a half coiled snake with the head of a woman represents not the root of all evil but instinctual knowledge and other alternative ways of knowing that fuel transformation" (2005c, 120–21).

In acts of desconocimiento, we lose sight of our gifts and fall into a pit of dysconsciousness, where we uncritically accept the existing order of things as given.[15] But we are the children of Eve, the original metaphysic, as well as of La Llorona, the wailing woman who demands agency and will not be silenced. We are mobility and flexibility: our survival has depended on our ability to adapt, and this is threatening—other people would like to be as malleable and as strong as we are.[16] Through learning to navigate our day-to-days, we have gained

14. Aja Y. Martinez's book *Counterstory* (2020) works as both a guide to resisting others' narratives in pursuit of our own and as a map of the method and methodology to get this work done.

15. From Joyce E. King's use of the term *dysconscious* (cited in Kim and Olson 2017, 135).

16. From Hector Torres's interview with Anzaldúa (Torres 2007); also, see Dr. Cedillo's discussion of proprioception in the interview with her in this chapter.

a strong sense of our self, powerful connections to each other and to our environments, and intuition that we trust. We do not accept the common narrative of a woman with agency as culpable for humans' downfall;[17] rather, we embrace our unique abilities of floricanto, making words dance, and of commanding audiences in the home, the classroom, and the polis.

I'd like to end with a parting word from the great poet Pat Mora, a mantra of sorts for those of us heeding the call to lead, in whatever capacity that means. Mora writes:

> We need you
> and your stories
> and questions
> that like a fresh path
> will take us to new vistas. (2010, 151)

References

Anzaldúa, Gloria E. 1982. "Speaking in Tongues: A Letter to Third World Women Writers." In *This Bridge Called My Back: Writings by Radical Women of Color*, edited by Cherríe Moraga and Gloria Anzaldúa, 163–74. New York: Kitchen Table, Women of Color Press.

———. 2000a. "Doing Gigs: Speaking, Writing, and Change." Interview by Debbie Blake and Carmen Abrego, 1994. In *Gloria Anzaldúa: Interviews/Entrevistas*, edited by AnaLouise Keating, 211–34. New York: Routledge.

———. 2000b. "Turning Points." Interview by Linda Smuckler, 1982. In *Gloria Anzaldúa: Interviews/Entrevistas*, edited by AnaLouise Keating, 17–70. New York: Routledge.

———. 2000c. "Within the Crossroads: Lesbian/Feminist/Spiritual Development." Interview by Christine Weiland, 1983. In *Gloria Anzaldúa: Interviews/Entrevistas*, edited by AnaLouise Keating, 71–127. New York: Routledge.

———. 2005a. "Geographies of Selves—Reimagining Identity." In Gloria Anzaldúa, *Light in the Dark / Luz en lo oscuro: Rewriting Identity*,

---

17. For more on counternarrative as decolonial praxis, see Martinez 2018.

Spirituality, Reality, edited by AnaLouise Keating, 65–94. Durham, NC: Duke Univ. Press.

———. 2005b. "Gestures of the Body—Escribiendo para idear." In Gloria Anzaldúa, *Light in the Dark / Luz en lo oscuro: Rewriting Identity, Spirituality, Reality*, edited by AnaLouise Keating, 1–8. Durham, NC: Duke Univ. Press.

———. 2005c. "Now Let Us Shift . . . Conocimiento . . . Inner Work, Public Acts." In Gloria Anzaldúa, *Light in the Dark / Luz en lo oscuro: Rewriting Identity, Spirituality, Reality*, edited by AnaLouise Keating, 117–59. Durham, NC: Duke Univ. Press.

Cedillo, Christina V. 2015. "Habitual Gender: Rhetorical Androgyny in Franciscan Texts." *Journal of Feminist Studies in Religion* 31, no. 1: 65–81.

Keating, AnaLouise. 2000. "Risking the Personal—an Introduction." In Gloria Anzaldúa, *Gloria Anzaldúa: Interviews/Entrevistas*, edited by AnaLouise Keating, 1–16. New York: Routledge.

Kim, Dae-Joong, and Bobbi Olson. 2017. "Deconstructing Whiteliness in the Globalized Classroom." In *Performing Antiracist Pedagogy in Rhetoric, Writing, and Communication*, edited by Frankie Condon and Vershawn Ashanti Young, 123–58. Fort Collins: Colorado State Univ. Open Press.

Lara, Irene. "Bruja Positionalities: Toward a Chicana/Latina Spiritual Activism." *Chicana/Latina Studies* 4, no. 2 (Spring 2005): 10–45.

Limón, Graciela. 1994. *The Memories of Ana Calderón: A Novel.* Houston: Arte Público Press.

Martinez, Aja Y. 2018. "The Responsibility of Privilege: A Critical Race Counterstory Conversation." *Peitho* 21, no. 1: 212–33.

———. 2020. *Counterstory: The Rhetoric and Writing of Critical Race Theory.* Urbana, IL: National Council of Teachers of English.

Mora, Pat. 2010. "Ode to Teachers." In *Dizzy in Your Eyes*, 151–54. New York: Random House.

Torres, Hector A. 2007. "Gloria Anzaldúa: The Author Never Existed." In *Conversations with Contemporary Chicana and Chicano Writers*, 115–45. Albuquerque: Univ. of New Mexico Press.

Winder, Tanya. 2015. *Words Like Love.* New York: West End Press.

———. 2017. *Why Storms Are Named after People and Bullets Remain Nameless.* N.p.: self-published.

7

Latina Leadership and Lessons Learned from the Women of the Local 890 and the Cold War–Era Empire Zinc Mine Strike

Michelle Hall Kells

Abstract

This chapter aligns the story of the women of the Local 890 with the journey of conceptualizing and implementing the Salt of the Earth Recovery Project with a team of graduate students. Through the construction of community writing workshops and the development of the Salt of the Earth Digital Cuentos archive, our team engaged with local citizens, activists, and scholars in a deliberative process toward a collective vision for the preservation and restoration of the historic union hall in Bayard, New Mexico. I extend this story to include reflections on the work of mentoring new leaders in the generative and restorative space of community activism and writing. Working and living together in the space of what I can best describe as the divine tension between strength and vulnerability represents, in my perspective, the soul of Latina leadership.

Introduction

This story begins in 1966 with me sitting in the back seat of my grandmother's white Chevy Impala with my two sisters and my nine-year-old aunt, and we are driving through the barrios of Oakland, California. It was a road trip about which we were sworn never to speak. As we cruised the back alleys of the Bay Area inner city, I

139

2. Mural at the union hall of Local 890, International Union of Mine, Mill, and Smelter Workers, Bayard, New Mexico, July 2017. Photograph by Michelle Hall Kells.

watched, over the tufted red-leather seats and through the towering bouffants of their Clairol-enhanced auburn hair, my grandmother and mother navigating a world strangely new to me. I was only eight years old, but I knew by the secretive nature of our journey that what we were doing was something transgressive, dangerous, and forbidden. We pulled up to a faded yellow bungalow on the edges of Oakland to visit my eighteen-year-old aunt, weeping and blue-eyed, and her bawling baby, who I would learn for the first time was my new cousin. The family secret. Somewhere, indelibly etched in my mind, remains the memory of my teenage aunt and her new baby living in the shadows of family ostracism.

Some fifty years later I found myself driving over the Gila Mountains to meet with the leaders of the Local 9424 of the United Steelworkers Union to see the decommissioned union hall made famous during the 1950s Empire Zinc Mine strike in Bayard, New Mexico. I started asking questions about the women of the Local 890, who held the picket line during the strike, as I finished writing *Vicente Ximenes, LBJ's Great Society, and Mexican American Civil Rights Rhetoric* in April 2016 (Kells 2018). I was writing the final drafts of the manuscript for the book when I read the stirring news in the *Albuquerque Journal* that the iconic Local 890 in Bayard, New Mexico, had voted to decertify the union after more than seventy-five years. My curiosity and concern were piqued. I realized that I needed to explore more deeply how the epic Empire Zinc Mine strike of the early 1950s had shaped Vicente Ximenes's rhetorical imagination and inspired his work as a community organizer and founder of the first chapter of the American GI Forum in Albuquerque in 1950.

Over the next six months, it became clear that this project was more than academic; I was searching for hope in the face of overwhelming despair at the outcome of the presidential election in 2016, the loss of a nation's soul, and the looming specter of white nationalism. This chapter focuses on the parallel journey of reconciling loss (both personal and national) with the launching of the Salt of the Earth Recovery Project to explore the moral courage of the mexicana leaders who changed the rhetorical imagination of Cold War America.

The Women of the Local 890

The Local 890 chapter of the International Union of Mine, Mill, and Smelter Workers of Hanover, New Mexico, comprising fourteen hundred members who were predominantly Mexican American and Mexican-origin laborers, staged a strike near Silver City, New Mexico, that lasted fifteen months, from October 1950 to January 1952. The erosion of ancestral communities and the rise of company towns, as illustrated in this historic case, provided a catalyst for political activism among Cold War Mexican American communities. The cultural and political reverberations of the Empire Zinc Mine strike have extended well beyond a small mining community nested in the Gila Mountains of New Mexico. The workers' grievances included racial discrimination, toxic work environments, no-strike contract clauses, and inequitable power sharing between labor and management. The dramatic showdown between the women and local law enforcement agents and the resulting incarceration of forty-five women, seventeen children, and a six-month-old baby shocked people locally and nationally.

Women took a leading role in the Empire Zinc Mine strike to confront enduring harassment, intimidation, incarceration, and numerous civil rights violations by the dominant Anglo power structure. The legacy of loss and suffering of the Local 890 workers still resonates in this small mining community of southern New Mexico. The gaping hole in the landscape outside the quaint and nostalgic Old West town of Silver City is a startling reminder of the tremendous costs, human as well as environmental, of the multinational copper-mining industry on the high-desert landscape of New Mexico. The job action of the Local 890 men and women captured so much national attention that independent film producers Paul Jerrico and Sylvia Jerrico were inspired to make a film about the incident, *Salt of the Earth* (1954). As the only film to be banned (and still remain on the blacklist of so-called subversive propaganda targeted by Senator Joseph McCarthy's infamous Committee on Un-American Activities), *Salt of the Earth* sought to humanize mexicano laborers, expose exploitive work conditions, interrogate the environmental impact of the mining industry, and challenge the local white hegemonic political climate.

I felt immediately inspired by the Empire Zinc Mine strike story when I first saw *Salt of the Earth* soon after joining the faculty of the University of New Mexico (UNM) as an assistant professor and teaching a course on Mexican American civil rights rhetoric in 2006. However, I didn't feel a deep community connection and civic responsibility moving me to preserve this story until ten years later, when I started conducting research in Silver City in April 2016 in the wake of the decertification of the Local 890 union hall. I felt both a professional and civic responsibility to help protect the hall when I saw the luminous story of collective sacrifice in the vibrant murals painted inside and outside it during my own search to find hope amid despair over the collapse of our national vision for universal justice, liberty, and inclusivity. The urgency to recover the narratives, murals, and artifacts related to the Local 890 became even more evident when I saw the site where the Empire Zinc Mine strike took place, a bridge on the edge of the Central Mining District, now relegated to obscurity and covered in weeds, litter, and graffiti. What was once invisible to me became vibrant and visible.

As Stefani Baldivia and Kendall Leon observe in chapter 5 in this collection, the act of navigating and curating archives of memory is both rhetorical and political. Constituting an archive for the public sphere involves, Baldivia and Leon assert, "recognizing that stories make change." Hence, in this chapter I align the story of the women of the Local 890 with the hermeneutic project of conceptualizing and implementing the Salt of the Earth Recovery Project with a team of graduate students. Through the construction of community writing workshops and the development of the Salt of the Earth Digital Cuentos archive, our team engaged with local citizens, activists, and scholars in a deliberative process toward a collective vision for the preservation and restoration of the historic union hall in Bayard, New Mexico.

Since the coming of the COVID-19 pandemic, we are witnessing the tragic impact of a public-health crisis on our most vulnerable communities. In a *New York Times* op-ed in April 2020, a month after the declaration of a national emergency, UNM graduate student Sunnie Rae Clahchischiligi wrote, "The coronavirus virus outbreak in the Navajo Nation is showing that nowhere is as remote as it might have once seemed. And the reservation is not prepared. My nation is held together by a culture of togetherness—but that tradition of gathering also makes the spread of the virus worse."

Indigenous communities blighted by the contagion of Anglo-European settler colonizing and empire building more than five hundred years ago remain vulnerable to twenty-first-century pandemics and the genocide of environmental racism. In every corner of this nation, in every community on this planet, we are looking for a universal story that promotes global healing, wholeness, and hope. The mobilization of Native women leaders during the Standing Rock Protests of 2016 is reflective of the collective resistance, advocacy, and leadership demonstrated by women labor activists (Estes 2019). We are looking for a common language to teach in a world that has become more divided, more polarized, more threatening, and more unjust. The environmental and public-health impacts of colonization and of an ecology out of balance were evidenced in social and political violence well before the COVID-19 crisis.

La Huelga: The Archive as Habitat

The story of embodied activism by the women of the Empire Zinc Mine strike has lived for almost seventy years in a kind of liminal space between fact and fiction, a space obscured by what could be considered strategic rhetorical silence. The expansive list of intolerable living and working conditions in racially segmented job duties and pay, the lack of sanitation for mexicano housing, the glaring racial divisions between mexicano labor and Anglo management motivated mobilization for la huelga. The Grant County authorities asked the governor to send in the National Guard as soon as the strike began in October 1950. An injunction enforced by local law enforcement preventing the men from holding the picket line pressed the workers either to act or to concede to corporate pressure to end the strike. In response to this tactic, though, the women of the Local 890 took the lead and held the strike line until the laborers' demands were met. Many of the workers, including women, spent several months in jail and paid heavy fines. Mexicanas and Mexican American women, like other women of color, were active change agents in twentieth-century US civil rights reform.

With the production and release of the historic film *Salt of the Earth* in 1954, local lore, political expediency, and social convention ultimately effaced the "real" lives of the "real" women who held the picket line and helped to bring la huelga to a successful close. The US government banned *Salt of the Earth* upon its release, but local civil rights activists such as Vicente Ximenes and the newly formed American GI Forum's Albuquerque chapter immediately recognized the important implications of the events depicted in the film for organizing Mexican Americans. The producers of *Salt of the Earth* resisted the stereotypical representations of the region, enlisting local union members and residents in the screen writing, acting, and production of the film.

Gabriel Meléndez argues in "Who Are the 'Salt of the Earth'?" (2007) that the "red-baited and blacklisted Hollywood filmmakers who came to Silver City, New Mexico to film *Salt* . . . were not absorbed in exotica, nostalgia, or romance, the standard elements that had been applied successfully in films about New Mexico and *Nuevomexicanos*" (117). The end result is a gripping homespun story about labor, gender, race, border politics, and civil rights conditioned by the forces of history, culture, and economics. The events of the fifteen-month Empire Zinc strike are narrated from the perspective of Esperanza Quintero, a wife, mother, and activist who calls for "sanitation not discrimination." A portrait of Benito Juárez, liberator and revolutionary of Mexico, holds an honored place in her home. The roles of women engaged in the deliberative process of union organizing, agenda setting, work stoppage, strike maintenance, and gender-role negotiation distinguished this movie from the standard fare offered by McCarthy's blacklisted Hollywood filmmakers.

Rodolfo Acuña notes, "The so-called Salt of the Earth strike is the best-known Chicano strike. It inspired a classic film that received worldwide acclaim but was banned in the United States" (1972, 278). The rhetorical situation of the events surrounding the strike was conditioned by the anticommunist hysteria of the McCarthy era. The success of the Local 890 represented a collective affirmation for all Mexican American laborers in the region who sought redress for discriminatory work conditions. Ultimately, the labor strike and the film *Salt of Earth* provided a clear and visible case of Mexican American political activism in New Mexico. The strike offered a model for direct action, organization, collective activism, and deliberative processes. Ten years later, *Salt of the Earth* gained popularity in the Chicano movement of the 1960s as a model of paideia. As Meléndez notes, "In the mid-1960s, *Salt* became an important cultural and educational document that served to educate and raise the consciousness of a generation of university students," including the early organizers of the United Mexican American Student Association in 1968 (2007, 122). The teleological value of these connections, exemplified by *Salt of the Earth*, extended into the civil rights era of the 1960s with national policy making on behalf of Mexican Americans.

Over the next seven decades, the film and the historical event have become conflated, with the fiction of the film script functioning as a trope, rhetorical avatar, or celluloid metonymy. Some of the women strikers eventually reconvened for the fortieth and fiftieth anniversary conferences commemorating the strike. The overall silence about the lives of the "real" women of the Local 890 after the Empire Zinc Mine strike is clear. There are no memoirs or manifestos recounting the ideological underpinnings of these women's collective action. There are no essays or pedagogical treatises advancing their organizing strategies. Robin Wall Kimmerer reflects in *Braiding Sweetgrass: Indigenous Wisdom, Scientific Knowledge, and the Teachings of Plants* (2013), "Stories are among our most potent tools for restoring the land as well as our relationships to the land. We need to unearth the old stories that live in a place and begin to create new ones, for we are storymakers, not just storytellers" (341). Confronting the trauma of extraction industries on human and "more-than-human" communities, Kimmerer looks to language and storytelling as restorative practices.

Exemplifying the deep need to fill this void and promote new story making among emerging leaders, Ana Milena Ribero and Sonia C. Arellano articulate the ethical dimensions of Latina leadership in their essay "Advocating Comadrismo: A Feminist Mentoring Approach for Latinas in Rhetoric and Composition" (chapter 1 in this collection). The emergent themes of comadrismo delineated by Ribero and Arellano are profoundly evidenced in the narratives of the Empire Zinc Mine strike leaders who came to tell their stories through the Salt of the Earth Recovery Project. As suggested by Ribero and Arellano, these women cultivated and demonstrated deep kinship ties, enduring empathy, and sustained collaboration with one another. Consistent with Ribero and Arellano's emergent themes of Latina leadership, findings from the Salt of the Earth Recovery Project also suggest that the ethic of querencia, concern for home and community, was a catalyzing value among the Local 890 women activists during the strike.

The Salt of the Earth Recovery Project

It was my principal goal as chair of the Salt of the Earth Recovery Project to cultivate the conditions to encourage civic literacy and deliberative democratic practice through the formation of community writing workshops by inviting local citizens to write their own narratives. In brief, I wanted to construct a platform, a space, for community members to exercise their own voices. I hoped to enact what the ancient Greeks called the "agora," where citizens could engage with each other in the messy work of citizenship to tell their stories, to advance their own rhetorical positions, and to determine together the fate of the now empty Local 890 union hall.

Moreover, as an academic researcher and civil rights scholar who has engaged in the slow research of empirical inquiry, I was determined to keep the findings of my research free, open, and accessible rather than buried in the annals of history or bogged down in the lengthy, mystified, and protracted process of scholarly publication. Someday perhaps there would be a book about this journey of research, but, more importantly, it was imperative to me to keep the Salt of the Earth Recovery Project current, relevant, transparent, and inclusive, not locked away in the ivory tower of the academy.

Above all else, the stories, the murals, the artifacts, and archival materials needed to remain the intellectual property of the community. Hence, my team and I painstakingly imagined and designed the Salt of the Earth Digital Cuentos writing workshops as both an organic and digital archive using "old school" as well as "new school" modalities and generated workshop materials in English and Spanish. The Salt of the Earth Recovery Project was a team effort from the outset through the collaborative leadership of four graduate students: Steven Romero, Zakery Muñoz, and Kelli Lycke-Martin, all MA students at

UNM, as well as Elvira Carrizal-Dukes, a doctoral candidate at the University of Texas at El Paso.[1] Each of these emerging scholars exercised a strong authorial role both through the development and the design of the Salt of the Earth Recovery Project as a group endeavor as well as through their own individual scholarly projects related to the Empire Zinc Mine strike.

We held four community writing workshops throughout the summer of 2016, including an initial workshop in May in collaboration with the UNM Center for Regional Studies. We held the Salt of the Earth Digital Archive community writing workshops at the Western New Mexico University Library, the Silver City Public Library, the Silver City Museum, and the Bayard Public Library. The graduate students and I structured a set of writing-consultant-assisted "stations" for the workshops to support each participant through the story-writing process, beginning with an invention protocol by means of a writing prompt that invited free-writing and brainstorming processes, followed by revising, editing, word processing, digitizing, and finally assisting each participant in scanning photos and other archival materials and taking "selfies."

During one of our writing workshops in the garden courtyard behind the Silver City Museum, my team and I were busy working with local community members when a law enforcement officer in a bulletproof vest strode through the area. She made eye contact with me as she walked by, but she did not speak. She walked directly to the museum curator who was chatting with the community writing workshop participants and asked if he had seen a person of interest running through the area. The officer spoke to no one else about the person under pursuit. This behavior puzzled me at the time. Why would an officer giving chase not speak to everyone in the area or investigate the site more thoroughly—and not even peek around the corner or peer down the street?

---

1. See the Salt of the Earth Recovery Project profiles at https://saltoftheearth recoveryproject.wordpress.com/project-profiles/.

Without further conversation and with what seems to have been a code word exchanged between her and the curator, the officer turned around and left the community writing workshop as intently as she had arrived. Were the local Silver City authorities expecting a protest during the community writing workshops? Silver City Museum's curator had confided in me that the public announcement of the museum's sponsorship of the Salt of the Earth Recovery Project had been contested by several detractors in Silver City. What the young female officer found that Saturday morning in July was a gathering of citizens scattered about the vivid green grass telling their stories to one another: the son of the first Mexican American sheriff in Grant County sitting in a wheelchair, scrolling through the Digital Cuentos archive, and two young Bayard natives—a young Chicano UNM student and his Chicana girlfriend, a student at New Mexico State University—writing together. Our presence was radical, bold, subversive, and transgressive. We were together engaging in the practice of deliberative democracy. This is embodied rhetoric.

Testimonios: Recovering Rhetorics of Presence

I remain inspired by the moral courage of the leaders of the Local 890 and their descendants in Bayard who are keeping the story alive. This story continues to reach across generation, class, race, gender, and national boundaries. The power of acts of moral courage such as the Empire Zinc Mine strike extend through our collective consciousness to stir our souls when we need them most. After more than two decades of researching civil rights rhetorics and after writing two books on the Cold War Mexican American civil rights movement, I maintain that the Empire Zinc Mine strike in Cold War–era New Mexico represents el alma of the post–World War II Mexican American civil rights movement and el corazón of the Chicana movement that followed decades later.

The women labor activists of the Empire Zinc Mine strike mobilized to protect la querencia, the well-being of their families and community. They sought to sustain the ways of life of la comunidad, la dignidad of workers, la solidaridad of the union, and la autoridad of one another as mexicana leaders. The histories, memories, and stories of their collective rhetorical action remain inscribed in archives and the union hall of the Local 890, which remains empty on the edge of the village of Bayard. The Local 890 union hall is one of the few landmark sites of this important historical period. Hence, the impetus to advocate with the community through the Salt of the Earth Recovery Project remained pivotal to our efforts throughout the project. The goal to restore and preserve the Local 890 union hall remained at the center of this cross-institutional, cross-regional, and cross-generational project.

As Paul Ricoeur argues in *Memory, History, Forgetting* (2004), "Everything starts, not from the archives, but from testimony" (137). We lose our national stories, like our own familial narratives, one frayed strand at a time until the fabric of collective identity is unraveled, and no one is left to weave themselves into the story or to witness how the intricate tapestry of belonging is woven and maintained. Since the Local 890 union hall was first established in Bayard soon after World War II, an old army barracks dragged over the mountains from Deming, it has been the center of social life of the Central Mining District. For some seventy years, it was the site of union meetings, Lady Auxiliary events, wedding receptions, baptism and graduation celebrations, and quinceañeras. The Local 890 union hall has embodied the cultural and social values of the community across generations—a crucible of querencia. The small circles of mexicana solidarity that lived inside the Local 890 union hall for seven decades and played out in the public sphere during the Empire Zinc Mine strike still reverberate powerful representations of Latina leadership that merit our close attention.

The love and reverence for family, home, place, community, and landscape resonate as an organizing theme in the stories of the early Empire Zinc Mine strike of the 1950s. After two-thirds of a century, those stories ripple across time in the sites, images, and narratives surrounding the preservation and protection of the Local 890 union hall, especially through the public art of the murals painted by local youth and artists. The Cold War–era civil rights and labor rights movement that was catalyzed in Bayard and Hanover, New Mexico, in the early 1950s vibrated concurrently across the nation and across social groups. Chicano activists such as Corky Gonzalez and Cesar Chavez as well as Chicana leaders such as Dolores Huerta and Gloria Anzaldúa came of age in the Cold War era. The soul of the United States began shifting like a great collective dance when the women of the Local 890 took to the picket lines and stood together in la huelga, exercising a rhetoric of resistance through the enactment of la autoridad, la comunidad, la solidaridad, y la dignidad.

This is the story that needs to be remembered and should be preserved with this historic union hall. This is the reason for launching the Salt of the Earth Recovery Project. I believe that the leadership demonstrated by the women of the Empire Zinc Mine strike represents one of the most compelling and inspiring moments of civic activism in US history. These leaders' legacy and sacrifice remain inscribed in the murals and paintings of the Local 890 union hall. These murals and paintings are the testimonios, the resonances breaking the silence. And this is the very purpose of the Salt of the Earth Recovery Project: to celebrate the lives, labor, and leadership of the women and men of the Local 890. As Laura Gonzales boldly explores in chapter 3 in this collection, the reflective process toward self-understanding is critical to building coalitions among Latina leaders.

Rachel Juarez Valencia (2018), the lone woman in the strike who was still living at the time of our project, offered her powerful testimonio when she came to write her story for the Salt of the Earth Recovery Project. Sitting with our team at the Bayard Public Library on a sun-drenched New Mexico morning in July, Rachel came to tell her story. But she did more than that. As semis carrying sheets of processed copper from the nearby pit mine rolled through downtown, Bayard's local citizens streamed into the Bayard Public Library carrying old pictures, union posters, and other memorabilia. Rachel watched her friends and neighbors working with us and then began helping many of the workshop participants revise and edit their own stories. As participants uploaded their finished stories and scanned vintage photos for the Salt of the Earth Digital Cuentos website, Rachel then asked us to help her tell her story:

> Sometime during the summer, as the women were picketing, the district attorney Thomas Foy, gave the sheriff and some deputies permission to break the women's picket line. We didn't anticipate the violence that would come. As I was going around the circle, one of the cars that a deputy was driving caught me by surprise. As it was moving fast, the only thing I could do was hold on to the hood of the car the best way I could. I was able to hold on for approximately fifty feet. At that time, I knew I was either going to go under the car or I had to throw myself to the side of the road, which I did.
>
> As I lay on the ground, I could see some women coming to get me. I could see that a car had completely run over Mrs. Consuelo Martinez, an elderly lady of about seventy-five at the time. The women dragged me back to the side of the rode and the deputies started to arrest us. Some of the men who had been overseeing us, dragged Mrs. Martinez to the side of the rode so they wouldn't run over her again. One of the men was shot on the leg because he was trying to help us. One of the deputies threw me in the back of his car and he took me to the Watts clinic in Silver City. I had a dislocated shoulder. They took care of it at the clinic and released me. The deputy drove me to the court house and into the jail. The jail cell where they put me was very overcrowded. The women moved the children and teenagers to the front of the cell, which had slats, so they could breathe better.
>
> An elderly lady named Bersabe Rosales was placed on a bed because she was ninety-years-old at the time and she was passing out. My dad heard about the violence in Hanover at his job at Kennecott in Santa Rita through the radio. He knew that I was supposed to be there and left his job to go to the court house to see what was going on. He did not know I was hurt and was hoping I was not jailed. They let us out after many complaints from the community who became outraged about having women and children in jail because we had already spent three to four hours in the crowded jail cells. My father had to sign release papers and was given a court

date as was everybody who had been jailed. The strike ended with the violence and the jailing of the union officials and the women and the children. I can still see the jail cell from the street to this day because it's in the center of the court house and I can see the window to the cell where we were. (Valencia 2018)

Like many of the women of the Local 890, Rachel Valencia has lived out her life close to the mining district and the jail that confined her. She continued living close to the circles of women who supported and protected her at that time. The violence of the Empire Zinc Mine strike and the structural racism and sexism in the Central Mining District never really ended. Although the collective trauma gripped survivors such as Rachel, the community prevailed. Creating and protecting habitats where their families and loved ones, their communities and their own private stories, could safely exist constituted an organizing force for the women of the Local 890.

Querencia

As we worked together with the citizens of Silver City and Bayard to help them give accounts of their own experiences of the Empire Zinc Mine strike, I began recalling more vividly my own childhood memory of my mother and grandmother navigating Oakland to find my banished aunt. I realized at that moment some unspoken lesson passed down through generations of women: an intrinsic human need to nest, to create a habitat within which to thrive, to work, to love, to give birth, to protect, to flourish, to tell our stories, to make our lives meaningful, and ultimately to die close to our precious few. This need, I believe, is what catalyzed the women of the Local 890 to risk their lives, their livelihoods, and personal safety during the Empire Zinc Mine strike.

Likewise, I believe it was the same need that moved my grandmother and my mother to bundle us little girls in the back of my nana's Chevy, "to circle the ships" against a violent storm, to lock arms and hold firm together, and to defy my grandfather's expulsion of the young lovers from the family. In 1966, the love affair between my mexicano uncle and my Irish aunt transgressed the explosive racial and class lines dividing working-class whites like my grandmother's burgeoning Irish Catholic family and the working poor brown/Black communities struggling to survive in Oakland. This indelible lesson would shape my politics and my own journey as a leader, a scholar, a writer, and a teacher in myriad ways. The violent racial discrimination playing out in the streets of Berkeley, Oakland, San Francisco, Watts, and Los Angeles at the time, with the images of broken Black and brown bodies streaming into our living rooms on the nightly news, was quietly and insidiously reproducing itself within my own family.

As an eight-year-old, I had neither the intellectual nor the discursive resources available to me to articulate the rupture dividing my grandmother's family. The split was discernible, nevertheless, like a wedge dividing our home. As most of my working-class family leaned right through the 1960s and on through the 1980s, paying off their mortgages, raising their children, and voting for Nixon and Reagan, I found myself leaning farther and farther left.

I made regular summer pilgrimages to visit my tíos and their four children throughout my childhood and youth, eating fresh sourdough tortillas with los Gallegos and their extended family in their Bay Area home. The radiator of their old station wagon overheated during an ill-fated road trip I took with my tíos through the San Joaquin Valley, a misadventure for which my uncle would tease me for decades, lightheartedly blaming my poor directions as the reason for getting us hopelessly lost and stranded somewhere out in the sunbaked fields between Stockton and Sacramento. There was some unspoken bond that connected me to them, perhaps stemming from the unquestioned loyalty my grandmother demonstrated to me by her bold transgressive act. Ultimately, I would name my own son "Jacob" in honor of my uncle's father, Jacob Gallegos. And over those formative years of my young life, I gravitated and identified—emotionally, culturally, and spiritually—in some unspoken solidarity with mis tíos, mis padrinos, mis primos.

I think it is the universal human condition that deep within us all is a child who wants to go home again to our communities, our familias, our gente. In my grandmother's house, we are Oakies and Portuguese; Irish and Philippine; Mexican and Venezuelan; Polish and African; Vietnamese and Swiss. We are poor, and we are rich; we drive pickup trucks and Porsches; we are nurses and firemen; gay and straight. We vote Democrat, and we vote Republican. This cultural consciousness is formed in the crucible of community. We are a raucous rabble—a turbulent community. And in this terrible time of national whitelash and militarized border politics, we are living, metaphorically and literally, in a frail and fractured house, an American family abode crumbling at its very foundation.

Decades after this transgressive road trip to Oakland, as I engage the personal narratives and historical artifacts that give witness to the individual and collective stories of the Empire Zinc Mine strike, my understanding of this nearly irrepressible need to cultivate generative habitats in our communities, our workplaces, our classrooms, and the public sphere inspires me. Through the Digital Cuentos of the Salt of the Earth Recovery Project, I begin to see the powerful role these citizens played in conditioning their own rhetorical habitats within a hostile and repressive Cold War moment. The women of the Local 890 then and now have enacted the kind of community memory that Christina Ramirez describes in chapter 10 in this collection. As Ramirez asserts, "Possibly with or without our knowing, these backstories become the motivation to continue our work." In the face of overwhelming despair and unrelenting oppression, the women of Local 890 persisted. The Salt of the Earth Recovery Project continues to inspire new public discourses and stimulate new scholarship about Latina leadership.

After learning about the Salt of the Earth Recovery Project, Sayre Quevado, the National Public Radio documentarian for *Latino USA*, recently launched a journalistic investigation to interview community members for a documentary on the historical events surrounding the Empire Zinc Mine strike. Likewise, then graduate students Elvira Carrizal-Dukes, Kelli Lycke-Martin, Steven Romero, and Zakery Muñoz launched their own related scholarly research projects. Elvira created a YouTube video documentary of ninety-nine-year-old Local 890 union

3. Mural at the union hall of Local 890, International Union of Mine, Mill, and Smelter Workers, Bayard, New Mexico, July 2017. Photograph by Michelle Hall Kells.

member Arturo Flores, which Governor Michelle Lujan Grisham of New Mexico lauded in January 2019. Kelli launched a study into state and national historic-preservation efforts for the Local 890 union hall. Steven received the UNM Center for Regional Studies Fellowship in 2019 to construct the Salt of the Earth Community Literacy digital community curriculum to support Chicanx studies programs nationally. Finally, Zakery received the UNM Center for Regional Studies Fellowship in 2020 to examine New Mexico constitutional-era public rhetoric and the erosion of heritage languages in the state.

The concept of "querencia," this notion of rhetorical habitats as safety zones, circles of belonging and sanctuary, resonates deeply throughout the archive of personal stories and historical fragments. The lessons learned from the women of the Local 890, the takeaway insights that seem especially relevant to us as educators and scholars in this era of unfettered market capitalism, virulent sexism, and resurgent

4. Mural at the union hall of Local 890, International Union of Mine, Mill, and Smelter Workers, Bayard, New Mexico, July 2017. Photograph by Michelle Hall Kells.

white nationalism, point to the necessity of exercising la solidaridad, la dignidad, la comunidad, and la autoridad in all our various spheres of belonging and influence. These stories show us how a shared vision of solidarity, a respect for human dignity, a celebration of community, and a reverence for our own authorial voices can empower new Latina leaders to create habitats of survival in hostile climates. These narratives remind us of the urgency to form small circles with each other, to engage the power of radical intimacy. The testimonios, the artifacts, the murals, and the images of the women of the Local 890 stand collectively to reinforce the value of holding our ground and drawing a circle in the sand where we are bold enough both to work assiduously and to dance unabashedly in the face of adversity and the threat of oppression. Our bodies, our labor, our scholarship, our classrooms, our neighborhoods, and our gente represent home ground that demands not only our relentless attention but also our sacred protection.

References

Acuña, Rodolfo. 1972. *Occupied America: The Chicano's Struggle toward Liberation.* San Francisco: Harper and Row, Canfield Press.

Clahchischiligi, Sunnie Rae. 2020. "Nowhere Is Remote Anymore." *New York Times,* Apr. 20. At https://www.nytimes.com/2020/04/20/opinion /coronavirus-navajo-nation.html.

Estes, Nick. 2019. *Our History Is Our Future: Standing Rock versus the Dakota Access Pipeline, and the Long Tradition of Indigenous Resistance.* New York: Verso.

Kells, Michelle Hall. 2018. *Vicente Ximenes, LBJ's Great Society, and Mexican American Civil Rights Rhetoric.* Carbondale: Southern Illinois Univ. Press.

Kimmerer, Robin Wall. 2013. *Braiding Sweetgrass: Indigenous Wisdom, Scientific Knowledge, and the Teachings of Plants.* Minneapolis: Milkweed Press.

Meléndez, Gabriel. 2007. "Who Are the 'Salt of the Earth'?" In *Expressing New Mexico: Nuevomexicano Creativity, Ritual, and Memory,* edited by Felipe Gonzales, 115–38. Tucson: Univ. of Arizona Press.

Ricoeur, Paul. 2004. *Memory, History, Forgetting.* Translated by Kathleen Blamey and David Pellauer. Chicago: Univ. of Chicago Press.

Valencia, Rachel Juarez. 2018. "Digital Cuentos." Salt of the Earth Recovery Project, Dec. 10. At https://saltoftheearthrecoveryproject.wordpress .com/.

Part Three

Pedagogies and Mentorship within and beyond Academia

8

Counterstory por mi Gente

Color-Blind Racism, Assimilation,
and the American Dream

Aja Y. Martinez

Abstract

This essay explores Chicanx identity in academia through critical race theory (CRT) counterstory. A turn to CRT is an interdisciplinary approach that allows writing programs, faculty, and writing program administrators to ready the field of rhetoric and composition for the increasing number of diverse students enrolling in higher education. CRT challenges the institution's status quo injustices toward racial minorities and works to expose institutionalized and systemic racism as it exists and continues to flourish in American institutions. Furthermore, CRT counterstory is theorized methodology with potential for both scholarship and pedagogy in rhetoric and composition. An interdisciplinary method, CRT counterstory recognizes that the experiential and embodied knowledge of people of color is legitimate and critical to understanding racism, which is often well disguised in the rhetoric of normalized structural values and practices.

Introduction

Back during my final year as a graduate writing instructor—when I still lived in the Southwest—I had a student by the name of Ricardo Ramirez, who on the first day of class during roll call asked that I call him "Rick."[1] Rick was a diligent student, a student athlete who read all assigned readings and made sure I was aware of this with his thorough class participation. On one occasion, Rick approached me at the conclusion of class and asked if we could discuss further a couple of the assigned readings during office hours. I agreed, and Rick arrived at my office ten minutes early for his appointment the very next day.

He peeked around my office door and knocked politely on the doorframe. Looking up from the scattering of articles on my desk, I waved him in.

"Hi, Rick. Go ahead and take a seat," I said, gesturing to the seat across from me.

"Hello, Ms. Prieto. How are you?"

"Call me Alé or Alejandra. Ms. Prieto sounds so formal," I responded congenially. "And I'm doing really well. How are you?"

"I'm okay. I feel like my schedule has really filled up now that our season has started. I thought last semester was hard when we only had practice and conditioning to worry about, but now that games are part of my schedule, I'm feeling a little overwhelmed."

"Yes," I answered, "I'm always so impressed with all you student athletes; it's like you have a forty-plus-hour-a-week job in addition to school, but you all are always my best and hardest-working students," I concluded with a smile.

Rick gave a little sigh and looked out the window for a second, then smiled and said, "Yeah, *I* feel like I work really hard, and I guess I'm glad to know you think I do, too, because that's not the usual feedback I get from a lot of other profs. They tend to treat me with suspicion and sometimes outright dislike. Like I'm gonna try and get away with something."[2]

---

1. My research in counterstory crafts characters written as composites of many individuals. Characters represented in my counterstories do not have a one-to-one correspondence to any one individual I know. Accordingly, the characters crafted for this essay involve a scenario and dialogue conducted between my composite characters Alejandra Prieto and her student Rick Ramirez.

2. See Marhiri and Van Rheenen 2010.

Rick's expression darkened, and he continued, "In fact, I had a professor last semester who straight up told me, 'Don't think you're gonna get special treatment in my class just because you're on the baseball team!'" Rick looked up at me with a frown as though it were I, Alejandra, not the professor from last semester, who had just accused him of seeking special treatment.

"Yikes, Rick. I'm sorry to hear that," I responded.

His expression softened, and he offered, "I know. I'm sorry. I know not everyone is like that. I'm just sick of being treated like people *know* something about the way I am or even who I am just because I belong to a group—student athletes, that is. We work hard, but it always feels like our reputation as athletes precedes us, and then people come at us with all their prejudices. In fact, that's really why I'm here today. I want to discuss some ideas from the last two readings you assigned; prejudice is definitely a topic these authors wanna talk about."[3]

Rick's Surprising Objection to Bev Tatum's "Disturbing" Assertions

I pressed the ignore key on my buzzing cell phone and reached across the desk to place it in my purse; I wanted to be sure Rick had my undivided attention. I then fished the two course readings Rick referred to from the bottom of the scattering of student essays I was grading that now covered my desk.

"So," I began, "if it's prejudice you want to talk about, then I'm guessing you'll want to start with Tatum's 'Defining Racism: Can We Talk?'" (in Tatum 1997, 83–98).

"Yeah," Rick replied. "I honestly think that lady's dead wrong. I mean, does she honestly believe only white people can be racist?"

I gave Rick a slight smile, trying not to come across as too maternalistic. The truth of the matter was that I had been assigning this

---

3. See Tatum 1997 and Bonilla-Silva [2003] 2018. I assign excerpted versions of Beverly Tatum's and Eduardo Bonilla-Silva's works in first-year composition courses. The excerpted essays can be found in Rothenberg 2007: see Bonilla-Silva [2003] 2007 and Tatum [1997] 2007.

reading for the past five years of my teaching career, and I had come to expect this response from most of my students who read it. In fact, I had developed somewhat of a ready-made response for this typical student resistance and reading of Tatum's argument, but generally the only students who had ever been vocal about their disagreement with Tatum (not to mention their overall dislike of the essay) were white. It's not that I hadn't ever taught the Tatum essay to students of color, but the response I had been conditioned to receive from this demographic was either complete silence during course discussion or support and celebration of Tatum's claim from those who felt more empowered to speak (generally graduates of high schools with strong ethnic studies programs). So Rick's objection was a first, of sorts, for me.

"Okay, Rick, the Tatum reading it is. Her essay is usually a controversial one."

"Well, yes, Ms. Prieto."

Hmm, I thought, *so he's decided to call me "Ms. Prieto" anyhow. He must come from a "La Maestra" household—where the teacher is regarded with grave respect.*[4]

"That's exactly it," Rick continued. "I was pretty disturbed by what the author implies."

"Oh yeah?" I responded.

"Well, let me rephrase that," Rick said. "She didn't *imply* only whites could be racist; she right out said it. She even titled one of her essay's sections 'Racism: For Whites Only?.'"[5]

I smiled to myself. Rick was right; we *do* think we can *know* something about others without really knowing anything about them at all. We're so entrenched in the idea that we can somehow assess a person based on appearance alone,[6] and this seems to be especially so if you identify with the person in some way. In my stereotyping of Rick,

4. See Elizondo Griest 2008.
5. Tatum 1997, 127–30.
6. See Rodriguez [1982] 2004.

a Mexican American moreno like me,[7] I had anticipated his reaction to Tatum's essay would be the same as mine. However, I had to remind myself that I had first encountered Tatum's argument as a graduate student, a point at which I was being awakened to institutional racism and other subtle forms of racism I had remained readily oblivious to for many years, especially back when I was an eighteen-year-old first-year student.[8]

"So, basically, Tatum gives a new definition for the term *racism* and separates it from prejudice. Is this what you take issue with, Rick?" I asked.

"Well, yeah, sorta," he began, his expression a bit strained. "I just always thought of racism as the really bad kind."

"What do you mean?" I prompted. "Give me some examples."

"You know, like the kind from back in the day when they used to hang signs in windows saying certain groups weren't allowed inside, cross burning on people's lawns, calling people racist names to their faces, that sort. And people of all races are capable of calling each other terrible racist names—"

"Oh, so you mean the racism we associate more with the Jim Crow era?" I asked.[9]

Rick gave me a curious look, then, looking down at his folded hands in his lap, he muttered, "Yeah, I think so. I mean, I don't really know too much about who Jim Crow is . . ."

Oh! I thought. "Hey, Rick, that's not a problem. Our American history class curriculum seems to be more concerned with telling the nicer details in our nation's history. The messy stuff gets glossed over sometimes, and depending on who your teachers were and what books were being used, it's very likely you didn't really get much information on what the Jim Crow era was. You can think of it as a racial era bookended by the two 'civils' in our nation's history."

---

7. In Chicanx urban slang, "morena/o" means a dark-featured or dark-skinned person.

8. See Martinez 2009.

9. See Bonilla-Silva [2003] 2007 and [2003] 2018.

Rick gave me a questioning look, so I elaborated.

"I mean the post–Civil War to the civil rights era. In terms of the way racism operated during that span of time, it was characterized by the actions and laws you already described and was in fact called 'Jim Crow.' But as far as there ever being a real person named Jim Crow, I myself am not sure if there ever was, but the name did get assigned to a Disney character once."

Rick's eyes bulged, and he choked on the water he was sipping. "Really?" he asked.

"Yep, in the movie *Dumbo* [Wilfred Jackson et al., 1994], there are some shuckin' and jivin' crows, all black of course, and the leader is named 'Jim.'"

"Oh," Rick responded dully, seemingly unimpressed. "Well, I'm sure it's just coincidence, and if not, Disney probably didn't mean anything by it. I mean, when was that movie even made?"

"Good point," I admitted. "I think it was released in the 1940s when the racial ideology was certainly one more accepting of this sort of naming and stereotyping in mainstream film. So, certainly, back then themes and topics that were the norm might seem more shocking to an audience today. Take, for instance, the Disney film that Tatum refers to in the beginning of her article. Let's turn to that section and go over it together," I suggested.

Rick took out his copy of the essay and turned to the section I was referring to.

"Would you mind reading the section out loud, Rick, and I'll follow along."

"Sure," he replied, and began: "'Several years ago, one of my students conducted a research project investigating preschoolers' conceptions of Native Americans. Using children at a local day care center as her participants, she asked these three- and four-year-olds to draw a picture of a Native American. Most children were stumped by her request. They didn't know what a Native American was. But when she rephrased the question and asked them to draw a picture of an Indian, they readily complied. Almost every picture included one central feature: feathers. In fact, many of them also included a weapon—a knife or tomahawk—and depicted the person in violent or aggressive terms. Though this group of children, almost all of whom were White, did not live near a large Native American population and probably had had little if any personal interaction with American Indians, they all had internalized an image of what Indians were like. How did they know? Cartoon images, in particular the Disney movie *Peter Pan* [Clyde Geronimi, 1953], were cited by the children as their number-one source of information. At the age of three, these children already had a set of stereotypes in place. Though I would not describe three-year-olds as prejudiced, the stereotypes to which they have been exposed become the foundation for the adult prejudices so many of us have.'"[10]

Rick looked up from the essay and frowned.

"What's up, Rick? What's the frown about?"

"Well," he started, "I get what she's saying about how these three-year-olds could be influenced by this cartoon, but, I mean, do you really think this sorta thing is even something they'd remember all the way into adulthood? It all seems kinda far-fetched."

"Well," I replied, "how long has it been since you watched Disney's *Peter Pan*?"

"I don't know, probably not since I was little kid. Maybe when I was in kindergarten. Yeah, actually, kindergarten or first grade would make sense 'cause my parents couldn't afford a TV back then, so if I saw any of those movies, it was always at school. Teachers used to show us movies all the time."

"Right," I noted. "Well, I think what you're describing is exactly what Tatum is also taking issue with. The fact that even in schools the information we get from cartoons, movies, TV shows, and other mainstream media sources is oftentimes pretty limited in terms of accurate and informed portrayals of certain races or ethnicities. This is especially so if we're showing films that represent the racial ideology

10. Tatum 1997, 124.

of another era when it was less objectionable to portray Native Americans and African Americans in racially stereotypical and animalistic forms. And when parents, but teachers in particular, don't follow up these sorts of messages conveyed by such texts with more accurate and contemporary information through course textbooks or discussions, then it becomes reasonable to assume this misinformation *very much* informs a child's perception of certain groups. Especially if, as Tatum (notes in the passage you read, the child has little or no contact with the group this media source is stereotypically portraying. You follow me?"

Rick nodded uncertainly, clearly not convinced.

"Okay, let's back up to those elementary-school days when you were watching those films," I said. "Now, think about your education concerning Native Americans. What do you recall learning?"

"Just in elementary school?" Rick asked.

"Well, actually, let me revise that; think about your entire primary- and secondary-school career. What did you learn about Natives?"

Rick paused to consider my query for a bit and then responded, "I mean the obvious answer is first contact, you know, when Columbus, the pilgrims, and all those people first got here."

"Right," I said, a little bothered that he was conflating the arrival of Columbus and the pilgrims, but I said nothing more to allow him to continue.

"And then we did learn something about the Trail of Tears, but I can't really recall the details because I think someone came in just once in middle school to talk to us about it during Native American Appreciation Month—"

"Heritage Month," I interjected.

"What? Oh, you mean instead of appreciation?"

I nodded.

"Okay then, *Heritage* Month," Rick said with a dismissive shrug.

He paused at this point and seemed to be inventorying his mind for another instance, but after several moments had passed, I asked, "Is that all?"

"Yeah, I think so," he answered.

"Well again, Rick, your experience is not atypical for most American schools and history courses for that matter when it comes to comprehensive histories of minoritized groups. I mean, take, for instance, your people. Your 'Race Literacy Narrative' [see appendix A for the assignment instructions]," I gestured to his assignment at the top of the pile of student essays on my desk, "says you identify as Mexican American."

"Yeah," Rick responded. "I mean, that's the box I check on forms, but I'm definitely more American than Mexican. I mean, I was born here after all and have only been to Mexico a couple times." Rick looked thoughtful for a moment and continued, "To be honest, I get that question a lot because people can't ever really place *what* I am. I guess I don't look like the typical Mexican."

"What do you mean?" I asked with a quizzical look on my face.

"I mean that I'm tall for a Mexican. Six two to be exact, and most people don't tend to think of us as tall. I've also been told my features are more European. Growing up, my grandma always said that even though my skin is dark, at least I have a narrow nose and a strong square jaw like our Spanish relatives."[11]

"You have family in Spain?" I asked.

"Well, no, not any that we still know, but my grandma always said that's mainly where our bloodline traces back to, and that's in Europe, so I'm assuming Spain is where I get my European features. It's just logic," Rick finished matter-of-factly.

"Yes," I replied, "and it's interesting that your family kinda makes up for your skin color with your European features."

At this remark, Rick shifted in his seat, and his eyes took on an expression that looked both questioning and defensive at once.

I scrambled to explain myself by saying, "Take my family, for example. I also have a grandma who would say strange things about

11. See Villanueva 1993.

skin color. She used to assure my mom that my skin would lighten up someday, and she'd scold me for getting so dark during the summers. My grandma would tell my mom not to let me spend so much time outside, and I grew up feeling ugly—not as good or as pretty as my light-skinned cousins, who were endearingly referred to as güeras and blanquitas."[12]

"Well, I never said *my* grandma's comments were strange," Rick interrupted with a defensive tone to his voice. "She's just old, and that's the way she is. In fact, that's just the way things are in general in a Mexican family. It's not a big deal; I don't let it get to me."[13]

"Right," I responded, inwardly embarrassed at having overstepped my boundaries in my attempt to identify with Rick. "Well, getting back to my original question," I said, externally attempting not to show my embarrassment, "do you remember learning much about Mexican American history in school?"

Again, Rick thought for a moment and said, "I guess all I can really recall is stuff about the Mexican-American War, something about revolutionaries like Pancho Villa and then a little about Cesar Chavez. But again, the details are fuzzy 'cause the stuff on Chavez was probably during a *Heritage* Month speech."

"Okay," I said, doing my best to regain my "teacher persona." "So, relating your experience back to Tatum's point, do you see how limited information, paired with misinformation offered by something like a Disney cartoon, could lead to the formation of inaccurate notions, prejudice if you will, about a whole group of people? Especially when teachers and parents aren't doing anything to supplement children's education with less-fantastical and stereotyped stories of who these people are, especially contemporarily?"

Rick still looked unsure, so I offered, "Why don't we take a look at the part of *Peter Pan* Tatum is referring to?"

12. Rodriguez [1982] 2004 as well as Caldas and Gonzales, chapters 2 and 3, in this collection.

13. See Bonilla-Silva [2003] 2007 and [2003] 2018.

Rick shrugged and said, "Okay, sure. I haven't seen that movie in forever, though."

"That's perfect," I responded. "Then you'll be able to view it as an adult within the context of the conversation we're having, which is a totally different context from when you last viewed it as a kid."

Rick said nothing but peeked at the cell phone slightly sticking out of his pocket, likely checking the time or if he'd missed any calls or texts. Meanwhile, I pulled up YouTube.com on my computer and typed in a search: "Disney's Peter Pan What Makes the Red Man Red?" The first hit was a clip of the scene in which Peter Pan, Wendy, her brothers, and the Lost Boys go to the "Indian" camp and encounter the Chief, his daughter, Princess Tiger Lily, and many other tribe members. I turned my monitor at an angle so both Rick and I could view the screen and pressed *play*.

Rick and I Explore Media Representations of Tatum's Argument

The clip begins with the Chief announcing in perfect "Hollywood Injun English" (Meek 2006, 95) that he will teach the "palefaces" all about the "Red Man." To which a Lost Boy asks, "What made the Red Man red?" The "Indians" then launch into song and dance all about why the "Red Man" is red (Wallace and Churchill 1953). Throughout the clip, a variety of representations of "Indianness" are expressed, such as a smorgasbord of Native artifacts drawn into the scene: totem poles, teepees, bonfires, mohawks, feather headdresses, peace pipes, and drums. There is a general lack of variety in how the "Indians" are drawn, with the options being either short and squat or tall and rangy—the only exceptions being the Chief, who is stern-faced with an enormous and imposing brown body, and his daughter Tiger Lily, who adheres to all classical ideals of beauty and is in fact identical to British Wendy, with the exception of the exoticizing elements of brown paint constituting her complexion and braids and a feather in her hair (Gilman 1985; Bordo 1993, 9–11).

After the short clip concluded, I looked expectantly to Rick, who simply shrugged.

"So," I began, "did you observe anything in the clip that might contribute to a young child's formation of stereotype and future prejudice against Native Americans?"

"I guess." Rick responded noncommittally. "I just don't see what the big deal is. I mean, like I said before, this movie was made back when racial stereotyping was more acceptable—"

"Yes," I interrupted, "but that's not the problem. The problem is that these films, with their racial ideology from another era, are being shown *today* to an audience who is young, impressionable and who is not being taught much about how this is not an accurate or respectful portrayal of Native American people."

"Okay, fine," Rick responded, a slight rise in tone to his voice. "But at the end of the day this movie is made for *entertainment* purposes alone and should not be taken so serious. I mean, look at where the whole thing is set, Never Land. It's fantasy, not real, and of course not meant to be taken *literally*."

"Right," I countered, noting this was beginning to feel like an actual debate, "but think about it this way: If the film is set in a fantasy world, where mermaids, swashbuckling pirates, fairies, and boys who never grow up exist, how does it make sense to place Native Americans in the mix? What's the message being conveyed there? What would a Native American person feel when encountering a representation of herself portrayed in such over-the-top terms alongside creatures and characters that don't actually exist?"

Rick was silent, his eyes downturned, scanning Tatum's essay, so I proceeded, "Are you a fan of Dave Chappelle?" Rick's eyes immediately flicked up to meet mine, and he said, "What? I don't see the connection."

"Let me show you something else here on YouTube," I said, quickly typing "Dave Chappelle Native Americans" into the search browser. This brought us to a clip from Chappelle's stand-up show titled *For What It's Worth* (1994). In the clip I now showed Rick, Chappelle talks about meeting a Native American at a gathering of "fifteen hundred Native Americans." The comedian adds, "They were all gathered in one place; the place was called Wal-Mart in New

Mexico." Chappelle tells the audience he feels bad for Native Americans; he says "they get dogged" openly because everybody thinks they're all dead, extinct, nonexistent. He is thus amazed to meet one in real life. Upon this meeting, Chappelle recounts that he excitedly professed to the Native man, "I studied you in social studies," asking, "You're a hunter-gatherer, right?" Because it's comedy, and because Dave Chappelle is good at his job, Rick's moody disposition lifted, and he laughed out loud several times yet was still careful to steal sidelong glances at me, likely gauging my reactions to his own mirthful reactions. At the conclusion of the clip, Rick smiled, and I returned the smile.

"So, the connection," I began, "is that Tatum's point is in this clip proven. The reason Chappelle has material to write about Native Americans and the reason he knows his audience will laugh is that there is an overall social understanding of how Native Americans have been stereotypically portrayed. Think about it, Rick: How many of the same exact themes are shown in both the Disney and Chappelle versions speaking to 'what Indians are like'?"

Rick pondered this for a bit and responded in a deflated sort of way, as if I had just punctured the fun of the situation: "I guess."

"Does this help in your understanding of Tatum's argument?" I ventured.

"Well, no, not really," Rick answered, "because I still don't understand how she can get away with saying only white people are racist. I've heard so many minorities, including people in my own family, call white people terrible names—"

"I don't think that's what she means, Rick. It's kinda like the question people who aren't Black usually come up with regarding why Black people are the only ones allowed to call each other 'nigga' when no one else is given immunity to do so—at the end of the day, it all roots back to power."

Rick's eyes asked me to clarify.

"Okay, Rick, turn to page five of Tatum's essay. In this section, she provides a definition for prejudice. I see you have the exact sentence I'm referring to highlighted in your copy. Would you mind reading it?"

"'*Prejudice* is a preconceived judgment or opinion, usually based on limited information. I assume that we all have prejudices, not because we want them, but simply because we are so continually exposed to misinformation about others.'"[14] Rick looked up, silently asking if he should read on.

"Good," I answered, "so, according to Tatum's definition, this is the form of discrimination you seem to associate with racism, but Tatum defines it as prejudice, not racism. Now, turn to the next section, where she really defines and distinguishes racism from prejudice. She quotes David Wellman in his assertion that racism is a 'system of advantage based on race' and elaborates with the definition of racism used by antiracist educators and consultants termed 'prejudice plus power.'[15] Do you see how this definition is set apart from our more common understanding of racism that would limit it to racial slurs or other blatantly hateful actions? It *is* all those things but also more subtle actions, plus *power*— a whole system of it."

I Show Rick the Midwestern University Point System as an Example of Systemic Racism

"For instance," I said, turning back to my desktop and searching through files for the document I now required, "universities as functioning institutions have *systems* in place when it comes to admitting students. I'm sure you have experience with this through the application form you filled out to attend in the first place."

"Oh, right," Rick replied, "all the paperwork?"

"Yep," I said, having found the file I wanted and pulling it up for us both to view on the computer screen. "What I'm showing you here is a point system that a midwestern university *used* to adhere to when measuring applicants for undergraduate admission."

"What do you mean 'used' to? They don't use it anymore?"

Ah, I thought, *he misses nothing.*

14. Tatum 1997, 5.
15. Tatum 1997, 126; see also Wellman 1977, chap. 1.

"Right," I continued. "As of 2003, they no longer employ this particular point system, or at least one section of it, due to an anti-affirmative-action lawsuit brought against the university.[16] But, before we venture into that messy business, let's first go over the document so I can explain the categories." (See appendix B.)

"Okay," Rick replied as he scooted his chair closer to the desk.

"Based on a 150-point scale, generally an applicant scoring upwards of 100 points is said to have been guaranteed admission.[17] The first category of measurement concerns GPA. This is a pretty standard measurement and is something I'm sure most universities consider."

Rick nodded his agreement, so I continued.

"In this particular category, a student with a C average would earn 50 points, which, considering the 100-point goal, is a pretty good deal."

Rick nodded again.

"Now, a student with a perfect 4.0 is assigned 80 points, which puts the student in a real good position for admission, considering there are still nine categories to acquire points. Moving on to the next category, the university considers a category called 'School Factor,' which measures the difficulty and prestige of the applicant's high school."

"You mean like whether the person went to a college prep or not?" Rick asked.

"Yep, but also how your school measures up in standardized tests like the ones instituted by No Child Left Behind. You know how some schools, based on these tests, have been labeled 'failing,' while others are deemed 'excelling'?"[18]

"Yes," Rick nodded. "Actually, it's kinda funny. I went to both kinds of schools. I grew up in a pretty poor all-Mexican part of town, but when I was twelve, my family and I moved to a new neighborhood,

16. See Richardson and Lancendorfer 2004.
17. See Perry 2007, 181.
18. See US Census Bureau 2010.

and I went to school in a waaaay better part of town. When my parents and I moved out of the neighborhood where I grew up, I saw some significant changes. For example, in my old neighborhood, everything seemed old, and the things the city departments needed to take care of were not being attended to. My school was also not the best-looking thing in the world. It seemed as if everything we had was old and used. When we moved to a better part of town, everything seemed new. The schools were new with a lot of technology that was very helpful, and the campus was *clean*. Another significant thing I realized was that it seemed like a lot more people were better educated than I was at that point. I did well in all my classes growing up, but when I moved, it seemed like what we were learning at my old school was not even close to what other kids were learning."[19]

"Yes," I said. "That's a really great way to illustrate how this measure is used. And just out of curiosity, what was the racial and class makeup of the new neighborhood you moved to?"

"Mostly white and, I guess, middle to upper class," Rick answered.

I nodded, pretty confident that would be his response. "So then the way the School Factor measurement works in this midwestern university system is that students who went to schools like the ones in the first neighborhood you lived in are assigned zero points because their school is deemed a level-0 difficulty, whereas students who went to schools like the one in the next neighborhood you lived in are assigned five points for having attended what's considered a level-10 difficulty school, and this all boils down to what neighborhood the student was fortunate enough to grow up in. Again, out of curiosity, why did your family move to this more affluent neighborhood?"

Rick began to look suspicious but responded, "My dad got a better job and ended up getting paid more. We could afford to live in the better neighborhood."

"Ah, I see," I said, "then I think this is a good time to transition to the other essay you came to see me about. We can discuss it in

19. See Martinez 2009.

conversation with both Tatum's definition of racism and the midwestern university point system as an example."

Both Rick and I retrieved our copies of Eduardo Bonilla-Silva's article "Color-Blind Racism."

Rick and I Put Bonilla-Silva's Four Frames of Color-Blind Racism in Context

"I think the frame of Bonilla-Silva's term *abstract liberalism* best fits the point system we're looking at here and even Tatum's assertion that only those who benefit from racism are those in a position of power," I said.

"Yeah," Rick replied, "I guess that's a good place to start with his article, seeing as I didn't really understand that frame. I mean, the others were easier, like the frame of naturalization of racism. I've heard my extended family claim they still live in the neighborhood we moved out of because it's 'natural' for Mexicans to want to live with other Mexicans and whites to live with whites, and I guess in some ways I can see their point. Sometimes, that's just the way things are."[20]

"But your family moved into a white neighborhood," I pointed out.

"Yeah, but my dad made more money, so it made sense for us to move," Rick reasoned. "Okay," I nodded, mentally noting how his rationalization proved precisely Bonilla-Silva's point about the myth of naturalization.

"And then there's cultural racism, right?" Rick continued.

I nodded my assent.

"So, I got that one too. I guess that frame works like the prejudice Tatum is talking about? You know, 'cause it makes assumptions about whole groups of people but really kinda judges them based on cultural stereotypes, like saying Mexicans don't value education."[21]

"Right," I answered. "Good, Rick, that's exactly it."

"But," Rick interrupted, "I pretty much agree with this one."

20. See Bonilla-Silva [2003] 2007 and [2003] 2018.
21. See Bonilla-Silva [2003] 2007 and [2003] 2018.

"What do you mean?" I asked, inwardly dismayed and not sure I really wanted to hear what he meant.

"I just think that the level of education being taught has to do with the way the majority of students in the schools were brought up to value and appreciate it. In most Mexican families, *not all but most*," he was quick to add, likely noting the objection on my face, "education really does not play as big of a factor as, say, working. Especially the families who come to the country to make money and live the way they want. They could care less about the education their children receive as long as they are bringing home the money. On the other hand, white families strive for their kids' school success. I'm not saying that there are not Mexican or even black families that don't do this for their kids, 'cause there are those families out there. I'm just saying that a *majority* of the families that do it are white."[22]

Wow, I silently mouthed.

Rick looked pleased at my silence, likely assuming he'd rendered me speechless, which he had but not because I was convinced by anything he'd just said. In fact, I was a little heartbroken to hear all of these culturally racist assertions coming from a young morenito like Rick. I wanted to point out the fact that his beliefs fit perfectly into the cultural racism frame to which Bonilla-Silva referred, but I didn't know how to say this without Rick thinking I was calling him a racist—and against his own people that. I remained silent, and Rick took this as his cue to continue.

"The last frame he talks about is minimization, which I also get because I've seen people use what Bonilla-Silva refers to as the 'race card' all the time."

"Let me interrupt you there," I said, no longer able to let him misread Bonilla-Silva's argument. "Bonilla-Silva is saying people of color are often accused of 'playing the race card' when they point out racially motivated discrimination, especially the more subtle or systemic forms like what operates in this midwestern university point

22. See Martinez 2009.

system. These accusations happen because there is some sort of post–civil rights commonsense belief that discrimination is no longer a central factor affecting marginalized peoples' life chances. I've heard people say on countless occasions, 'It's better now than in the past' or 'There is discrimination, but there are still plenty of jobs out there.' I mean, this frame allows society to accept things like what we were talking about earlier—the absence of history about Native Americans and Mexican Americans in our education system or the racial stereotyping of minoritized people in Disney films—and if a person of color were to make a big deal about this, he'd end up accused of being 'hypersensitive,' of using race as an 'excuse,' or of 'playing the race card.' Bonilla-Silva does not support those who would accuse people of color as 'playing the race card' simply for speaking out about discrimination and injustice."

"Oh," Rick said quietly, his eyes turned downward to his hands in his lap.

Shit, I thought, *back off, Alé; bring it back to the text—don't scare him away.*

"How about if we return to the midwestern university's point system and put these frames, in particular abstract liberalism, into context? I wanna make sure you get this one before you leave my office today since you said that was the one you were struggling with."

"Sure," Rick said with a noncommittal shrug.

"So," I began, "if you compare the two first point categories we already discussed, I want you to consider them with the key words Bonilla-Silva offers as characteristic of abstract liberalism—*individual, choice,* and *equal opportunity.*"

"Okay," Rick said, and I could almost see the cogs in his mind turning.

"If you think about the first category that deals with GPA, how much of this category has to do with an individual who has his own choice and equal opportunity?"

"Well," Rick responded, "I think that category is all about the individual and his choices. Everyone has the same opportunity as the next person to either choose to do their schoolwork or not, right?

If you get bad grades for not doing your work, not showing up for school, and being a generally poor student, then that's all on you. What can a teacher really do if you refuse to do it for yourself?"

"Okay, Rick, sure. I'm with you most of the way. However, what about the student who is homeless? Or the student who is hungry? Or the student whose parents work the night shift and so is expected to care for younger siblings in the evenings? Would any of this affect the student's ability to complete schoolwork? If you don't know where your next meal is going to come from, if you don't know when you'll have time, or if you don't even know if you'll have a place to lay your head at night? We don't know everyone's story, Rick."

"I guess. I never really considered those factors, but at the same time there are people who have bad lives like that and still make it happen. They just work hard and make it."

"Yes, Rick, those people do exist, but keep in mind they're the exception, not the rule." Rick said nothing. "Now, let's move along to the second category, which is School Factor. As we already discussed, this is basically determined by how prestigious a high school the applicant attended, and from your experience what does this depends on?"

"Well, I guess for the most part it depends on what neighborhood you live in—"

"Right," I interrupted, "and going back to our key terms, how much individual choice and equal opportunity does a high school student have in choosing what neighborhood he is going to live in and thereby choosing what school he will attend?"

"Not much, I guess," Rick reluctantly admitted, but a light bulb seemed to turn on over his head, and he said, "but now that I think about it, there were a few kids at my prep school on scholarship, and I know they were bussed in from other neighborhoods. So even though they didn't live in the best place, they still made the choice to come to a better school," he finished triumphantly.

"Ah," I said, "but does that really represent equal opportunity for *all*? Why weren't all the kids from the poor neighborhood at your school? Why only a few?"

"That's easy," Rick said. "Values. The others must not have wanted it as bad."[23]

Alejandra Comes to a Realization

I sighed as it became clear that my way of reasoning was not something Rick was ready to hear. Rick's "Race Literacy Narrative," his first essay for the semester, which I had just read and begun grading, engaged an overall theme that expressed a sense of academic accomplishment and success achieved through his effort (see Villanueva 1993). *Of course!*, I now thought to myself. Rick had made clear early on the importance for him of the abstract liberal ideology of the individual, and I had just challenged this notion to which he clung, likely so as not to lose the tenuous footing and purpose an underrepresented student encounters in a system that assumes all students come to the doors of the institution equally equipped with the same cultural capital (see Oldfield 2007). Rick's narrative essay was a success story told to detail the struggles he and his family faced in their quest to get him an elite American education. I recalled now his focus on the notion of overcoming the odds of the racial status quo in order to become successful as an *individual* in society and to become a student who embodies the American Dream. I remembered his invocation of personal sacrifice, and his discussion of how he has been influenced and inspired by his parents' struggles and goals involving their decision to immigrate to the United States and how he feels the pressure to "make good" on this sacrifice. Rick stated in his essay, "The best form of repayment to my parents is if I achieve the American Dream" (see Martinez 2009).

How insensitive I was to assume a first-generation and first-year student was ready to have his outlook challenged in such a way after he admitted to the training in white middle- to upper-class ideals he had undergone during secondary school. At this point in his academic career, Rick was surviving, doing his best to navigate a system not originally intended for him, and he was a smart tactician to realize

23. See Martinez 2009.

that you don't bite the hand that feeds you; you just learn to play by their rules until—until when? I suppose I hadn't really questioned the rules or even noticed the system until my first year in graduate school, until my race, my class, and my difference were shoved under my nose. I thought back to those early days of graduate school, only five short years ago, when all I wished to do was stay afloat and blend in with the other students. Yet neither my professors nor my peers would let me be. They made sure, in both blatant and subtle ways, to point out my difference, and it was at this point that I began to know myself, but only through my relation to others (see Moya 2002). I came to realize that assimilation would not be permitted because assimilation was not for the brown (see Castillo 1995). No matter how hard I worked, how hard I tried to be "like them," I was only spinning my wheels, putting forth a whole lot of effort and getting nowhere. So I chose another route, a route with pathways cleared for me by Gloria Anzaldúa, Chérrie Moraga, Beverly Tatum, Eduardo Bonilla-Silva, Adela Licona, Victor Villanueva, Jaime Mejía, and Carmen Kynard—to name a few. But at that point of consciousness, I was no longer eighteen; my experiences in this system had not just begun.

Un Abrazo

Emerging from my reverie, I smiled warmly at Rick, who this time had taken his cell phone completely out of his pocket and was scrolling through the interface. I glanced at the time on my desktop and realized an hour had passed, so I concluded our meeting by asking Rick if he had any other concerns about the essays for us to address. He said he didn't, eyes still on the phone, so I thanked him for coming in and encouraged him to continue the "good habit" of visiting during office hours, fearing silently that I had lost the opportunity to mentor him by scaring him away with ideas he was not ready to consider, much less embrace. As Rick got up to leave, I also rose and walked around my desk to where he, with his back to me, was gathering his bag and water bottle from the floor. When Rick straightened and turned toward the door, his expression shifted from a slight frown to surprise. I suppose he hadn't realized I was no longer in my chair behind the desk. We both stood there for a moment; Rick seemed to be sizing me up, likely wondering what I wanted—or rather that's the message I gathered from his questioning eyes. Yet for a moment I caught a glimpse of something familiar in his eyes, something or someone I knew, perhaps from another time. As the silent moment became increasingly awkward, Rick made to skirt around me and his now unoccupied chair, but the space was so narrow that he tripped on the chair leg, and I reached out to steady him before he could fall. As he straightened, now a sheepish look occupying his face, I embraced him in a hug, un abrazo, which he did not return. In fact, he stood there, arms straight and stuck to his sides, but I hugged him anyway because it was at this moment that I recognized who I had glimpsed in his eyes a moment ago—it was me, all of who I was and all of what I believed years ago when I too was a first-generation and first-year college student. I loosened my embrace, and Rick made a beeline for the door, muttering something sounding like "thanks, have a good day" before he was gone. I knew he was not ready to return the abrazo, but I was hopeful that someday he could; however, I felt satisfied knowing I was ready to embrace him and all that he represents. *Tú eres mi otro yo*,[24] I thought.

References

Bonilla-Silva, Eduardo. [2003] 2007. "Color-Blind Racism." In *Race, Class, and Gender in the United States*, 7th ed., edited by Paula S. Rothenberg, 113–19. New York: Worth.

———. [2003] 2018. *Racism without Racists: Color-Blind Racism and the Persistence of Racial Inequality in the United States*. 5th ed. Lanham, MD: Rowman and Littlefield.

Bordo, Susan. 1993. *Unbearable Weight: Feminism, Western Culture, and the Body*. Berkeley: Univ. of California Press.

24. This phrase is inspired by the Maya-Quiche mantra used to begin classes in Tucson Unified School District's raza studies: "Tú eres mi otro yo / Si te hago daño a ti, me hago daño a mi mismo / Si te amo y respeto a ti, me amo y respeto a mí mismo" (You are my other self / If I hurt you, I hurt myself / If I love and respect you, I love and respect myself).

Castillo, Ana. 1995. *Massacre of the Dreamers: Essays in Xicanisma*. New York: Plume.

Elizondo Griest, Stephanie. 2008. *Mexican Enough: My Life between the Borderlines*. New York: Atria Books.

Gilman, Sander L. 1985. "Black Bodies, White Bodies: Toward an Iconography of Female Sexuality in Late Nineteenth-Century Art, Medicine, and Literature." *Critical Inquiry* 12, no. 1: 204–42.

Marhiri, Jabari, and Derek Van Rheenen. 2010. *Out of Bounds: When Scholarship Athletes Become Academic Scholars*. Bern, Switzerland: Peter Lang.

Martinez, Aja Y. 2009. "'The American Way': Resisting the Empire of Force and Color-Blind Racism." *College English* 71, no. 6: 584–95.

Meek, Barbra A. 2006. "And the Injun Goes 'How!': Representations of American Indian English in White Public Space." *Language and Society* 35, no. 1: 93–126.

Moya, Paula M. L. 2002. *Learning from Experience: Minority Identities, Multicultural Struggles*. Berkeley: Univ. of California Press.

Oldfield, Kenneth. 2007. "Humble and Hopeful: Welcoming First-Generation Poor and Working-Class Students to College." *About Campus*, Jan.–Feb., 2–12.

Perry, Barbara A. 2007. *The Michigan Affirmative Action Cases*. Lawrence: Univ. Press of Kansas.

Richardson, John D., and Karen M. Lancendorfer. 2004. "Framing Affirmative Action: The Influence of Race on Newspaper Editorial Responses to the University of Michigan Cases." *Harvard International Journal of Press/Politics* 9, no. 4: 74–94.

Rodriguez, Richard. [1982] 2004. *Hunger of Memory: The Education of Richard Rodriguez*. New York: Bantam.

Rothenberg, Paula S., ed. 2007. *Race, Class, and Gender in the United States*. 7th ed. New York: Worth.

Tatum, Beverly Daniel. 1997. *"Why Are All the Black Kids Sitting Together in the Cafeteria?" And Other Conversations about Race*. New York: Basic.

———. [1997] 2007. "Defining Racism: 'Can We Talk?'" In *Race, Class, and Gender in the United States*, 7th ed., edited by Paula S. Rothenberg, 105–12. New York: Worth.

US Census Bureau. 2010. *2010 Census Interactive Population Map: Nogales, AZ*. Washington, DC: US Department of Commerce, 2010. At https://www.census.gov/quickfacts/nogalescityarizona.

Villanueva, Victor. 1993. *Bootstraps: From an American Academic of Color.* Urbana, IL: National Council of Teachers of English.

Wallace, Oliver, and Frank Churchill. 1953. "What Made the Red Man Red?" Song on *Walt Disney's Peter Pan.* Walt Disney Records.

Wellman, David. 1977. *Portraits of White Racism.* Cambridge: Cambridge Univ. Press.

Appendix A: "Race Literacy Narrative" Essay Assignment

The first essay of the semester will ask you to explore your life as it relates to the way race is conceptualized here in the United States. You will look at your own history and experiences and aim to discuss how class, power, privilege, homophobia, disability, etc. may tie into and affect your own race literacy. Ideally, you will pick an event in your past, either positive or negative, and will explore it with the purpose of coming to some kind of statement, or insight about how race works in this country and how this affects you and your own conceptions about race towards/about those around you.

The purpose of this assignment is to open up for the class a dialogue about an issue that is often misunderstood, misappropriated, or completely dismissed in this country during the era in which we currently live. Since writing can serve as one of our most powerful human instincts, this assignment should serve the purpose of helping you explore a social issue that presently affects us all, but you'll explore it in an environment where we as a class can learn about each other while speaking to groups of people who, in other circumstances, may not normally listen. This ties nicely to the idea that teaching is a powerful human tool and we all owe it to ourselves to discover who we each are as individuals in a diverse classroom setting. You will use mainly descriptive detail, vivid scenes, and reflection to support some central issue or question. To varying degrees, you can opt to analyze and comment on some cultural/societal aspects related to race, in much the same way as Amy Tan and George Lopez do with language in their work.

So, you want to tell a good story, with plenty of vivid, specific, concrete detail, about how your identity/identities have been shaped due to the historical and current (mis)conceptions we have about race in the United States. Try to hang your smaller details on some larger idea or point that emerges as you brainstorm. This larger idea should eventually emerge as an exploratory claim/argument, or speculation about the function, purposes, and/or social importance of a race literacy. Remember this is your story, so don't shy away from telling truths as you know them . . . in other words tell it like it is, not as you think I or your peers want to hear it. This essay should depict some of your experience in your voice.

You may take off in one of these several directions:

- You can start by exploring the question, "When did you first realize you were different?"
- You might look at an influential person or people who helped or hurt the shaping of your race literacy.
- You might look at a significant event in your life, whether it happened directly to you, or even if you just witnessed it.
- You can explore the cultural/ethnic values and attitudes toward issues of race from the culture/ethnic group with which you identify.
- You might talk about becoming literate about America's ideas toward race. How did you learn how race is talked about, thought about, and acted out in this country? What are the assumptions and stereotypes with regard to race as applied to certain groups and how did you learn about them?

We will workshop your essay for both effective "evidence" and "focus" or controlling idea. The main object, after all, is to share your experience(s) with your audience—the class—with as much detail and insight as possible to make this the best learning experience possible.

Appendix B: A Midwest University's Admission Point System

Office of Undergraduate Admissions Point Sources (100 Points Possible)

ACADEMIC FACTORS		OTHER FACTORS	
GPA		**Geography**	
GPA	Points	Residency	Points
2.5	50	Michigan	10
2.6	52	Underrepresented MI County	6
2.7	54	Underrepresented State	2
2.8	56	**Alumni Status**	
2.9	58	*(Assign only 1 option)*	
3.0	60		
3.1	62	Status	Points
3.2	64		
3.3	66	Legacy *(parents/stepparents)*	4
3.4	68	Other *(grandparents, siblings, spouses)*	1
3.5	70	**Required Essay**	
3.6	72	Essay Quality	Points
3.7	74		
3.8	76	Outstanding Essay	1
3.9	78	Not Outstanding Essay	0
4.0	80		
School Factor		**Personal Achievement**	
		(Assign only 1 option)	
Quality	Points	Level of Achievement	Points
0	0		
1	2	State	1
2	4	Regional	3
3	6	National	5
4	8	**Leadership and Service**	
5	10	*(Assign only 1 option)*	
Curriculum Factor		Level of Achievement	Points
Difficulty	Points	State	1
-2	-4	Regional	3
-1	-2	National	5
0	0	**Miscellaneous**	
1	2	*(Assign only 1 option)*	
2	4	Criteria Met	Points
3	6		
4	8	Socio-economic Disadvantage	20
		Underrepresented Racial/Ethnic	20
Test Score		Minority Identification or	
(Assign only larger point value)		Education	5
ACT	SAT I	Points	Men in Nursing	20

ACT	SAT I	Points
1-19	400-920	0
20-21	930-1000	6
22-26	1010-1190	10
27-30	1200-1350	11
31-36	1360-1600	12

Criteria Met	Points
Socio-economic Disadvantage	20
Underrepresented Racial/Ethnic Minority Identification or Education	20
Men in Nursing	5
Scholarship Athlete	20
Provost's Discretion	20
	—

5. Image of a midwestern university's admission point system. This university uses this 150-point system in evaluating applicants. University officials say that this score sheet is a guideline and that each application is handled on a case-by-case basis.

9

¿Estamos locas?

Narratives of Resistance in an English PhD Program

Raquel Corona and Nancy Alvarez

Abstract

This chapter is a collaborative endeavor between two Latina graduate students who critically reflect on key experiential moments they have encountered as they journey through a doctoral program in an English department at a college in New York City and as they teach at various types of institutions. One may assume that living and working in such a diverse and liberal area of the United States would provide a safer and more socially just work environment, but even there the institutional structures of higher education and the values of the academy oppress students of color. This chapter takes a close look at the crucial issues at stake when Latinas hold various subjectivities in the context of graduate school through reflexive moments highlighting those struggles in the writers' personal lives. Navigating the challenging terrain of higher education as a Latina is a constant exercise in reflexivity and flexibility. Mentorship by faculty and peers may help Latina graduate students feel less isolated, while also helping them recognize and fight against harmful microaggressions that run rampant in graduate programs in the United States.

Introduction

"Have you met Raquel? She's Latina." Back in 2015, Nancy had finished her coursework and was on campus only once a week to attend a dissertation-writing workshop. Almost every week that semester some-one would ask her if she had met Raquel and made sure to inform her that Raquel was Latina. Nancy's initial reaction was a big smile and the response "No, not yet." Likewise, Raquel was often asked the same about Nancy. Faculty would say, "I have to introduce you to Nancy." Raquel would also respond with an agreeable smile and nod and say, "Oh, really?" After a few weeks, Nancy stopped smiling and would just arch her eyebrow. Why did it seem like everyone was so excited for Nancy and Raquel to meet when the only thing they could tell Nancy about Raquel was that she was Latina?

Word eventually got around that Raquel was interested in writing studies, just like Nancy, and so it made more sense that we should meet. Both of us were pleased to know that there was another Latina in the doctoral program. And yet it felt odd when others celebrated the fact that there were two of us now. ¡Dos Latinas! ¡Dos Latinas in an English doctoral program in Queens, New York (one of the most diverse boroughs in New York City)! Had diversity and the great affirmative-action quota been achieved because there were two of us now? Were two of us enough?

Systems of oppression would have us believe that having two Lati-nas in one program was *more* than enough. These systems would even go as far as to argue that we should be happy to see the Latina contin-gency represented. At this particular moment, we have to ask questions of ourselves and question others' intent in connecting us: "Am I crazy, or is this weird? Should we be happy to have the system somehow chal-lenged and turned on its head? How did *both of us* manage to get by? What does it mean for anyone to ever believe that it is enough?" What we hope our stories illustrate is that having two Latinas in one space is far from enough! It is not enough precisely because, despite being brought together owing to the fact that we are Latina, we are actually vastly different. Latinxs in the United States come from myriad coun-tries and cultures in Latin America, and many have spent most or all of their lives in the United States. What complicates this variety fur-ther is that our racial makeup is just as diverse. Therefore, our chapter documents our experiences as doctoral students navigating graduate school with our peers and colleagues and in various teaching positions in higher education. We are from Latinx ethnic groups rarely represented in scholarship within rhetoric and composition. We document these experiences with the belief that being able to circulate more and more of these narratives may help Latinas and students of color feel less lonesome and less "crazy" in their own doctoral journey.

In the chapter's title and throughout, we reference the larger narrative discussed in an ethnographic study of twenty-two self-identified Black and Latinx doctoral students. Ryan Evely Gildersleeve, Natasha Croom, and Philip Vasquez (2011) found a consistent social narrative among their participants, which they called "Am I Going Crazy?!" This narrative entails a self-analysis process imposed on Black and Latinx students by various forces (peers, faculty, institutional structures, etc.) that is quite harmful to them because it questions their presence and abilities in graduate school. The researchers argue that the social narrative of "Am I going crazy?!" demonstrates "that the culture of doctoral education is dehumanizing and marginalizing for Latina/o and black students" (99)—meaning that it's "normal" to feel crazy because what we are doing as students of color is, in fact, "crazy" and out of the ordinary.

Before telling our stories, we want to acknowledge the complications associated with our use of the term *crazy* and its implications for undermining the reality of mental illness, especially in Latinx communities. In the case of our narratives specifically, we mean to honor the difficulties of those who are "othered" in the context of the institution of higher education. We know that those difficulties only multiply when individuals are managing disabilities of any kind, and other scholars have spent a considerable amount of time addressing issues of neurodiversity in academia.[1] We do not mean to diminish the actual concerns of mental illness, but we also do not want to dismiss the reality of how living under the systems of oppression in academia have an impact on us and our mental well-being. Our goal is for our stories to

---

1. For more on this topic, see Price 2009, Yergeau 2013, and Cedillo 2018.

provide a way for these kinds of narratives *not* to be deemed deviant or crazy. Our wildest dream is that we could somehow be accepted in both spaces (our homes and academia) and no longer be seated at the margins of both, where language such as *crazy* is attributed to things that are not actually related to mental sanity or illness. Sharing our stories as part of a collection that focuses on the stories of Latinas in academia is one way to begin this process.

Another part of this process is considering what this notion of "crazy" means in the context of our schooling and general life upbringing. Similar to how Christine García and Cristina D. Ramírez share in their respective essays in this collection (chapters 6 and 10), we would like to consider the significance of la facultad as proposed by Gloria Anzaldúa. In her well-known book *Borderlands / La Frontera: The New Mestiza* ([1987] 2012), Anzaldúa writes: "La Facultad is the capacity to see in surface phenomena the meaning of deeper realities, to see the deep structure below the surface. . . . Those who are pushed out of the tribe for being different are likely to become more sensitized (when not brutalized into insensitivity). . . . When we're up against the wall, when we have all sorts of oppressions coming at us, we are forced to develop this faculty so that we'll know when the next person is going to slap us or lock us away. . . . It's a kind of survival tactic that people, caught between worlds, unknowingly cultivate" (60–61).

And so the act of being delineated as "crazy" by the oppressors is really just something that checks their privilege against us. They force us to go against this deeply embedded knowing; our facultad is present to protect us as we navigate these varied worlds. There is this disjuncture between oppressor and oppressed because what we know as real is something they ask us to question and then make us feel as though we have it wrong. We have essentially questioned all logics associated with the greater structures of the institution. In Christina García's essay for this collection, she interviews Christina V. Cedillo, who describes how "literacy is . . . closely related to Anzaldúa's concept of 'la facultad.' It's not instinct; rather it's a powerful praxis based in spatial and embodied rhetorics" (chapter 6). In our experiences, this knowing is based specifically on the spatial context of our engaging with graduate peers but also an instinctual response to questioning ourselves just to check on our own understanding of what is transpiring in that space. Our body and our minds communicate something to us about questions we have received from others in the particular space of graduate school. Cristina Ramírez's use of this same definition in this collection (chapter 10) is powerful to encounter because she reminds us that this knowing also occurs in the classroom space when we are considering who and what we're teaching and for what greater purpose. Her experiences reveal what kind of service we can provide to students when we can fine-tune our response to la facultad and believe in it and make decisions according to it. Unfortunately, being in the position of students, we had to work toward developing this literacy, as Cedillo so eloquently tells us in Garcia's chapter. As students, we are/were still working through how we are/were being perceived by others as outsiders and what it means/meant for our own definitions regarding our identity in the academy if all anyone ever really sees/saw of and in us is/was our Latinidad.

An additional meaning we would like to attribute to the notion of "crazy" is the gendered way this word is infused in defining how women behave and respond to others. Usually when a woman is seen responding in a particularly emotional or impassioned manner, she is immediately seen as aberrant and deemed "crazy." There was a time when women were relegated to mental health facilities and institutions for simply having to manage hormones and the effect of those hormones on their bodies and minds (Chesler 2018). We are sure that our different approach to writing about our experiences as graduate students will continue to relegate our experiences to the margins of the academy—"crazy" or, as they say in our home language, Spanish, "loca." We are already seen as the locas of our respective Latinx communities, overeducated women who have supposedly chosen their careers and education (and a tremendous amount of student loan debt) instead of choosing marriage and children. As Anzaldúa states in *Borderlands / La Frontera*, "Educated or not, the onus is still on woman to be a wife/mother—only the nun can escape motherhood. Women are made to feel total failures if they don't marry and have children"

([1987] 2012, 39). One of us is seen as an "old maid" because she is nearing her midthirties with no man or children in sight, while the other is a divorced single mom. Whereas our personal lives have, for lack of a better word, "failed," according to the standard Anzaldúa describes, our careers are on track.

We would like to believe we are our mothers' and grandmothers' wildest dream as financially independent women who are pursuing careers we love while achieving what few can, a doctorate degree. However, we find it hard to fully embrace that idea because of the socialization process in our Latinx community, where women should not (or cannot) center their lives on their careers and education but must instead focus on their romantic prospects and families. We are not convinced we would ever be fully held up in our community as being successful or as not having failed somehow. But both our chapter and our lives are living proof of what bell hooks describes as being situated in the margins, a "site of radical possibility, a space of resistance," "a central location for the production of a counter-hegemonic discourse that is not just found in words but in habits of being and the way one lives" (1989, 149). Therefore, the documentation of our lives in textual form and our literal presence as Latina faculty in our respective academic departments and as Latina students in our graduate school recenter the entire conversation.

Moreover, Ana Milena Ribero and Sonia C. Arellano's essay "Advocating Comadrismo: A Feminist Mentoring Approach for Latinas in Rhetoric and Composition" (chapter 1) allows us also to rethink the ways that our community was bringing us together and that we did not find each other. In fact, it was not easy for us to engage as students or come to know each other because one of us was in the dissertation-writing phase and the other was in coursework, yet we were quick to question why a white institution and professors within it were trying to bring us together. In context now, though, it looks as if these people might have been attempting to have us support each other through our graduate journey, and in the end our being brought together enabled us eventually to create this essay. Unfortunately, our respective experiences in higher education did not allow us to take comfort immediately in being brought together because we were trained to believe that each of us would be the only Latina present in a graduate program. We were also taught never really to build community in an environment that values independence and meritocracy. Despite these beliefs, we eventually did come together, and in our collaboration on this essay we saw comadrismo in action.

Finally, our use of the term *Latinx* is intentional. We had conversations about our own gendered noun and pronoun use and what this term means for us in the context of our research. When speaking about ourselves and women who identify as women, we use the word *Latinas*. However, we decided it was important to use *Latinx* rather than the traditional *Latina/o* when speaking of people of Latin American heritage because we want to be inclusive of all genders. Our stories challenge and push at the established and traditional notions of what women are and can be within our own communities, so we think it is appropriate to choose the term that also does not comply with the masculine or feminine gendered word usage of the Spanish language. Our hope is that the use of the word *Latinx* releases us and our work to permit a more robust sense of how gender might be imagined in the future.

Nuestros Cuentos

Although brief author bios of us are already included in this collection, we thought it was imperative for us to go beyond them so that our readers can get a sense of who we are and why we are on this doctoral journey. When we started writing this essay in the fall of 2018, Nancy (who began her PhD in 2011) was about to defend her dissertation, while Raquel (who began her PhD in 2015) was in the dissertation-writing stage. At a glance, we found that we had lots in common: (1) we were Latina doctoral students at the same university and were pursuing degrees in English; (2) we were writing dissertations focused on rhetoric and composition in our department; (3) we were also former adjunct writing instructors in full-time, non-tenure-track positions in community colleges; and (4) we are first-generation New Yorkers. But this is where our similarities end. We led very different lives before deciding to take the leap into our PhD program, and we continue to live different lives in different parts of the city, but we have experienced so many of the same microaggressions in all areas of academia. We have often asked ourselves and each other, "¿Estamos locas? Is this normal?," when discussing the kinds of issues we encounter in academia. Sometimes the answer to both questions is yes. We are crazy for wanting to be a part of an institution that constantly ignores our existence and/or marks our bodies as bodies in need of help. We are crazy for not walking away from it all when times get tough. We are crazy for showing up time after time, even when faculty, colleagues, classmates, conference attendants, and our students have made us feel as if we have nothing to contribute to the field of rhetoric and composition. We are just those locas who refuse to quit and insist on smiling when others seem uncomfortable.

In an effort to add more Latina doctoral student narratives as counterstories[2] into the realm of Latinas in academia,[3] we have decided to share brief stories about our experiences as undergraduate students, graduate students, and instructors. What we realized after getting to know each other is that even though we are living very different lives in different parts of the New York City area, we have encountered similar experiences on our journey to the English PhD. We decided to tell our stories in three parts that describe the battles we have faced on this journey. Through these batallas, we hope to show other Latina doctoral students examples of the challenges we have faced and how we were able to push through in order to continue toward our goals. We also hope that faculty and others who read this chapter gain insight into how the doctoral journey is different for everyone, seeing that there is no one way to be or become a doctoral student. We honor our journeys and everything we have overcome to get to where we are now.

2. For more on this topic, see Solórzano and Yosso 2002 and Martinez 2013.

3. For more on this topic, see Latina Feminist Group 2001; Kamimura, Gloria, and Castellanos 2006; Howard Hamilton et al. 2009; Gutierrez y Muhs et al. 2012; Torres 2016.

La Primera Batalla—Choosing English as a Major

We begin by sharing narratives of how and why we became English majors who decided to pursue doctoral degrees. Our stories are very different, but they converge in similar places. Although Raquel's parents did not interfere in her selecting English as a major, she found that some of her professors were not as welcoming as she had hoped. Nancy's experience was the complete opposite. Because her parents did not encourage or approve of her pursuit of an English major, she felt insecure about her abilities, even when professors tried to encourage her. What we gather from our stories is that mentorship could have helped us find our way sooner than we did. But not just any kind of mentorship. If we would have seen Latina professors in action in our classrooms and had they shown us what was possible, perhaps we would have carried less doubt about ourselves.

Making a connection with a professor and building what Steven Alvarez (2017) describes as confianza can open so many doors for students of color. In "Diving for Pearls: Mentoring as Cultural and Activist Practice among Academics of Color" (2002), Gail Y. Okawa reflects on the mentoring relationship between two faculty members of color, Geneva Smitherman and Victor Villanueva, and their graduate student mentees. Okawa interviewed Smitherman and Villanueva about their own experiences as students of color and what they feel they bring to their mentoring relationships with students of color.

Villanueva describes how his own "need to know" informs how he mentors: "There is a knowledge that is assumed, the kind of thing that Gramsci says the middle class knows by a kind of osmosis. Mentoring, then, is something beyond the teaching. It is the making explicit what is implicitly known, assuming nothing of tacit understanding of academic or white or white middle-class workings, no matter who ends up being the mentee. And mentoring means being able to enter into an intellectual friendship" (Okawa 2002, 514). Villanueva's "need to know" leads him to build confianza with his mentees by sharing knowledge that blurs the line between insider and outsider. When a mentor is there to inform and support his or her mentees, the mentees learn and feel less alone in their academic journey. In addition, Okawa writes, "mentoring for Smitherman and Villanueva instilled in them a belief that it may be possible to make change, to establish their own worth within the context of the academy and the profession. This becomes a collaborative, activist practice" (524). The mentees are inspired by mentors who have begun to clear the road ahead and come to believe they can also do part of the work that is needed to make that road smoother and wider. Villanueva adds that he also gains from the relationship he develops with his mentees: "[They] have allowed me to learn, to feel a sense of doing something tangible for people of color, and to feel a sense of community in an environment that is so often alienating" (528). Through mentorship that respects students' cultural and linguistic diversity, mentees can learn to accept their own identity and languages. If the mentees decide to pursue careers in education, they can take what they have learned and use it to nurture linguistic diversity within their future students.

Raquel

I was born and raised on Long Island (the suburbs near New York City). My parents were born in the Dominican Republic but spent the majority of their lives in the United States, so they could be defined as a little more "assimilated" to American culture (as much as I hate the use of that word), and both of them speak English. I went away to college at Cornell University and knew immediately that I was going to be an English major. I loved writing poetry and reading extensively. I initially imagined I would go on to get my doctorate degree right after getting my bachelor's degree. I was on this particular path when I began my junior year and enrolled in the department-required course for students who were going to be writing a thesis. I remember being excited and challenged by the course. It was one of the smallest classes I had ever taken; there were maybe ten of us in a small room with couches. We were reading the traditional American works of Herman Melville, and I was finally introduced to the famous line in "Bartleby, the Scrivener": "I prefer not to." But everything changed after the professor returned my first writing assignment. She was concerned about my aptitude and wondered how I had managed to get accepted into the honors program with its required thesis. I went to visit this professor in her office hours for weeks. It was there that she introduced me to Strunk and White's *The Elements of Style* (1972). (Yes, she handed me a copy to keep, and, yes, this copy is still in my book collection as a reminder of what introduced me to and also kept me out of the academy.)

I remember the professor being so surprised by my writing that early on in the semester she reached out to the director of the honors program to inquire about me and attached a sample of my writing for the director to review. I wish I could remember more details about it, but I have a strong recollection of receiving a copy of the email she sent to the director and being appalled and scared. My investment in her course, my work to improve my writing, and my requests for her assistance during office hours—all of that had not mattered. At the end of the semester, when I got my final grade for the course, I sent her an email message explaining why I did not deserve a C. She must have had enough of fighting me because she never replied to my message and changed my grade to a B–. My experience with this faculty member left me disillusioned about my interest in academia and questioning whether I was ever meant to pursue further education in English. After that semester, I decided to withdraw from the honors program. I was exhausted. I did not have the Ivy League writing chops to pursue an undergraduate thesis, and I knew I did not want to continue fighting white faculty to be accepted in the field. I had spent so many years in this effort already, working so hard but barely ending up with a B– in most of my English-literature courses; I just did not have it in me to consider more education where I knew that all I would do is continue fighting. I instead found solace in my creative-writing courses, where I never failed to excel and had the ability to write to my heart's content in a form that spoke to me much more than the stuffy academic jargon required of traditional literature courses. Like Bartleby, in an odd way, I had announced to the English literature field, "I prefer not to" continue being stifled and harmed by the ridiculous standards and convoluted use of the English language.

While at Cornell, I joined a sorority my sophomore year and was an extremely active leader on campus (involved in orientation, the larger Greek community, and the Multicultural Affairs Office). I transitioned my desires and hopes of staying in higher education to the other side of the house, where I received the support to get through my bachelor's degree: student affairs. After leaving Cornell, I spent six and a half years as a residence-life professional at two different schools. After that, I returned to the New York City area and began training to teach intensive remedial English courses. Despite training for three months, I felt as though being a remedial English teacher was not the best role for me, and I moved back into administrative student support by becoming an adviser and eventually the coordinator of this special program. During this time, I managed to get the opportunity to teach as an adjunct in the English Department at the same City University of New York (CUNY) institution where I was working. Ever since leaving residential life, I had been intent on figuring out my interest in teaching, and despite not feeling as though I could teach remedial students, I wanted to see how I would fare with students taking credit-bearing English courses. The moment I got in front of that introductory literature class in fall of 2013, I knew I was standing in the place I was always supposed to be. I fell in love with teaching this really special student population that I was so passionate about at an institution that was dedicated to its open-access mission. It was because of this experience teaching as an adjunct for more than three years that I was inspired to go back to school and get a doctorate degree. I wanted to be and continue to learn with these students.

However, I knew that even professors at community colleges have to hold a doctorate degree. I wasn't sure about whether I wanted to do research or not, but, if anything, I could get my doctorate degree in creative writing and possibly write nonfiction as a dissertation. However, I eventually accepted admission to the only institution among those I applied to where I would have to write one of those academic dissertations. I was excited nonetheless because from conversations with alumni and faculty I had learned that the institution was flexible about student research interests and the possibility of a nontraditional or more interdisciplinary dissertation project. If there was anything I was committed to in regard to graduate school, it was ensuring that I had faculty who would support my research interests and not expect me to focus on their research agenda.

Nancy

I was born and raised in Queens, New York. My parents were born in El Salvador and fled their home in the late 1970s when the civil war threatened their safety. My parents were undocumented residents in the United States for years, and their fear of being deported shaped my childhood. I loved school as a child, but I couldn't imagine college as a real possibility for myself. My parents were open to the idea of my attending college, but they also wanted me to work. English had been my favorite subject throughout high school, and the thought of reading and writing as a college student excited me. But my parents thought that studying English would not lead to a prosperous career, so I went to a for-profit secretarial school that helped me land a full-time secretarial job by age eighteen. From then on, I did not have a traditional undergraduate journey. After earning my associate's degree at the for-profit college, I was academically dismissed twice from a four-year university before I found myself at a local community college. Two English professors noticed me and suggested that I declare English as a major. No one had ever before encouraged me to become an English major. It took me a year to finally gather the courage to take their advice and declare English as a major. In total, it took me eleven years to finish my undergraduate program, and I graduated with my bachelor's degree in English literature at age twenty-eight.

When I found the Language and Literacy Program created by Mina Shaughnessy at the City College of New York, I thought it was a perfect fit as I considered teaching adult literacy. When I found out that I had been accepted into this program, I dismissed my above-average GPA as the reason for my acceptance and convinced myself that affirmative action had given me a hand. As Victor Villanueva writes, "He sees sense in Affirmative Action. He is sometimes grateful. He is often leery" (1993, 13). I walked into my first class feeling grateful to be there but also embarrassed and not good enough, even though I wasn't the only person of color in the classroom. I fulfilled the Latina quota, I was sure, even though there was another Latina sitting right next to me in class. I figured the program needed both of us in case one of us dropped out. A year later my Latina classmate dropped out, and I had straight As. She decided to join the Peace Corps and pursue other dreams instead of finishing the program. Her departure helped convince me that I had been right—there's got to be two Latinas. When Raquel joined the English PhD program at our university, I remembered this moment and thought, "Again, there has to be two of us in case one of us drops out."

During the last semester of my master's degree program, I took a leap of faith. I decided to apply to a PhD program that a former classmate had recommended. She loved her professors and their work in writing centers, and I was interested. I had begun tutoring at the writing center of a local community college, and I loved the students there. Working with those students made me want to become a pro-fessor. I applied to only one program and was thrilled when I heard I had been accepted. The following fall I began my doctoral journey and also taught my first writing course as an adjunct instructor at City College. On my first day of teaching, I didn't feel fully prepared, and my voice shook violently as I stood in front of the classroom and stared at my first batch of students. I wanted to cry. I wanted a "real" professor, an older white male or female, to come and tell all of us what to do. I had never met a Latina English professor in my thirteen years of college, and I didn't know how to perform the role as I saw faces that looked like mine staring at me for answers. All semester I wondered if my leap of faith had been a mistake. I decided to stop teaching, stop tutoring, and just focus on learning.

La Segunda Batalla—Becoming Doctoral English Candidates

According to the National Center for Education Statistics, "In fall 2015, of all full-time faculty at degree-granting postsecondary institutions, 42 percent were White males, 35 percent were White females, 6 percent were Asian/Pacific Islander males, 4 percent were

Asian/Pacific Islander females, 3 percent each were Black females and Black males, and 2 percent each were Hispanic males and Hispanic females" (2017, 255). The total percentage of Latina full-time faculty is so small, and it encompasses *all* Latina faculty across all disciplines, which makes the percentage of possible Latina English faculty even smaller.

The silver lining to consider here is that the percentage of Latinx (there are no statistics available that show the difference between genders) majoring in English at the undergraduate and graduate levels is increasing. Between 2009 and 2014, the number of Latinx English majors earning bachelor's degrees rose from 7 percent to 10.5 percent of all English majors, making it the highest increase of all minorities majoring in English during that time period (Humanities Indicators 2016, fig. II-18d). During that same period, there was also an increase in the number of Latinx graduate students earning a master's in English from 5 percent to 7 percent (Humanities Indicators 2016, fig. II-18c) and of Latinx graduate students earning doctoral degrees in English from 3 percent to a bit less than 4 percent (Humanities Indicators 2016, fig. II-18f). Although these percentages may not seem extraordinary, when compared to the statistics for other minorities, the numbers for Latinxs are higher. In addition, because Latinas are graduating at a higher rate than Latinos for associate's degrees, 21 percent versus 15 percent, and bachelor's degrees, 47 percent versus 37 percent (Carnevale and Fasules 2018, fig. 3.3), there's a chance that more Latina professors are in the works.

With the increase in the number of Latinxs in college, we entered our PhD program with high hopes. We were going to learn to become English professors, and we would become the professors we had needed throughout our undergraduate careers. Both of us knew that embarking on PhD degrees would require a lot of work, but we were not prepared for the microaggressions we encountered just for being Latina. As born and raised New Yorkers, we assumed that racism would not play a role in or interfere with our educations. We were wrong. Our interactions with our classmates took an emotional toll on us in how we understood ourselves as doctoral students.

Nancy

I began my doctoral program in the fall of 2011. After my first week of coursework, I immediately wanted to drop out. I felt out of place and a little bit lost. I was intimidated by my mostly white classmates and how they could easily quote writers I had never even heard of. I felt as if I were back in prekindergarten. When I began elementary school, I didn't speak English and was in awe of how my classmates could easily sing songs in English that I had never heard before. This time in my life at graduate school was eerily familiar. Hardly any of my classmates spoke to me, just as in prekindergarten, so I chose silence over saying the wrong thing—again, just as I did in prekindergarten. As a child, I didn't learn to speak English until I was in kindergarten. As an adult student, I spoke English, yet I still felt as if my language was not good enough and, worse, as if my words had no value.

I thought about affirmative action again. I felt unprepared for my coursework and wondered if I had been chosen to fill a quota. After a few weeks, I reached out to one of two professors of color in my department at that time. I told her how I was feeling, and she handed me a copy of a recently published article, "'Am I Going Crazy?!' A Critical Race Analysis of Doctoral Education" (2011) by Ryan Evely Gildersleeve, Natasha Croom, and Philip Vasquez. Reading that article made me feel less lonely. I asked her if she knew whether affirmative action was the reason I had been accepted into the doctoral program. She said that it had not played a role. I wanted to believe her, so I did. I put my all into my coursework and decided that I wouldn't let any of my classmates see me as someone who didn't belong. The following semester I began working at the writing center and tried to open up a little bit. I met two more professors who took time to get to know me. I felt seen, and that meant everything. I wish professors knew how much a smile or some sort of acknowledgment means to students of color, especially graduate students of color because there are so few of us. Graduate programs are overwhelmingly white across all disciplines. We are often overlooked by classmates and professors, who see us as foreigners or even invaders.

During the spring semester of 2012, the professor who eventually became my dissertation adviser was unable to attend a national conference, but instead of skipping it altogether, she asked me if I would attend the conference in her place. My first instinct was to say no, but I was practicing being brave, so I accepted. This professor vouched for me and negotiated with my university and the host of the conference so that I could attend in her place. At this point, I was feeling better about my place in the doctoral program, but I was not all that confident about representing the professor at this conference. The list of invitees included academics I admired, and her name fit on that list so much better than mine. And yet I attended the conference, met some of my academic heroes, and also met other Latina doctoral students. Before attending this conference, I had never met any. This conference made me believe that I could be part of something bigger in my field. I didn't have to hide and blend in with my cohort. I had a voice and could use it to present at conferences and share my experiences with others.

When I returned from that conference and told my peers about it, many asked out loud why I had been chosen instead of them. They even listed reasons why they were more qualified than I was to attend. I didn't know how to respond to their passive aggression. Honestly, I think now that this professor knew that I needed this experience more than the others did, that maybe I would benefit in ways that they wouldn't, or that I would appreciate the experience more. But at the moment my classmates' questions made me feel as if perhaps I couldn't and shouldn't share any of my successes with them. Again, I thought about affirmative action and wondered if any of my achievements would ever feel like mine. I considered adopting silence again.

Raquel

I began the PhD program in 2015, and it was in my second year that I encountered an incident that stays with me today. I want to recount this incident because it occurred outside the traditional space of the academic classroom. I think it's important to continue discussing what

Nancy mentioned: holding in your head the idea that you have been accepted into graduate school simply to fulfill an affirmative-action quota. In my case, the idea came up in the context of the socialization process among graduate students, which also coincides with graduate peer-to-peer mentorship and leadership. This incident occurred when I was asked to be the graduate student representative on the department's faculty search committee that year. A few weeks into the search process, I was asked (though it felt more like an interrogation) by a fellow graduate student how I had been chosen to be on the committee. This student was in the exams stage at the time; she was a white, cis-heterosexual woman, married with children, and living on Long Island. I wish I could remember what I said to her, but I'm sure it was something along the lines that I was just approached by a faculty member. I didn't know how to put into words the reasons I was approached instead of her without sounding condescending; not wanting to treat her the way she was currently treating me, I didn't say any of the real reasons given to me for the committee members' choice:

1. They saw me as capable of representing the department in a manner that would reflect positively on the graduate student population *and* the institution overall.

2. I was already a graduate student leader in the department. I had worked with a fellow student who was in the dissertation phase to create a graduate student organization for the English Department. I had recruited other graduate student peers to serve and worked hard to consider student interests and needs in implementing the program. The faculty thus saw me putting forth all this unpaid labor and being genuinely interested in the graduate student experience within the department and at the institution. They imagined I would be a good person to continue providing graduate student insight on potential candidates because I was already working to gain their input on other aspects of the program.

3. I was one of the students who sat on the interestingly odd divide between the camp of rhetoric and composition and the

camp of literature in the field of English (not only with my research interests but also in my work as a graduate student leader). Faculty saw me navigate that complexity as a student leader in the department.

And, to be fair to myself, I had other qualifications that the faculty may not have been aware of but that were directly linked to my abilities previously outlined. I was available and flexible enough to take on this kind of responsibility because I was often on campus and was still on fellowship. A serious time commitment was needed to interview candidates and take part in the hosting committee's other duties, which included attending meals and bringing candidates to the graduate student meeting. I suppose that because they saw me actively planning and organizing events for students and still taking coursework, they knew that my schedule was amenable to being on campus often. There is no funding available to students after coursework at my institution, so many of our older graduate students (third year and beyond) work for other colleges in New York City and on Long Island. In addition, I had extensive search experience, having gone to conferences to interview candidates, sitting on search committees, and even running my own search process in my previous positions in higher education. The peer who questioned why I was chosen to be on the search committee had no idea that my previous professional experience gave me an incredible amount of insight, and despite the search process being for an academic position that I had never been privy to, I still knew what it was like to do a search in the context of higher education.

I assume her question was supposed to reveal to me that I was chosen because as a graduate student of color I met the expected affirmative-action quota. What did I do after experiencing this question about the department's choice of me as the graduate student representative to sit on the department's search committee? I spoke directly to the director of graduate studies and the department chair about making these opportunities open to all graduate students and having them submit applications to faculty, who would choose fairly which student(s) should represent the department. This process would allow the department to communicate what kinds of students they are looking to have on these committees. I don't know if my feedback was ever implemented or taken into account. But I found it hard to explain to certain faculty that despite my being an exceptional or stellar graduate student in the department (for a variety of reasons), they needed to take into account the narrative that this exceptional status still seemed to communicate to some fellow students: namely, that I am excellent only *because* I'm a woman of color. This is why I insisted on having the department take time to communicate general standards for working on service posts as a graduate student. I wanted publicized standards to show my peers that as a Latina I wasn't just fulfilling some ridiculous diversity target but that, in actuality, I fulfilled most or all of the guidelines and expectations the faculty had of any graduate student representing the department.

La Tercera Batalla: Joining the Ranks

Several scholars of color have discussed being mistaken for anything other than faculty either on their campus or when attending conferences (see, e.g., Gutierrez y Muhs et al. 2012). As adjunct instructors at various institutions across the boroughs of New York City, we have resembled the student demographic more than the faculty profile. For example, in March 2018 the CUNY Office of Institutional Research and Assessment reported that during the fall 2017 semester 32.3 percent of all undergraduate students identified as Hispanic/Latinx, 25.6 percent as Black, 21.1 percent as Asian/Pacific Islander, 20.7 percent as white, and 0.3 percent as American Indian/Alaska Native (CUNY 2018). These statistics are significantly different for graduate students at CUNY, where 48 percent identified as white, 18 percent as Hispanic/Latinx, 17.1 percent as Black, 16.2 percent as Asian/Pacific Islander, and 0.2 percent as American Indian/Alaska Native (CUNY 2018). One would assume that within the twenty-four colleges that make up CUNY, there would be more faculty of color, considering the locations of those institutions and the students they serve. According to a CUNY report on its workforce demographics in 2016, only 12.1 percent of all faculty across CUNY institutions identified as Hispanic/Latinx, while 54.1 percent identified as white (CUNY 2016).

During the fall 2018 semester, both of us were full-time non-tenure-track faculty within CUNY's community colleges. At our respective colleges, we have found that our colleagues and our students are often quick to mistake who we are on campus. These mistakes are often covered up with assertions that our "young" appearance is what led to the erroneous assumption, not the fact that we are brown women. Because both of us are in our midthirties, it would be a compliment to be mistaken for being in our early to midtwenties, but we know what the real deal is behind these compliments: we do not look like your average English professor. We are not bearded white men wearing tweed blazers with suede elbow patches. We are not white women. But we are here to say and show that there's more than one way of looking like an English professor, and our students and colleagues are learning.

Raquel

One time I was mistaken for a student by a white woman with whom I shared an office when I was an adjunct. She gave me an odd look one day as I walked into my office looking to get access to my desk, where she had a student seated. I was initially annoyed that she seemed unwilling to have the student move. It wasn't until she apologized a week or two later, admitting that she had believed me to be a student, that I could process that a white-presenting woman was incapable of sincerely believing that I could be doing what she was doing: teaching community college students. This same woman later went through the search process with me for the openings on our campus, asked me what my yearly salary was, and then said she had a feeling the amount would match what she was already receiving by working at two different schools concurrently—the implication being that it did not matter if she had not gotten the position because we were making an equal amount of money.

Another moment of mistaken identity occurred when I was walking to the staff bathroom, and a different white woman, a full-time faculty member, said, "The student bathroom is around the corner." I responded by jingling my keys and smiling. If I have been taught anything as a woman in higher education, it's that smiling and laughter always help offset the awkward microaggressions that hit you at almost any point in your day. She replied by complimenting my youth and saying she mistook me for a student. This interaction is a reminder that my presence sets askew a space that hasn't held a body and person like me previously. As an adjunct and a graduate student, I am in a precarious situation, vulnerable at all times, so in what ways could I actually have a conversation with this faculty member without compromising myself (and my financial livelihood)? Suffice it to say, I wonder if my presence, my existence, helped these women to reconfigure the possibilities of how the professoriate can look when it represents the student population of the institution itself. This full-time faculty member has ever since then been my advocate and supportive of me in the department. But I am still left wondering: To what extent does social justice work have to continue to be done in departments with faculty who really need to consider and discuss some of the biases they hold?

Nancy

When I was working as an adjunct instructor at a predominantly white Catholic college in New York City, I was often mistaken for a student by colleagues and students alike. One day a white male adjunct instructor walked past my classroom during a lecture, stopped, walked backward a few steps, and watched me teach for two seconds. He continued to do this regularly, until one day he just walked into my classroom and asked me in front of my students if I was a Spanish professor. I replied that I wasn't, and he said that he needed a Spanish speaker to translate paperwork for him. I shook my head and could not say the words that I wanted to say. When he left, my students expressed surprise at the interruption, and all I could say was, "You see?" In my first-year writing course, we had been discussing racism and language rights. My predominantly white classroom of students just nodded their heads. They understood.

I am currently working at a community college that is a Hispanic-serving institution. I find that I do in fact look more like a student than a professor because many of the students I encounter are single moms trying to make the best of their situation. I think they find it comforting that I can understand their priorities. Their children, our children, will always come first. Sometimes papers take longer to get written, but they are written. I have embraced looking like my students because I have decided this means that I look like a hardworking mom, which doesn't bother me at all. I think my students are curious about me because I look like them. Instead of fearing me, which is what I thought students should feel toward their professors because that's what I had always felt, my students respect me and see me as role model. I tell them about my eleven-year journey to earning my bachelor's degree, and I motivate them to keep going in their education because time will keep passing by anyway.

Even though I have learned to accept that I look like a student on my community college campus, I have to admit that I took offense at a recent incident there. I was grading papers in a staff room at the community college, and a male student had the gall to ask me if I belonged in that staff room. I said yes, and he asked me if I was sure. I nodded and kept grading my papers. When I encountered him again a few weeks later, he asked me, without any sort of greeting or explanation, what my job title was. I wondered about his limited experience in the United States and wondered if he assumed that professors couldn't possibly look like me because he hadn't had one yet. I asked him if I looked suspicious to him and why he was questioning me in that manner. I don't think he expected me to question *him*. I told him that I was a professor and that his interrogation was rude. He apologized, and I moved on. This encounter continues to trouble me, though, as I wonder how I could have made our interaction a teachable moment for both of us. This is a reminder of how important representation is for students. We academics of color serve not only as examples of what students can aspire to but also as examples of what a more just society can look like. There is enough room for faculty of color as well as scientists, accountants, doctors, and lawyers of color.

Remaining en la Lucha: Meaningful Mentoring for Latina Doctoral Students and Emerging Faculty

In considering what it would mean to provide appropriate mentoring for Latinxs as they encounter various obstacles on their journey to the doctorate degree, we thought it would be helpful to showcase important moments in our own experiences that highlight the kind of mentorship Latinas need. Although we appreciate and respect our mentors, we have to mention that our mentors are not Latinas. Raquel's mentor is Latino, and Nancy's is a white woman. There are no Latinas teaching in our university's English Department.

Raquel

I am currently in the beginning of the dissertation phase and developing a prospectus. I have an adviser who self-identifies as Latino and used to be a writing program administrator on our campus. I recently had two meetings with him about my project that I think really encompass what kind of mentoring we should consider developing in the future. The first conversation concerned the significance of my work in the current time frame and how important it will be in the field. We also had a discussion about my first semester as a full-time lecturer at a community college and my own reservations about seeking a professor position that required more research and focused less on teaching. It led to a moment that allowed us to have a really meaningful conversation about what it means for a person of color to "dream" of being a professor. We are not raised in communities where this is even part of our imagination. We are also part of an educational system that does not allow us to fully believe that we can and will be able to do that. What is key about this moment for the purposes of mentoring is the fact that he could so honestly reveal that this was another place from which my concerns came and that the question I was trying to answer for myself was: Am I allowed to reach for more? This conversation was illuminating and important for me

6. Raquel Corona with her mentors after successfully passing her oral exam two years ago. Photograph courtesy of Steven Alvarez.

as I continued to consider the kinds of full-time professor positions I wanted to apply to in the future.

Recently, this same mentor and I had another eye-opening conversation. He asked me genuinely how I was doing, and I was only able to say, "I'm tired." He is one of the few people in my life who actually understands what my life is like now and responded, "I know you're working hard, and you're working in a teaching position that requires more labor, and you're trying to write consistently." When I replied to this comment with a smile and said, "Everyone works hard," he stopped me. He didn't smile back; instead, he said straightforwardly, "No, not everyone works hard." He reminded me that the kind of labor I do as a woman of color is different, that it is actually "more," and that I have made a false assumption. Despite my experience in the workforce and knowing fully that everyone around me does not necessarily have the same work ethic or commitment, I was still disillusioned as a graduate student in higher education. My mentor had to take a moment in a Skype conversation to metaphorically take my hand and sit me down with these false notions and ideas to remind me that everyone isn't doing what I'm doing. I truly believe this is how you keep Latinxs and other budding scholars of color in the field: (1) Tell them you see them and you see their work and their determination and their exhaustion. For some reason, their experience is different from that of other graduate students they're surrounded by, and you need to confirm that difference for them. (2) Remind them that their work is valuable to the field. (3) And, finally, tell them that they can dream beyond the borders they have developed and the disciplinary ones placed around them. They can imagine a position or career different from the one they thought they were just lucky to get (or the system told them they were lucky to have gotten).

Nancy

Near the end of my dissertation journey, I realized that I would have never gotten to this point in my career without thoughtful mentoring from my dissertation adviser, a white woman. She has not only opened doors for me but also held them open. I could list all of the ways that she has supported my work, but I want to mention two things specifically.

In 2014, I was accepted to present at a regional conference when my son was only six months old. I wanted to attend this conference because a classmate and I had worked really hard on the research project that we wanted to present, but it seemed as if the universe was conspiring against me. My husband (at the time) wanted me to skip the conference and stay home; my mother wanted me to leave my son with her and go to the conference without him; and my university said that my son couldn't ride in the university-sponsored vehicle because of liability/insurance reasons. I wanted to be with my son, and I wanted to attend the conference, but I saw no way of achieving both goals since I don't drive. Thankfully, my adviser offered a solution: she would drive both my son and me to the conference. She was also presenting a paper there, but she could have easily traveled with others or in that university-sponsored van. She and another professor instead helped me transport my son to Rhode Island so that I wouldn't have to choose between missing presenting my research at the conference and missing my son. So many people were against my

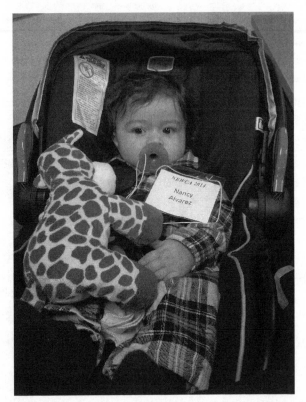

7. Six-month-old Benjamin at the Northeast Writing Center Association's annual conference, March 2014. Photograph by Nancy Alvarez.

son traveling with me for various reasons, but my adviser supported my decision, and that was all I needed. She made me feel as if I could do both: be the kind of mother that I wanted to be *and* be the kind of academic that I needed to be.

After that conference, I felt confident enough to travel with my son to national conferences and presented with him in my arms or in the arms of audience members. My family expected me to choose my child over my academic pursuits, but my adviser supported my decision to do both, and I continue to do both to this day. I believe that the main role of an adviser should be to show you what's possible in your academic journey and not to block your path or create any unnecessary hurdles. For a Latina, the hurdles are already there; no one should add more, especially not your adviser-mentor-friend.

When my marriage came to an end in 2015, my adviser was one of the women who were there to help me pick up the pieces. Part of me wanted to quit the doctoral program so that I could focus on reestablishing my new life as a single mother, but because of her support, I didn't quit. She let me take my time. She encouraged me but never made me feel like a failure when my dissertation stopped progressing for months. From 2015 to 2019, I worked on publications, hustled between numerous jobs, won a dissertation grant, and reached other personal goals. My adviser understood that I was on my own personal journey and didn't make any demands on my time. I never felt shamed for completing my degree in eight years instead of four. Her support was vital to my finishing this degree, and I am lucky to have had her as my adviser.

Recommendations for Faculty and Peers

As we came together to consider the significance of our batallas, we wanted to provide some important recommendations for both faculty and our graduate peers based on what helped us on our doctoral journeys. We feel that mentorship from faculty should be intentional. Our graduate student peers should also feel that they can ask for specific mentorship or guidance from their mentors. To be better mentors, faculty need to

1. Consider and acknowledge the true reality of intersectionality. We need to approach the mentoring of students of color and Latinxs with a more nuanced understanding of the full spectrum and interconnections of challenges and obstacles they may have to overcome. What our stories in this chapter document is that despite both of us being Latinas, we have vastly different backgrounds, not only in English, education, and ethnic particularities but also in our personal life circumstances. We ask faculty to consider the full identities of their students and meaningfully spend time understanding the key

challenges and obstacles their students may be facing. This requires being open and observant and asking students questions rather than making assumptions and pursuing only one way to resolve graduate student concerns.

2. Remember and tell students that the doctoral journey is not meant to look any particular way. Basically, it is going to look however it is going to look. One of our mutual mentors constantly reminded Nancy of this when her journey became more challenging and she wasn't able to keep to the timelines she had set for herself. There should be some freedom in the way students pursue this journey, and they need to know that they can succeed in the way that best suits them. Faculty often feel they need to mold graduate students as though we are formless, despite our years spent earning college degree(s), working full-time jobs, and managing our home lives. It is important for faculty to know that what is going to work for one student may not work well for another. Take the time to get to know us.

Latinx graduate students need to

1. Realize that there is a wealth of resources out there, try to get involved beyond campus, and make connections elsewhere. Sometimes our home institutions look and function in very odd and particular ways. Although it is expensive to attend conferences, there are opportunities that help graduate students present their work to others in their field. Mentors can offer assistance in navigating conferences and in meeting other graduate students and circles of scholars of color. We have gone into a lot of debt, even with travel stipends offered by our university, in order to attend conferences, but we feel that the cost of it all has been worth it. In addition, we are currently members of the Latinx Caucus of the National Council of Teachers of English/Conference on College Composition and Communication. We have met many of the contributors

to this volume at Latinx Caucus meetings. Attending these meetings has given us a larger understanding of the field and put us in contact with other scholars whom we can ask for assistance in navigating confusing situations at our home institutions.

2. Make comadrismo a resource for peer mentorship. We have put into action Ribero and Arellano's key concepts for building comadrismo just by writing this chapter collaboratively. We very much value and see each other as comadres who have knowledge about the institution of higher education as well as about all kinds of matters related to life beyond the classroom. When discussing the key theme of kinship in comadrismo, Ribero and Arellano state that "this kind of kinship can be built through an effort to get to know and to mentor the whole person. Comadres should create space for conversations about issues outside of academia" (chapter 1).

An example of comadrismo occurred to us a few years ago when we were talking on campus and came upon the topic of children. As a single woman unsure about having children, Raquel felt insecure about having a conversation with a single mother because she was tired of hearing people tell her that she needed to have children. She was unsure what to expect, but until this day Nancy's words stay with her: "You don't have to have children. One day you'll know for sure whether you want them or not, and then you'll make your decision. For a long time, I did not want children, but then came the point that I knew I did." Raquel was waiting to be made to feel guilty for not necessarily wanting them, but Nancy instead comforted her in such a realistic manner. Raquel has been surrounded by women her entire life and even joined a sorority full of them, and none of them was ever this objective or allowed her the freedom to figure out for herself alone this great question in her life. That was the moment she knew that Nancy was different and looked forward to interacting with her and getting to know her more. This great question has nothing really to do with academia per se, but it was a personal and emotional matter of great significance to Raquel that Nancy helped her think through.

In addition, when Nancy found herself applying for full-time work within CUNY, she reached out to Raquel since Raquel had recently accepted a full-time position. Raquel offered her advice and even disclosed her salary in order to help Nancy negotiate her own. Nobody wants to talk about money with their colleagues, but disclosing this information is so beneficial when it comes to seeking work, especially for a junior scholar in the field. I would also say that it is especially important for a Latina when you consider the large wage gap between Latinas and white women and men that leaves us earning considerably lower salaries annually (Hegewisch and Barsi 2020). Because Raquel disclosed such valuable information, Nancy was able to advocate better for herself, which helped her get a fair salary. These conversations need to happen between comadres so that they can help each other not only survive but also thrive in real life outside academia.

Throughout our time together at St. John's University, we did not always have the opportunity to connect directly, but when we were at the same conferences, we supported each other. Raquel has a fond memory of Nancy supporting her first presentation at the annual Conference on College Composition and Communication. When they were at another conference together, Raquel supported Nancy's presentation. We had not made these arrangements in advance or even stayed in the same hotel room for these conferences because we had made friends with others in our respective cohorts, but we never really left each other out of reach. This is part of the kinship that allows us to know that we're a community and can find support in each other. We believe this feeling has only expanded since we came together to write this chapter. We have spent hours on the phone talking and getting to know each other. It is through this collaborative endeavor that Raquel has continued to be mentored through various practices in academia. For instance, in our first phone conversation Nancy made it clear that Raquel's name was going to come first in the chapter's byline. The way Nancy stated that fact and stuck to it was always so surprising to

Raquel. This was an example of the tangible support that comadrismo comprises. Since Nancy had a few publications already, she endeavored to pay it forward by not only mentoring Raquel through this process but also allowing her to get "more credit" in academia for this joint endeavor. Through modeling and informing Raquel of the way publishing works, she was mentoring her, as comadrismo asks of us, in the very same ways Ribero and Arellano were building a community.

This chapter, much like the purpose of this collection, brought together two very different Latinas who were able to commune and exchange their experiences in order to process their varying experiences at the same institution. We know that the act of creating community is how we make it through these rather stifling and overwhelming academic environments. Supporting each other in the past three years may not have been the sole reason we made it through graduate school, but it definitely provided each of us moments of feeling seen and heard that we could not have found elsewhere. For instance, no one else but another Latina can really know the deeply entrenched ideas of womanhood and even motherhood in the Latinx community, but we do not need to explain anything to each other because we see each other, fully and completely. That acknowledgment of what the other means usually results in the release of a breath we have been holding in as we journey through a world that requires so much explanation and rigid alignment.

References

Alvarez, Steven. 2017. *Community Literacies en Confianza: Learning from Bilingual After-School Programs*. Urbana, IL: National Council of Teachers of English.

Anzaldúa, Gloria. [1987] 2012. *Borderlands / La Frontera: The New Mestiza*. San Francisco: Aunt Lute Books.

Carnevale, Anthony P., and Megan L. Fasules. 2018. "Latino Education and Economic Progress: Running Faster but Still Behind." Center on Education and the Workforce, Georgetown Univ., Feb. 9. At cew.george town.edu/cew-reports/latinosworkforce/.

Cedillo, Christina V. 2018. "What Does It Mean to Move? Race, Disability, and Critical Embodiment Pedagogy." *Composition Forum* 39. At http://compositionforum.com/issue/39/to-move.php.

Chesler, Phyllis. 2018. *Women and Madness.* Chicago: Chicago Review Press.

City University of New York (CUNY), Office of Institutional Research and Assessment. 2016. "CUNY Workforce Demographics by College, Ethnicity, and Gender: Fall 2016 Instructional and Classified Staff." Fall. At http://www2.cuny.edu/wp-content/uploads/sites/4/page-assets/about/administration/offices/hr/diversity-and-recruitment/Fall-2016-CUNY-Workforce-Demographics_02062017.pdf.

———. 2018. "Total Enrollment by Race/Ethnicity and College: Percentages Fall 2017." At http://www.cuny.edu/irdatabook/rpts2_AY_current/ENRL_0016_RACE_UGGR_PCT.rpt.pdf.

Gildersleeve, Ryan Evely, Natasha N. Croom, and Philip Vasquez. 2011. "'Am I Going Crazy?!' A Critical Race Analysis of Doctoral Education." *Equity and Excellence* 44, no. 1: 93–114.

Gutierrez y Muhs, Gabriella, Yolanda Flores Niemann, Carmen Gonzalez, and Angela P. Harris, eds. 2012. *Presumed Incompetent: The Intersections of Race and Class for Women in Academia.* Boulder, CO: Univ. Press of Colorado.

Hegewisch, Ariane, and Zohal Barsi. 2020. "The Gender Wage Gap: 2019 Earnings Differences by Race and Ethnicity." Institute for Women's Policy Research, Mar. 10. At https://iwpr.org/iwpr-issues/employment-and-earnings/the-gender-wage-gap-2019-earnings-differences-by-race-and-ethnicity/.

hooks, bell. 1989. *Yearning: Race, Gender, and Cultural Politics.* Boston: South End Press.

Howard Hamilton, Mary F., Carla L. Morelon-Quainoo, Susan D. Johnson, Rachelle Winkle-Wagner, and Lilia Santiague, eds. 2009. *Standing on the Outside Looking In: Underrepresented Students' Experiences in Advanced-Degree Programs.* Sterling, VA: Stylus.

Humanities Indicators. 2016. "Racial/Ethnic Distribution of Degrees in English Language and Literature." Apr. At https://www.humanitiesindicators.org/content/indicatordoc.aspx?i=242#fig244.

Kamimura, Mark, Alberta M. Gloria, and Jeanett Castellanos, eds. 2006. *The Latina/o Pathway to the Ph.D.: Abriendo caminos.* Sterling, VA: Stylus, 2006.

Latina Feminist Group. 2001. *Telling to Live: Latina Feminist Testimonios.* Durham, NC: Duke Univ. Press, 2001.

Martinez, Aja Y. 2014. "A Plea for Critical Race Theory Counterstory: Stock Story versus Counterstory Dialogues Concerning Alejandra's 'Fit' in the Academy." *Composition Studies* 42, no. 2: 33–55.

National Center for Education Statistics (NCES). 2017. *The Condition of Education 2017.* NCES 2017–2144. Washington, DC: US Department of Education.

Okawa, Gail Y. 2002. "Diving for Pearls: Mentoring as Cultural and Activist Practice among Academics of Color." *College Composition and Communication* 53, no. 3: 507–32.

Price, Margaret. 2009. "'Her Pronouns Wax and Wane': Psychosocial Disability, Autobiography, and Counter-Diagnosis." *Journal of Literary and Cultural Disability Studies* 3, no. 1 (Jan.): 11–34.

Solórzano, Daniel G., and Tara J. Yosso. 2002. "Critical Race Methodology: Counter-Storytelling as an Analytical Framework for Education Research." *Qualitative Inquiry* 8, no. 1 (Feb. 1): 23–44.

Strunk, William, and Elwyn Brooks White. 1972. *The Elements of Style.* New York: Macmillan.

Torres, Lissette E. 2016. "Tigre del mar: A Boricua's Testimonio of Surviving a Doctoral Science Education." In *Envisioning Critical Race Praxis in Higher Education through Counter-Storytelling*, edited by Natasha N. Croom and Tyson E. J. Marsh, 21–41. Charlotte, NC: Information Age.

Villanueva, Victor. 1993. *Bootstraps: From an American Academic of Color.* Urbana, IL: National Council of Teachers of English.

10

Mestiza Pedagogies

Borderlands Teaching, Writing, and Community
Activism Informing Academic Work

Cristina D. Ramírez

Abstract

In this chapter, the author considers the first years of her teaching career, which took place at a middle school in El Paso, Texas, only one mile from the US-Mexico border. Using testimonio, she traces the events inside and outside the classroom that led her to develop and cultivate a mestiza pedagogy in the Mexican American community of Buena Vista. A mestiza pedagogy is an educational strategy that connects educators to their minority Latinx students at a much deeper level than teaching to the standards with required texts. It is a connection to or understanding of learning that uses what Gloria Anzaldúa calls "la facultad." As traced in this chapter, the cultivation of the author's own mestiza pedagogy led to her awareness of missing gendered and historical voices. Ultimately, the author, feeling constricted by teaching standards, chose to leave the public-school classroom in order to pursue a doctorate degree, conduct research, and write the stories of Mexican women journalists.

Un testimonio

> Teaching composition links us not only to our students'
> languages and literacies, but to their localities as well—the
> home, the community, la frontera, the border between the

public and the private, the nexus between the polis and the
personal.

—Michelle Hall Kells, "Understanding the
Rhetorical Value of Tejano Codeswitching"

The academic research that our fellow scholars conduct and engage
in, within our institutions and surrounding communities, always
holds a backstory of personal and professional connections. Possibly
with or without our knowing, these backstories become the motivation to continue our work as researchers, educators, and community
participants. Because of this belief, I have often asked myself how I
came to conduct research on the rhetorics of Mexican and Mexican
American women writers and to engage with and translate primarily
Spanish-language texts. What was my own exigence that led me to
this topic? What were the work and pedagogies I engaged with prior
to my academic career that contributed the most to my choosing this
path? In this reflection on Latina leadership that considers a narrative
of connectivity to research and pedagogy, I offer my border teaching
experiences, which are connected to my awakening to wanting to
write for minority student audiences. Paulo Friere notes in *Teachers
as Cultural Workers* (1998) that reflection on our teaching practices
is "a coherent and permanent 'discourse' of the progressive educator" (55). He notes that "testimony [is] the best way to call learners'
attention to the validity that is proposed for the attainment of what
is valued, for resolve in the struggle, with the goal of overcoming
difficulties" (55). From a Chicana perspective, however, testimony
becomes testimonio.

Testimonio allows Chicana scholars to critically engage in reflection and self-transformation. In their chapters in this collection, the
scholars Michelle Hall Kells (chapter 7) and Mónica González Ybarra
(chapter 11) critically use testimonio to ground Chicana academic
work. Dolores Delgado Bernal, Rebeca Burciaga, and Judith Flores
Carmona contend, "Testimonio is and continues to be an approach
that incorporates political, social, historical, and cultural histories that
accompany one's life experiences as a means to bring about change
through consciousness-raising" (2012, 364). In her chapter in this

collection, Ybarra states that testimonio functions "as a methodological tool [and] is a political choice that disrupts normative research and conceptualizations of knowledge while forcing the 'reinvention and radical reposition of power' . . . for both the researcher and participants" (citation omitted). Furthermore, testimonio creates and clears spaces for reflection, memory recovery, and transformation, much as Diana Cárdenas writes in "Creating an Identity: Personal, Academic, and Civic Literacies" (2004). For Chicana academics caught in a space that at times silences our subjectivities, testimonio is essential to our becoming well-rounded pedagogues and academics.

This chapter presents a short reflection on the beginning years of my teaching career and un testimonio of remembering a much younger version of my teacher self. Although it is sometimes painful to reflect on these moments, this testimonio from a twenty-seven-year veteran teacher recounts the ways I came to understand the teaching of literacy in the mid-1990s at Henderson Middle School, located one mile from the US-Mexico border in El Paso, Texas. This ethnographic narrative bridges my years as an intermediate public-school teacher of reading and writing and my awakening to feminist rhetorical recovery work that would emerge from the dried ink of my pen as a researcher and writer. My experiences run parallel to that of Chicana author Christina V. Cedillo, whose interview in Christine Garcia's chapter in this collection reveals that she also taught middle school and that her educational experience is also closely connected to family history (see chapter 6). In coming to know my own strengths as an educator, I reflect on my classroom practices through what I now call "mestiza pedagogy," showing how my practices led me to research feminist rhetorical recovery work.

First Steps: The Middle-School Classroom

At the age of twenty-four, a bit naive and uninitiated to life and teaching, I landed my first professional job as a public-school teacher. In the mid-1990s, Henderson Middle School enrolled a student body that was 92 percent mixed heritage and racially diverse. At that time, racial diversity and integration in this school were the norm. I was contracted by the El Paso Independent School District and hired by the school's principal, Ralph Chavez, to teach seventh-grade reading. Writing was designated to another course.[1] Before the beginning of the school year, in mid-July, I was handed a massive three-inch-thick curriculum binder, an equally dense teacher's edition of the adopted textbook, and the keys to my own classroom at Henderson Middle School.

Named for James Pickney Henderson, the first governor of Texas in 1846, the campus sits approximately one mile from the US-Mexico border. For the past two centuries, El Paso has served as a vital North American border town promoting trade and commerce. The city runs alongside the meandering Rio Grande, with sister city Ciudad Juárez, Mexico, as its intimate neighbor. This fenceless and wall-less border served as my everyday reality. Concentrating on daily survival as a first-year public-school teacher, I did not think much about the school's colonizing name or its geographic location in the center of this Mexican and Mexican American community. As I would quickly learn, the US-Mexico border had a direct, immediate impact on both the school and my classroom.

Two weeks after my hire and close to the start of the school year, the registrar's office handed me five course rosters, each with 28 to 30 student names. Doing the math, I realized that every day I would be teaching the essentials of English literacy to more than 125 students. A shiver of nervousness mixed with anticipation ran through my body just thinking of this immense responsibility. Reading the list of names—Claudia Esquivel, Ernesto Chavez, Elisa González, Leonel Hernandez, Elias Davis, Alejandro Martinez, Denisse Lopez, Enrique Sanchez, Eugenia Longoria, Leticia Flores—made me feel settled for the task ahead.[2] Almost every student on the list had a Mexican surname or a mixed Anglo-Mexican name. Although I did not yet know

1. Even at that time I did not understand the logic behind separating the pedagogical work of reading and writing. I see them as intrinsically linked. To learn to write, one must read; to learn to read, one must write.

2. All names have been changed to protect the identity of my former students.

8. Henderson Middle School, circa 1997. Photograph courtesy of Cristina D. Ramírez and Henderson Middle School.

any of the students personally, their names rang familiar to me because I had grown up with a Mexican American background at home and at church. Beneath my own Anglo education rested an "other" consciousness—what I call an "ancestral remembering." Using a term from Gloria Anzaldúa, I held a "conocimiento" on how to function in a border classroom filled with students whose identities, through their language and daily culture, were shaped by la frontera. My path as an educator and researcher had been paved by a long line of educators from both sides of the border. It reflects the US-Mexico border, both linguistically and ancestrally. My first teachers were my parents, Neil Devereaux and Sandra González, both of whom taught Spanish, my father in a university and my mother in a middle school. My aunt, Norma Hernández, served as another formidable example (for more on my aunt, see Ortiz-Franco 2017).

In the 1980s, at the University of Texas at El Paso my aunt Norma Hernández became the first Chicana in the United States to serve as dean of a university education program. Norma specialized in mathematics and bilingual education. Her aunt, Josefa González, crossed from El Paso into Ciudad Juárez every school day for twenty-five years, into the 1950s, to teach as a maestra normal. My heritage *is* the very definition of borders.

Because of my Mexican American and pedagogical heritage, I came to my first year in the classroom with a deep-seated sense of ancestral rememberings and cultural frameworks that would help me to understand and connect with my students' backgrounds and heritages. Each student had a unique history and testimonio of border crossings and family experience. My proximity to these experiences—such as my family's story of emigration from Mexico to find work, flee violence and war, and settle in this region—allowed me to relate more readily to my students' potentially painful family histories. I entered the classroom well aware of their environments at home, in which they likely spoke Spanish and frequently crossed borders to visit family and friends. Guided by an intrinsic understanding and cultural appreciation of my students and the demographics of Henderson Middle School, I worked to build a strong relationship with the Mexican American barrios of San Juan and Buena Vista, where the school was located, as I also helped students shape their appreciation for and love of reading.

My students, whom I would get to know in the months and years ahead, had long been mestizos. According to the local El Paso historian Fred Morales, the border region of El Paso and Ciudad Juárez has a history that stretches back to the fifteenth century with the Manso and Tigua Native American people. Members of these tribes mixed and interacted with the Catholic Spaniards when they arrived, such as Fray Alonso de Benavides in 1630, and later with the Anglo-Texans who began arriving in the region in 1821 (cited in Tijerina 1994, 2–3). This history of the region meant that my students' mixed-heritage identity—Indigenous, colonial European, and Anglo—was their strength, and it emerged at the doorstep of a border region that they crossed daily and that affected their learning and knowing. In "Becoming a Border Pedagogy Educator" (2007), Elizabeth Garza states, "Living and learning in the borderlands is a unique experience, in which the mutual influence of the Mexican and U.S. cultures has created a regional binational culture that combines aspects of both ways of life" (2–3). Both sides of the border and the inhabitants' understanding of both ways of being are inextricably linked.

Even twenty-five years ago—and this knowing reaches back much further—my students and their parents were well aware that social and economic progress meant learning standard English. Ana Castillo notes in *Massacre of the Dreamers* (1994) what these students and their parents knew: "The individual who adopts the prevailing [English] standards will be rewarded; the one who refuses is ostracized" (165). For this reason, parents from Mexico would leave their children with family in El Paso so that their children could learn English. This family practice has been a long-held tradition. So what elicited my nervousness about entering the classroom? I had graduated with a college education, majoring in English literature and minoring in both education and Spanish. In my testimonio here, I admit that my anxiety came from wondering whether I was adequately prepared for the task of balancing my students' cultural backgrounds with teaching them standard English.

Entering the school on the first day of classes, I was greeted with swarms of students, talking at the water fountain, congregating around lockers, and huddling together as they sought to make their own way in a new environment. I felt a wave of doubt about my own level of preparedness and lack of experience. Looking back and reflecting on my work at that school, I can say now that I enacted in my classroom what I call a "mestiza pedagogy." As Kendall Leon notes in "Chicanas Making Change" (2013), "[I know that] change is often achieved through subtle shifts in behind-the-scenes practices that in order to be recognized require adopting different heuristics" (171). These "different heuristics" are linked to Anzaldúa's concept of "la nueva mestiza," an understanding of two cultures, of living, speaking, and teaching in a space of both cultures. I carried inside me a mestiza consciousness that I took into the classroom, which, in turn, helped me to forge a mestiza pedagogy. This pedagogical approach introduces what Anzaldúa calls "la facultad" into the classroom, allowing

Chicana educators to connect with their students on a deeper level than just through the material in the curriculum.

Closely connected to facultad, mestiza pedagogy reaches beyond the training that teachers receive to enter the classroom. In the classroom, teachers are required to follow standards, curricula, reading lists, and managerial protocols, but a mestiza pedagogy offers teachers who can tap into this space a glimpse into how to connect with students. Anzaldúa notes, "*La facultad* is the capacity to see in surface phenomena the meaning of deeper realities, to see the deep structure below the surface" (1987, 60). For a mestiza pedagogy, this "deep structure" emerges as the cultural, linguistic, and community connection Mexican American students face in an Anglicized classroom. For teachers working from a mestiza pedagogy, "[la facultad] is an instant 'sensing,' a quick perception arrived at without conscious reasoning. It is an acute awareness mediated by the part of the psyche that does not speak, that communicates in images and symbols which are the faces of feelings" (Anzaldúa 1987, 60). I am not suggesting that a mestiza pedagogy does not require teacher training; on the contrary, a mestiza pedagogy is enhanced and perfected by teacher training.

A mestiza pedagogy requires an educator's own understanding of living at the crossroads of two or more cultures, of two or more ways of knowing, to be incorporated into a teaching approach. In turn, mestiza pedagogy is enabled by calling upon these internalized linguistic and cultural epistemologies to teach students in a way that respects and recognizes their multiple realities in the classroom. A mestiza pedagogy anticipates the students' contact zones, funds of knowledge, multiple cultures, and diverse linguistic practices that exist in the classroom and adapts quickly with culturally grounded approaches. These approaches include calling on familial and/or familiar practices, such as pláticas (Guajardo and Guajardo 2013), tapping into the funds of knowledge about events and activities central to the community around the school, and creating and constructing classroom traditions that appeal to all students.

A similar praxis to mestiza pedagogy is a border pedagogy. First articulated by Henry Giroux in "Border Pedagogy and the Politics of

Postmodernism" (1991), border pedagogy was initially understood as "a radical pedagogical practice." A "border pedagogy points to the need for conditions that allow students to write, speak, and listen in a language in which meaning becomes multi-accentual, dispersed, and resists permanent closure. This is a language in which one speaks with rather than exclusively for others" (52).

Since this initial articulation, education scholars have articulated a deeper understanding of border pedagogy (Garza 2007; Kazanjian 2011; Ramirez, Ross, and Jimenez-Silva 2016; Reyes 2016). Although border and mestiza pedagogies are similar in their approaches to teaching—both with an eye to understanding the multilayered, complex construct of student identity and then to foregrounding respect with critical teaching—a distinct difference between them is that the latter comes from a wellspring of cultural awareness that guides instructors to connect with students of color or other marginalized groups. In short, mestiza pedagogy is inspired and shaped by the previously noted concept of la facultad.

Coming into a Mestiza Pedagogy

During my early teaching career in the 1990s, I had neither read nor been introduced to some of the fundamentals of Chicana critical theory, rhetorical theory, or even critical educational theory. Being an avid reader, however, I did read Chicano fiction, such as *The House on Mango Street* by Sandra Cisneros (1984), *Lupita Mañana* by Patricia Beatty (1981), and *Bless Me, Ultima* by Rudolfo Anaya ([1972] 2012), among others. These texts would later allow me to connect with my Henderson Middle School students and to help them reach their own educational literacy, which rarely resembles Anglo or Eurocentric literacies. It has been more than twenty-five years since I took the courses "Fundamentals of Secondary Education," "Teaching Literature in the High Schools," and "Classroom Preparedness." However, I do not recall learning or reading about deeper community cultural principles in any of them. This points also to a shift in teaching practices over the years. For example, I did not know of Gloria Anzaldúa's *Borderlands / La Frontera: The New Mestiza* (1987) or the National

Council of Teachers of English resolution "Students' Right to Their Own Language" (1972, 1974). Overall, through my university training at the University of Texas at El Paso, I had been given a *practical* understanding of the Texas public-school classroom—for example, learning how to write lesson plans, create budgets, understand Texas educational standards, teach to the standardized test, and work with and adhere to administrative policies.

Looking back, I understand that the training I received at the bachelor's level was to give teachers the working fundamentals of how to manage a classroom and teach basic literacy to students. However, there was not a sense of thinking beyond these aspects of the classroom and the school district. For example, there was no mention of the significant impact that living only miles from the US-Mexico border would have on the reality of the classroom. This gap in my educational experience would become apparent during the first few weeks spent in the classroom.

Following Educational Standards: Disaster Ahead

My first (painful and disheartening) experience of cultural clashing between my Mexican American students and the standardized curriculum came when I taught the first novel on the list of required readings, *A Day No Pigs Would Die* by Robert Peck (1972). As a newly graduated student teacher, I was taught to follow the standards and approved curriculum, then known as Texas Essential Knowledge and Skills (TEKS), and to teach only what was on the shelves of the school's book room. Before starting the book with my students, I read through it, not having had the opportunity to do so when I was a college student. I noted that it had received the American Library Association's Best Book for Young Adults Award and thought it would be a great book with which to start the school year.

As a Texas Chicana, I could not make a cognitive connection to the book, yet I was expecting my students to make that leap. Even as I gave *A Day No Pigs Would Die* its first read, I had problems keeping my interest attached to the main character, Robert. At age twelve, Robert is a young Shaker boy growing up under the guise of his religiously strict yet illiterate father in rural Vermont in the 1920s. Because of his religious beliefs, Robert is taunted and teased at school. With such interweaving themes as coming of age, family, friendship, and isolation, the overall plot of this book shows how Robert, after saving a neighbor's cow in childbirth, earns a pig he would name Pinky. The pig would later prove to be barren and would then be slaughtered by Robert's father to help meet the family's needs. To this beginner teacher, having just left the standardized training grounds of higher education, this book seemed to hold the elements that would appeal to a group of seventh-grade students. I spent weekends planning the lessons, preparing the writing prompts that asked students to connect to the character's situation as a young adolescent boy learning some of life's lessons. However, I struggled in forming questions and connecting the book to my seventh graders living on the US-Mexico border. As I understand it now, the gnawing sense that didn't allow me to connect with the main character and that made me wonder how my students would make this leap was my own facultad. This facultad left me with deep confusion as to why I could not connect to the plot or to the character. I heard and sensed an unease within me but did not listen to it.

Classes at Henderson Middle School lasted fifty minutes. I was responsible for five classes, each with 28 to 32 students, and would prepare and teach the same reading and writing lesson to approximately 130 students throughout the day. Having only thirty-two copies of the book for all five classes, we would read aloud in each class, and then I would assign stretches of silent reading. As I had learned in the course "Teaching Literature in the High Schools," I started each period with a reading-and-writing reflection, using prompts such as those provided in the teacher's manual: "Discuss how Robert feels isolated from his peers and community. How does he deal with such isolation? Do you ever feel isolated at home? At school? In your own community?" The personal questions initially seemed to pique the students' interest in the overall theme, but after a week of reading the book I struggled to keep my students' attention. It was 1995, and the

Internet or other multimedia distractions had not yet penetrated our world, but regardless of any number of imaginative ways of interpreting the plot, keeping seventh-grade students' attention on a book that clearly didn't connect to their sense of self or resonate with their community experiences remained a daily struggle. Students were instead talking, passing notes, laughing, and falling asleep in class.

During a class discussion, I picked up a note that was being passed around, and it was full of drawings of flowers and hearts from "La Sleepy to La Chamaca." Taking another glance at the text, I saw the margins written up with Spanish and English text. Without missing a beat, I crumpled up the humorous and community connective writing, threw it away, and continued reading aloud. "That afternoon, Pinky and I went for a walk up on the ridge that parts our land from Mr. Tanner's. We didn't go too near the spot where old Apron and I met up. I don't hanker to ever see that place right away quick; and if it's never, you won't hear a howl from me" (Peck 1972, 19). While I read, I thought, "Yup, I've lost 'em." Finding it hard to concentrate and even make it through the day, I realized that I had become the teacher I had in my own schooling, the one who ignores the students' personal and community literacies, the one who occupies the margins of the classroom.

Was it my own management style that provoked this behavior? Even as a novice teacher, I sensed the strained attention my students were giving to the lessons. After only a week and a half of reading *A Day No Pigs Would Die*, the attempts to connect my Mexican American students, whose lives were tied to the border less than a mile from my classroom door, to the life of a twelve-year-old Shaker boy from Vermont in the 1920s were falling so flat and were going so badly that I considered stopping the book midread. This thought, I remember, brought a moment of panic. I was the newest teacher on my hall, so there was much to consider in not finishing a book with students whom I was given the task of teaching habits of literacy. By not reading this book to its end, I was modeling to my students that it was okay not to finish a book. On the end-of-year TEKS reading exam, students who don't read the text cannot respond well to the questions. Equally concerning, if I stopped the book midread, was I effectively communicating to the students that they couldn't or didn't have to connect with others through universal themes? Blindly following the TEKS, I had lost sight of why I had become an educator.

My priority as a reading teacher for seventh-grade students from border neighborhoods such as Durazno, San Juan, and Sambrano was to get them excited about reading. So much of the curriculum in US public schools is white, Anglo, and male, and *A Day No Pigs Would Die* fell right into this tired category. My students could not connect to the voice they were hearing on the page. For them and for me, this book perpetuated the insufferable cliché of the importance of white culture and the white teenage coming-of-age experience—in this case, that of a Shaker boy in the 1920s. My classroom was made up of Mexican American students who were missing and losing any connection with the characters, the geography, and themes (and rightly so). Deep down, I knew that this was not their fault.

Looking back now with sufficient theoretical knowledge, I realize this was my first classroom encounter with a contact zone (Pratt [1991] 2002). My students, even as seventh graders, knew that they were being duped. I had become the enforcer of the standards of the Anglo knowledge system, and they were resisting this assimilation. Pratt writes of the contact zone, "What is the place of unsolicited oppositional discourse, parody, resistance, and critique in the imagined classroom community? Are teachers supposed to feel that their teaching has been most successful when they have eliminated such things and unified the social world, probably in their own image? Who wins when we do that? Who loses?" ([1991] 2002, 15). Losing sleep at night and even beginning to question my choice of profession, I stood on the losing side of this struggle for both my students' identities and my own. I didn't understand at the time, but my senses, developed from birth and already well established through my mixed Mexican and American heritage, were pushing me toward an understanding of a mestiza pedagogy.

Shifting Curricular Course Midstream

In the early 1990s, when I started teaching, teachers still had relative control over their classroom curriculum. With this in mind, I took action. Midweek, I decided to have the class stop reading *A Day No Pigs Would Die* and start another book. Seventh graders aren't like adults. They are young, impatient humans growing into themselves, full of hormones, wonder, imagination, and angst about the world they are discovering. And if as teachers we don't tap into this transition, we can easily lose them. I had sufficiently considered the issue of ethnic and cultural relevance and knew from the facultad I carried (not from any theory I had read) that the students who "acted out" were communicating that they weren't connecting with the book. I harbored a similar disconnect.

With all the copies of the book packed again in a box, along with the teacher's manual, quizzes, and vocabulary sheets, I went to the book room to find another book. As I looked over the ones available, the book-room lady asked, "Finished the other book so quickly?"

"No," I said, "the students hated it. I'm looking for another book."

She asked, "Is that a reason to stop teaching it? It is a required text."

I peered from behind the shelves and said, "Oh, yes, it is." I kept looking and found a book on the list that I knew well: *The House on Mango Street* (1984) by Sandra Cisneros. "I'll take all thirty-five of this text, please," I said. Having previously read *The House on Mango Street*, I knew that Cisneros connects with her reader through her experiences as a young girl in the barrios of Chicago. Furthermore, because the central character is a female, the book would tap the imaginations of my female students to become writers and keepers of community knowledge one day.

The next day in class, copies of a new book rested in the middle of each desk. I stood at my regular spot at the doorway to my classroom and greeted my students as they shuffled in for their first class.

Laughter and loud talk filled the room as the last student scurried in. I looked out over the seated students as they waited for my instruction on what we were going to do for the day. Picking up the book and quickly leafing through the pages, the students asked a flurry of questions: "Is this our new book?" "What happened to the other one?" As a mestiza pedagogue, I knew that the previous book had missed the mark with my students. In "Culturally Relevant Texts and Reading Assessment for English Language Learners" (2010), Ann Ebe synthesizes the research that has been done on culturally connecting students in their literacy development. Ebe notes that "[Frank] Smith, who has studied reading from a psycholinguistic perspective, explains that reading starts with the background the readers bring to text. Readers come from diverse backgrounds with different ideas about the world so previous experiences and knowledge, also known as schema, affect how a reader comprehends text" (195, citation omitted). This research, which started around the time I began teaching, affirms my own understanding and my mestiza pedagogical approach.

This approach reflects an inherent understanding of students of color not connecting with culturally distant texts. A mestiza pedagogical approach advocates for students' identities, language, and cultural background to be reflected in what they read and learn. And although it is important to make connections with different cultures and backgrounds, especially in texts, this moment at the beginning of school—when I was trying desperately to get my students reading— was not the time to focus on connecting with Anglo culture. That morning and for the rest of my classes, I started the class by explaining that *A Day No Pigs Would Die* just wasn't working for us and that we were moving on to another text. I left my explanation there. It seemed to linger. Silence loomed, and then applause erupted.

In my training to become a teacher, I had learned the concept of writing to learn and writing to connect with the world. I started the reading with a writing prompt: "*The House on Mango Street* by Sandra Cisneros tells a story of a young girl growing up in the Latino section of Chicago. Living in San Juan here along the US-Mexico border, write about where *you* live. What are some notable things that you see, hear, and smell every day?" The students started writing immediately. Their pens whirled across the page. After writing, the students shared what they had written. They spoke of corner grocery stores, big and little sisters, tamales and buñuelos at Christmas, dogs running around in the neighborhood, crossing into Mexico on the weekends, and Catholic mass on Sundays followed by family reunions. Already they were speaking to Cisneros's vignettes in *Mango Street*. In *Sueños Americanos: Barrio Youth Negotiating Social and Cultural Identity* (2008), Julio Cammarota studies the education of Latino/a students and notes that "without the means to demonstrate their knowledge, students are quickly written off as failures because that is what schools expect of urban students of color" (134). At the time I began teaching, this writing exercise was called "pre-reading," which is actually the concept of writing to learn. Connecting more directly to my students' worlds, the discussion took thirty-five minutes of a fifty-minute class.

I suspended the enthusiastic talk in order to read from the book about Meme Ortiz (pronounced /mé-me/):

> Meme Ortiz moved into Cathy's house after her family moved away. His name isn't really Meme. His name is Juan. But when we asked him what his name was he said Meme, and that's what everybody calls him except his mother. Meme has a dog with gray eyes, a sheepdog with two names, one in English and one in Spanish. The dog is big, like a man dressed in a dog suit, and runs the same way its owner does, clumsy and wild and with the limbs flopping all over the place like untied shoes. Cathy's father built the house Meme moved into. It is wooden. Inside the floors slant. Some rooms uphill. Some down. And there are no closets. Out front there are twenty-one steps, all lopsided and jutting like crooked teeth (made that way on purpose, Cathy said, so the rain will slide off), and when Meme's mama calls from the doorway, Meme goes scrambling up the twenty-one wooden stairs with the dog with two names scrambling after him. (Cisneros 1984, 21–22)

A mestiza pedagogy is characterized by an intrinsic understanding of how language expands, creates, and connects with a quotidian space of orality and storytelling. A mestiza pedagogy also looks to uncover what students already know. As the days went by, we read many vignettes from *The House on Mango Street*, including "Hairs," "Boys and Girls," "My Name," "Cathy, Queen of Cats," and "Laughter." I guided my students in their writing and journaling to learn more about Cisneros and her writing style. We read the short sentences, which resonate and connect to a Mexican American oral culture, over again and imagined and witnessed Meme breaking his arm. Most importantly, from their reactions, many of my students began to see themselves in the pages of this book. They connected. They related. They read aloud. All children, as well as adults, love to be read to, and *House on Mango Street* warranted reading aloud. A major proponent of literacy and read-alouds, Jim Trelease notes in *The Read-Aloud Handbook* (2013) that reading aloud is the most important aspect of a child's literary training (4). Just as important as reading aloud is the choice of book. Trelease suggests that for the most effective read-alouds teachers should learn as much as they can about students' interests before selecting books. So the next book I introduced and read for my class wasn't on the required reading list but on the "supplemental list."

That next book was the Newberry Award–winning *Roll of Thunder, Hear My Cry* (1976) by African American children's author Mildred D. Taylor. Set in Mississippi in the Great Depression of the 1930s, *Roll of Thunder* tells the coming-of-age story of Cassie and the story of her family's struggle to stay independent in a community fueled by racism and jealousy and punctuated by social injustice. Mildred Taylor's stories are informed by life stories told by her father and other family members. These stories come to life off the page and are often painful to read because of the concrete discussions of racism and its material and emotional effects.

Speaking to students' reality of everyday life, *Roll of Thunder, Hear My Cry* opens with the students receiving their books for the year. The next scene brings out the reality of how resources are distributed between white and Black students across this country. As the students are being given their books, the character Little Man refuses his book from the teacher, Miss Crocker. My classes read aloud:

> "What's that you said, Clayton Chester Logan?" she asked. . . .
>
> His lips parted slightly as he took his hands from the book. He quivered, but he did not take his eyes from Miss Crocker. "I—I said may I have another book please ma'am," he squeaked. "That one's dirty." . . .
>
> "Dirty! And just who do you think you are, Clayton Chester? Here the county is giving us these wonderful books during these hard times and you're going to stand there and tell me that the book's too dirty? Now you take that book or get nothing at all." . . .
>
> Little Man bit his lower lip, and I knew that he was not going to pick up the book. Rapidly, I turned to the inside cover of my own book and saw immediately what had made Little Man so furious.
>
> Stamped on the inside cover of the book was a chart that listed previous students who had borrowed the book, their race [using a racial slur], and the condition in which the book was supposedly returned. The chart noted that an African American student had previously checked out the book, and Little Man did not want to check out the same book. (Taylor 1976, 22–25; ellipses indicate omission of text)

With every class that read this passage aloud, a silence permeated and lingered in the room. Reading this situation and seeing the racial slur on the page was a shock for my students. In the preface to the book, Taylor writes reflectively about the use of this language: "I have recounted events that were painful to write and painful to be read. . . . I must be true to the stories told" (1976, 7). In turn, reading these "fictional" accounts in Taylor's text opened critical spaces in my classroom to discuss the continued injustices that my students themselves faced. Although fictionalized, the harsh realities uncovered in the *Roll of Thunder* narratives were reflections of the realities of my students' own lives. Reading them provided my students with a point of departure for discussing racial issues.

In my first years of teaching and beyond, I looked for stories like *The House on Mango Street* and *Roll of Thunder, Hear My Cry*, those told of and by people of color, not because it was something I learned to do from theoretical or critical texts at the university but because I was developing a mestiza pedagogy. In *Teachers as Cultural Workers* (1998), Freire points to the connection that can and should be formed with texts that our students read: "In sum, the reading of a text is a transaction between the reader and the text, which mediates the encounter between reader and writer. It is a composition between the reader and the writer in which the reader 'rewrites' the text, making a determined effort to not betray the author's spirit" (30). As a mestiza pedagogue, I learned to select texts that would help students encounter some of their own realities and, in turn, connect with the text and grow as students with their own literacies.

Community Connection

As my teaching career at Henderson Middle School lengthened, I engaged in community literacy projects that reached beyond the classroom. These formative years and the outreach to which I was committed began to awaken and solidify my own impulses to become a researcher and scholar. As I became more confident as a young teacher in my twenties, my mestiza pedagogies expanded, and I reached out to the communities surrounding the school to design and involve myself with their projects. These projects included sponsoring weeklong book fairs, advertising them in the community, and holding them during parent conference nights. Each year I selected students whose parents would not (or could not out of fear or language barriers) come to campus. In having watched my Chicana mother forge relationships with other Latino families, I knew the importance of intimate bonds. Cammarota notes, "Trust, reciprocity, and respect—the central values in Latina/o family relationships—lay the parameters for the way in which Latina/o youth establish all kinds of relationships" (2008, 162). Intrinsically, I followed this learning.

Each month I would select two families a week to visit after school and set out to conduct home visits. Upon reaching their home and knocking on their door and speaking to the mother or father, I would always use my Spanish-language skills to connect with my students' families, asking about their child and their welfare. Families responded by opening their doors widely, asking me to have a seat in their humble living rooms, offering me a glass of water, and speaking openly about their lives as immigrants and the hopes they had for their child's education. In their often-native Spanish, the parents exposed their vulnerabilities and spoke of the lack of representation they generally felt in the school and school district. I understood their sentiment. "Lack of representation" within the literature and histories I taught and read was a theme I saw emerging in my classroom reflections and my ongoing education at the University of Texas at El Paso.

The River Remains a Reminder of the Border

After eleven years of teaching at Henderson Middle School, I parted ways with the school. Although it was very difficult to leave my students, I left behind an increasing burden of teaching to the standardized test in order to teach at El Paso High School, located in the central region of the city. From the fourth-floor window of my classroom, I could see the Rio Grande and the expanse of Ciudad Juárez. Seeing the US-Mexico border from my classroom served as a constant reminder of where I was and whom I was teaching. My classroom population, mostly Latino/a students from El Paso, was very little changed from the student population at Henderson.

However, my growing mestiza pedagogy, which at its core recognizes and connects to the intrinsic racial, ethnic, and gendered identities of my students, transformed me from seeking stories reflecting students' identities to teaching students to write in a way that they would be reflecting themselves. A mestiza pedagogue senses and recognizes the discomfort, disconnect, and occasional ambiguities of minority students learning and writing within an Anglo-centric writing, reading, and research curriculum. The astute pedagogue seeks out alternative ways of connecting with and reaching each and every student. When teaching high school seniors, my pedagogies shifted from drilling for standardized tests (what teaching had sadly become at the middle-school level) to guiding students to craft their own, authentic voices. Instead of having students write the standard research paper, I taught the multigenre research paper, inspired by pedagogies of the K–12 education scholar Tom Romano (2000, 2004).

Having learned about multigenre research papers in my English master's classes, I finally had the opportunity to teach this alternative structure to the straightforward, thesis-driven paper. Inherently a mestiza pedagogy, multigenre research papers constitute writings that are disjointed yet connected through multiple genres, which come together to make an argument for a given position. From a rhetoric-and-composition perspective, Julie Jung writes that "multigenre texts are by definition a composition of diverse genres and identities; they can potentially expose and thereby force us to contend with the silenced tensions," particularly within minoritized students' perspectives on academic writing and their perceptions of themselves in the world (2005, 33). When writing through multiple genres, students are encouraged to write in a different yet personal voice. As Jung theorizes, "Multigenre texts [are] one type of multivocal discourse where the inclusion of diverse genres adds another layer of 'vocality'" (2005, 33). My students found multiple ways to report on local historical events, such as the Farah strikes of the 1970s, the construction of Interstate 10 through El Paso, and even the historic construction of El Paso High School in 1916.

In my year of teaching at El Paso High, I found unconventional ways for my students to write about their identities and ideas of the world. The ways of "teaching to transgress" that bell hooks describes were prevalent in my classes: "Professors who embrace the challenge of self-actualization will be better able to create pedagogical practices that engage students, providing them with ways of knowing that enhance their capacity to live fully and deeply" (1994, 22). Moreover, the mestiza pedagogy and facultad that I had nurtured and developed through the years with my students also influenced me to theorize, narrate, and explore my own path of shifting perceptions. In the thousands of lessons that I had taught in public schools, I was always aware of a lack of representation of Chicanas and Mexicanas in literature accessible to students. In my quest to seek representation for Chicana and Mexican American women and girls, I eventually decided to leave the public schools of El Paso, in the process transforming my mestiza pedagogy into a research agenda of rescuing, uncovering, and representing Mexicana and Mexican American women in rhetorical history.

Forging a Mestiza Rhetoric

The summer before entering the doctoral program at the University of Texas at El Paso, I began researching the discursive role of women in the Mexican Revolution. Interested in my connection to the borderlands where my González and Hernández relatives have lived for more than a century, I took inspiration from the many oral stories that my abuela, Ramona González, would share about wanting to become a journalist but falling short because of the family's poverty in the 1920s. From these long talks, I too began to write. I started a young-adult novel on Latina identities set in El Paso High School, from which both my mother and abuela had graduated. Connecting this writing to my mestiza pedagogy and experiences teaching in borderland public schools, I saw that the purpose of the book was to reflect on how young Latino/a students struggle with their cultural identity along the Mexico-US border. In searching for a model for the abuela of the young Latina high school protagonist, I discovered I could not find any historical representation of Mexicanas (not surprisingly) in mainstream historical accounts of the Mexican Revolution.

Diving deeper into my research, I came across Shirlene Soto's book *Emergence of the Modern Mexican Woman: Her Participation in Revolution and Struggle for Equality, 1910–1940* (1990). Soto's research, which represents the early recovery work on gender in Mexico, illuminated some of the Mexican women who *did* participate in the struggle and those who wrote and published their writings in local and national newspapers during the struggle. Soto details the lives of these Mexican women who were politically active, each chapter concluding with female journalists from turn-of-the-twentieth-century Mexico: Larueana Wright de Kleinhans, Juana Belen Gutiérrez de Mendoza, and Hermila Galindo. The women in Soto's book stand out as trailblazers, revolutionaries, and activists who through their writing helped to define the realities of their fellow citizens caught in a government dictatorship and oppressive patriarchal structure. These stories transfixed me with wonder, and I enthusiastically pursued this newfound passion.

Recovery of Mexicana and Mexican American women stands firmly at the center of my own historical, rhetorical, and feminist studies. My own mestiza pedagogies, combined with the acknowledgment of a lack of identification to the texts I taught to my public-school students, led to my discovering additional voices of marginalized and silenced women writers deserving of recovery. The task that lay before me was not simply recovery of texts but also a literal crossing of the borders into Mexico, exploring nondigitized archives to find these women's voices and bring them to the fore. Castillo notes that Chicana historians "have the most unfortunate task of either examining our past using sources that obviously either omit or distort us and employing white male methodology, not writing about us at all, or of still using Western arguments and language to try to make a revisionist case with" the evidence available (1994, 216). Historically, this reality has been a burden. Yet looking at Castillo's statement from an alternative point of departure, I realize that scholars who are women of color now have the privilege, even obligation, to rescue, recover, and ultimately transform the landscape of history and the academy.

Being grounded in a mestiza pedagogy of connectedness to community, my research has now turned toward my own roots and family archives. Until I investigated my heritage, I did not realize that the frequent interpellations of facultad and mestiza pedagogy were appeals for me to come home. As I write this sentence, I have come full circle in feminine rhetorical recovery work and am focusing on the recently recovered writings of my own abuela, Ramona González (1906–95). With a collection of more than 750 pages of her writings, my historical and rhetorical recovery recuperates the published and recently discovered extent of Spanish- and English-language writings of Doña González.

For more than fifty years, these writings sat in a cardboard vegetable box, not emerging until 2014. These archives were donated by my family to and are permanently curated at the Latin American Benson Collection at the University of Texas at Austin. Mostly written in Spanish, my abuela's writings include forty-seven poems, ten short stories, four longer creative nonfiction pieces, approximately thirty-five fables, more than two hundred pages of dichos, and seventeen cuadros, a unique genre that González employed to discuss a single topic on a single page. The "Collected Writing of Ramona González" is the official title of her unpublished writings in the collection. Importantly, González published during the Chicano-dominated movement that mostly excluded women, and recovery of her writings is significant in understanding the history and gender dynamics of the Chicano literary movement.

González published her writing in the most significant university literary journal of the Chicano movement, *El Grito: A Journal of Contemporary Mexican American Thought* (1967–74), put out by Quinto Sol Publications (for those published works, see González 1973). González, an astute Chicana writer and rhetor, published in *El Grito* at a time when Chicano writers such as Rudolfo Anaya were receiving high praise and recognition for their writings, but Chicana writers struggled to have their work printed. Five of González's short stories appeared in "Chicanas en la literatura y el arte," a special edition of *El Grito* issued in 1973: "El tesoro enterrado," "El conjuramento," "Cuando tienes comezón," "La talaca," and "El camotero."

A historical analysis of this journal by Dennis López in "Goodbye Revolution—Hello Cultural Mystique" (2010) reveals that "the early contributions of Quinto Sol Publications proved vital to laying much of the ideological and institutional groundwork for the establishment of this Chicano Movement print culture" (187). My abuela, a Chicana literary writer, was also a rhetor working within and against the strict traditions of the Mexican patriarchy and the predominant white American culture. Doña Ramona possessed an innate understanding of feminist rhetorical historiographic theory. Feminist rhetorical approaches like hers resist the cultural and gendered status quo, instead pursuing the authentic lines and fissures of knowledge within her community. In the rhetorical approaches of the Mexican women I recover, spanning both my abuela's literary writings and my own rhetorical recovery work, I see all these struggles connecting, overlapping, and bridging both time and space.

Conclusion

After twenty-five years of teaching and engaging in critical pedagogies, I discovered that my own repository of knowledge—the writings of my abuela—had been waiting for me to recover them so that I could write about her stories, a situation that I refer to as ancestral remembering. As Anzaldúa writes of la facultad, it is like "'plunging vertically' into our selves." If heeded, facultad forces us to "pay attention to the soul, and we are thus carried into awareness and experiencing of the soul (Self)" (1987, 61, 60). From my early days as a middle- and high-school teacher in El Paso to my historical recovery of Mexican and Mexican American women's writings and finally to the engagement with my abuela's writings, my life's work and writings merge my ancestral past with my present scholarship. These three discrete phases of my career incorporate the blending of Anglo and Mexican American cultures and history. Through this testimonio, I have been able to listen to and reflect on my mestiza pedagogy, including those that I taught to my students, and to identify a new direction in my writing that involves my "returning home" to my own ancestral remembering.

As Latina leaders working, writing, and teaching in the field of rhetoric and composition, we exemplify for our young graduate and undergraduate students how to resist and overcome some of the suffocating realities of the academy. As a feminist recovery scholar, I encourage more Latina scholars to engage in rhetorical recovery of women's voices. This minority voice in the writing of history is underrepresented. Specifically, I refer to the recovery of texts in Spanish, English, and Indigenous languages that reflect the histories of Latinx, Chicanx, and Indigenous women. Such historical work is of vast importance, and much remains to be discovered and shared. By tapping into our own internal funds of knowledge, we counter centuries-old traditions of academic institutions refusing to recognize marginalized voices as knowledge. Reflecting on and listening to other Latina leaders in this collection, Stefani Baldivia and Kendall Leon conclude that "it is not enough to help our students or each other to learn to navigate or dismantle institutions; we need also to teach and model using the tools necessary to radically remodel the whitestream spaces that they inhabit." Although a much greater diversity of Latina voices has emerged in feminist rhetorical scholarship in the past decade, we need more. We need to tell our stories and those of others to explore and activate more and different kinds of theory and research. These rhetorical connections among Latina leaders who write from the borderlands and teach the connections to mestiza pedagogies are imperative in reshaping leadership roles in the academy to make them more inclusive and diverse.

References

Anaya, Rudolfo. [1972] 2012. *Bless Me, Ultima*. New York: Grand Central.

Anzaldúa, Gloria. 1987. *Borderlands / La Frontera: The New Mestiza*. San Francisco: Aunt Lute Books.

Beatty, Patricia. 1981. *Lupita Mañana*. Austin: Harcourt Brace.

Cammarota, Julio. 2008. *Sueños Americanos: Barrio Youth Negotiating Social and Cultural Identities*. Tucson: Univ. of Arizona Press.

Cárdenas, Diana. 2004. "Creating an Identity: Personal, Academic, and Civic Literacies." In *Latino/a Discourses: On Language, Identity, and Literacy Education*, edited by Michelle Hall Kells, Valerie M. Balester, and Victor Villanueva, 114–25. Portsmouth, NH: Heinemann.

Castillo, Ana. 1994. *Massacre of the Dreamers: Essays on Xicanisma*. London: Penguin, 1994.

Cisneros, Sandra. 1984. *The House on Mango Street*. New York: Vintage Books.

Delgado Bernal, Dolores, Rebeca Burciaga, and Judith Flores Carmona. 2012. "Chicana/Latina Testimonios: Mapping the Methodological, Pedagogical, and Political." *Equity & Excellence in Education* 45, no. 3: 363–72.

Ebe, Ann. 2010. "Culturally Relevant Texts and Reading Assessment for English Language Learners." *Reading Horizons* 50, no. 3: 193–210.

Friere, Paulo. 1998. *Teachers as Cultural Workers: Letters to Those Who Dare to Teach*. Translated by Donaldo Macedo, Dale Koike, and Alexandre Oliveira. Boulder, CO: Westview Press.

Garza, Elizabeth. 2007. "Becoming a Border Pedagogy Educator." *Multicultural Education* 14, no. 3: 1–7.

Giroux, Henry. 1991. "Border Politics and the Politics of Postmodernism." *Social Text*, no. 28: 51–67.

González, Ramona. 1973. "'El tesoro enterrado' and Other Stories." In "Chicanas en la literatura y el arte," special issue of *El Grito*, book 1:22–42.

Guajardo, Francisco, and Miguel Guajardo. 2013. "The Power of Plática." *Reflections* 13, no. 1: 159–64.

hooks, bell. 1994. *Teaching to Transgress: Education as the Practice of Freedom*. New York: Routledge.

Jung, Julie. 2005. *Revisionary Rhetoric, Feminist Pedagogy, and Multigenre Texts*. Carbondale: Southern Illinois Univ. Press.

Kazanjian, Christopher John. 2011. "The Border Pedagogy Revisited." *Intercultural Education* 22, no. 5: 371–80.

Kells, Michelle Hall. 2004. "Understanding the Rhetorical Value of Tejano Codeswitching." In *Latino/a Discourses: On Language, Identity, and Literacy Education*, edited by Michelle Hall Kells, Valerie M. Balester, and Victor Villanueva, 24–39. Portsmouth, NH: Heinemann.

Leon, Kendall. 2013. "Chicanas Making Change: Institutional Rhetoric and the Comisión Femenil Mexicana Nacional." *Reflections* 13, no. 1: 165–94.

López, Dennis. 2010. "Good-bye Revolution—Hello Cultural Mystique: Quinto Sol Publications and Chicano Literary Nationalism." *Crime, Punishment, and Redemption* 35, no 3: 183–210.

National Council of Teachers of English, Conference on College Composition and Communication. 1972. "Students' Rights to Their Own Language Resolution." At https://cccc.ncte.org/cccc/resources/positions/srtolsummary.

———. 1974. "Students Rights to Their Own Language." Apr. At https://cdn.ncte.org/nctefiles/groups/cccc/newsrtol.pdf.

Ortiz-Franco, Luis. 2017. "Norma Hernandez: A Pioneer." In *Women in Mathematics: Celebrating the Centennial of the Mathematical Association of America*, edited by Janet Beery, Sarah Greenwald, Jacqueline Jensen-Vallin, and Maura Mast, 293–302. Cham, Switzerland: Springer.

Peck, Robert. 1972. *A Day No Pigs Would Die*. New York: Laurel-Leaf.

Pratt, Mary Louise. [1991] 2002. "Arts of the Contact Zone." In *Professing the Contact Zone: Bringing Theory and Practice Together*, edited by Janice M. Wolff, 1–20. Urbana, IL: National Council of Teachers of English.

Ramirez, Pablo C., Lydia Ross, and Margarita Jimenez-Silva. 2016. "The Intersectionality of Border Pedagogy and Latino/a Youth: Enacting Border Pedagogy in Multiple Spaces." *High School Journal* 99, no. 4: 302–21.

Reyes, Reynaldo, III. 2016. "In a World of Disposable Students: The Humanizing Elements of Border Pedagogy in Teacher Education." *High School Journal* 99, no. 4: 337–50.

Romano, Tom. 2000. *Blending Genre, Altering Style: Writing Multigenre Research Papers*. Portsmouth, NH: Heinemann.

———. 2004. *Crafting Authentic Voice*. Portsmouth, NH: Heinemann.

Soto, Shirlene Ann. 1990. *Emergence of the Modern Mexican Woman: Her Participation in Revolution and Struggle for Equality, 1910–1940*. Denver: Arden Press.

Taylor, Mildred D. 1976. *Roll of Thunder, Hear My Cry*. New York: Phyllis Fogelman.

Tijerina, Andrés. 1994. *Tejanos and Texas under the Mexican Flag, 1821–1836*. College Station: Texas A&M Univ. Press.

Trelease, Jim. 2013. *The Read-Aloud Handbook*. New York: Penguin.

11

Testimoniando

Chicana/Latina Feminist Reflections on Embodied Knowledge, Literacies, and Narrating the Self

Mónica González Ybarra

Abstract

This chapter introduces the concepts of testimonio and testimoniando as central to Chicana/Latina feminist methodological approaches. Through testimonio and testimoniando, Chicana feminists reclaim their histories and experiences, positioning them as critical to literacy education. Using testimonio as a methodological tool, then, is a political choice that disrupts normative research and conceptualizations of knowledge while transforming possibilities for both researchers and participants.

Introduction

A Chicana mentor of mine once asked readers to finish the following sentence: "If my hands could speak, they would tell you. . . ."[1] At the time I responded, I wrote about my hands being descendants of hardworking, manual-laboring, mothering, and resistant hands—all of which is true. As I write this chapter now, a junior scholar navigating the often-toxic confines of academia, I recognize that if my hands could speak, they would also tell you how they are the median between my heart's work and the way I *do* literacy research in education. They would tell you how, when I write, they quiver because

---

1. Dolores Delgado Bernal, personal communication to the author, 2012.

much of my academic work comes with deep emotional reflection on my own educational experiences—too much of which is bounded by silenced/silencing memories. These experiences, many times, are not solely mine and are instead reflective of the educational experiences of generations of my family and community members. Their narratives, cultural and linguistic knowledge, are often overlooked and dismissed. My hands would tell you that these narratives, testimonios, make up my genealogy of empowerment, with the historical traumas and pain that transcend generations and become a "conflicted sense of pride" (Latina Feminist Group 2001, 25) in my academic accomplishments and cultural strengths of resistance, resilience, and survival.

Testimonios (the texts) and testimoniando (the practice of sharing and generating testimonios) have been a literacy practice central to my life—my family, my community, and my research with Latinx youth (DeNicolo et al. 2015; Ybarra 2018). As I was growing up, my grandfather would share testimonios with me about how he crossed the US-Mexico border by foot as a child (eleven years old) to look for work. He would tell me stories of how he and his brother used the stars to guide them and, despite getting deported multiple times, continued to make the journey back. My grandmother would share testimonios with me about her schooling experiences, specifically how she could not attend school past the third grade because the school with upper grade levels was too far, and for that reason she decided to pursue third grade for a second time. Testimonios of migration, schooling, and healing were the pedagogical practices of my grandparents and shaped how I understood who I was and the ways I made sense of the world. The Latina Feminist Group argues that genealogies are what make our scholarship and have "fueled our cognitive desires, the will to knowledge and comprehension" (2001, 25). It is from this understanding that I piece together what it means to center a methodology grounded in personal narratives, or testimonios.

Defining Testimonio

The genre of testimonio (Menchú [1984] 2010) is most notably recognized for its roots in Latin America, particularly for its use in documenting and voicing the experiences of people who have faced marginalization, persecution, and oppression by governments and sociopolitical forces (Brabeck 2003). Tied to a history of human rights struggle, testimonio incorporates sociopolitical, historical, and cultural experiences in an effort to elicit social change and greater social consciousness. It is understood as a performative text that purposefully and strategically connects individual experiences to a collective narrative—voicing the silences of the marginalized. Testimonio has evolved, illustrating personal, political, and social realities. Different from traditional narrative, life stories, and autobiography, testimonio calls for action based on personal accounts that situate themselves within larger sociopolitical contexts that transcend time and generations (Delgado Bernal, Burciaga, and Carmona 2012).

Framing Testimonio as a Chicana/Latina Feminist Method(ology)

Testimonio in education has become a methodological tool that incorporates the voices of Chicanx/Latinx communities and presents new forms of political agency, both of which allow for greater possibilities for exposing what has been silenced and unseen (Calderón et al. 2012). It challenges the notion of objectivity and calls for research to be situated within other(ed) epistemologies. As illustrated in the chapters by Laura Gonzales, Lorena Gutierrez, and Stefani Baldivia and Kendall Leon in this collection (chapters 3, 4, and 5), the power of testimonio can function within a community as a restorative practice to promote justice and healing as well as to build new knowledge. For Chicana/Latina feminists, our academic inquiries move "beyond quantitative versus qualitative methods, and [lie] instead in the methodology employed and in whose experiences are accepted as the foundation of knowledge" (Delgado Bernal 1998, 555). Using testimonio as a methodological tool, then, is a political choice that disrupts normative research and conceptualizations of knowledge while forcing the "reinvention and radical reposition of power" for both researchers and participants (Cruz 2012, 469).

Although the use of testimonio as a methodology is by no means limited to Chicana/Latina feminist researchers, we have taken it up in a way that "mirror[s] a sensibility that allows the mind, body, and spirit to be equally valuable sources of knowledge and embrace[s] an engagement of social transformation" (Delgado Bernal, Burciaga, and Carmona 2012, 365). Using testimonio as a Chicana/Latina feminist methodological strategy acknowledges that our bodies and experiences are valued sites of knowledge production and identity negotiation (Saavedra and Nymark 2008) that speak to collective community experiences—the experience of our communities. We, Chicana/Latina feminists, situate our research within the tensions and messiness of our own histories, traumas, and hopes because our academic work often centers on places, spaces, and community members who share these experiences. These experiences do not serve as masks that "can be put on or taken off" (Latina Feminist Group 2001, 4); rather, they serve as the base of who we are and how we live through our scholarly, political, and personal practice.

Chicana/Latina feminist scholars have had to continuously work in the margins (Anzaldúa 1987). Critiquing the scholarship deemed legitimate in the academy, Cindy Cruz explains that, "based on the standards of positivist inquiry, the narratives of women of color are considered too corporeal, too colored, and sometimes too queer to be considered publishable" (2001, 659). Within the institution, the knowledge, theories, and experiences of some are privileged and legitimized, whereas other(ed) epistemologies and theoretical frames are devalued, dismissed, and silenced. The academy thus has historically delegitimized queered and (en)darkened knowledges (Dillard 2000). As such, these other(ed) epistemological stances are imperative to problematize normative knowledge and the production of it, without apology and in a transgressive and political way (Saavedra and Pérez 2014).

Traditional social science research paradigms continue to work through normative, privileged, and oppressive ways of knowing, which continue to deem other(ed) epistemologies and frameworks as unscholarly, too personal, or too radical. These very methods, methodologies, and frameworks are what continue to dismember the bodies of women of color (Cruz 2001), hurting our souls and keeping us from feeling whole within the academy (Lara 2002). Cruz explains that the negations of women of color in these traditional genres have forced us to "develop alternative spaces and methodologies for the study" of our communities (2001, 658). As a result, by creating methodologies that are framed by an epistemology of the body, from the margins Chicana/Latina feminist scholars continue to challenge methodologies that have been used to oppress and misrepresent our communities. In the process, the personal becomes political in the sense that these very methodologies take up questions that are framed to relocate and center our communities within a discussion of marginalization, oppression, and resistance.

Centering the Body

Testimonio strongly aligns with the feminista tradition of theorizing from the body to break silences and name injustices to motivate social chance. Testimonio is a tool to document experiences and embodied knowledge that root themselves in our bodymindspirits (Lara 2002). Testimonios reveal our epistemological maps and how we come to make sense of our lived truths. They move us toward piecing together painful experiences to move us toward greater consciousness (Cervantes-Soon 2012). Testimonio, alongside Chicana/Latina feminisms, recognizes that memory is not just that of the mind and thus serves as a tool that challenges Western ideas of the body/mind split and positivist, objective research by motivating Chicana feminist scholars to examine the intersections of marginalization in our own lived realities and embodied knowledge (Calderón et al. 2012).

Using testimonio as a Chicana/Latina feminist methodology means framing research in a way that addresses multiple and intersecting layers of oppression, analyzing and presenting data using theoretical perspectives that value epistemologies from the margins, and embracing the knowledge that is centered in the sociohistorical imprint on our brown bodies. A methodology of em(bodied) knowledge means that we are no longer content being siempre en contra and that we are moving toward ways to make sense of our experiences of marginalization in productive and transformative ways (Anzaldúa

1987). Testimonio, as a methodology that centers bodied knowledge, not only recognizes the brown body as a source of knowledge and theory but also considers how the body is situated in the academy, always in resistance. Dolores Delgado Bernal suggests that in taking up a methodology rooted in our own sociopolitical historias, "Chicanas become agents of knowledge who participate in intellectual discourse that links experience, research, community, and social change" (1998, 560). In this way, a methodology of em(bodied) knowledge problematizes mainstream, normative research methods, theories, and paradigms that continue to legitimize and privilege Eurocentrism and white ways of knowing.

Testimonio as methodology challenges traditional research paradigms in that it disrupts who can produce knowledge, how it can be produced, and who can share it (Delgado Bernal, Burciaga, and Carmona 2012, 365). Particularly when taken up by Chicana/Latina researchers working with(in) Latinx communities, the methodological tool of testimonio has the potential to recenter the narratives, lived realities, and inequities of our communities. Working to reveal the layered and complex issues of identity and oppression that are rooted in pain and trauma, testimonio is a methodology that considers how knowledge is embodied and acknowledges that our communities work from complicated genealogies and structures of colonial and patriarchal legacies imprinted on the body (Latina Feminist Group 2001). Testimonio in educational research then allows for these often-silenced voices to be heard in a way that allows for new forms of political agency to disrupt normative and dominant conceptualizations of research (Calderón et al. 2012). With that, the political intention of testimonio as representative of a collective experience allows for Chicana/Latina feminist researchers in education to make the urgency of educational inequities visible (Delgado Bernal, Burciaga, and Carmona 2012).

Testimonio as Literacy

At its core, testimonio is a critical literacy practice that reveals what has been silenced and unseen within marginalized communities. Within

the reading, writing, orally sharing, watching, and witnessing of testimonio, testimoniando becomes a practice that names marginalized
experiences and invites others to share within the collective reality or
to act as allies in solidarity (DeNicolo et al. 2015). In other words,
testimoniando becomes the process that engages critical literacies
(Saavedra 2011). When we consider how coloniality reproduces texts
that aim to maintain systems of subordination, testimonio ruptures
the normalcy and silencing of these colonial structures by shedding
light on them. Conceptualizing testimonio as a critical literacy has
the potential to resist colonial literacies by centralizing conversations
on student experiences and knowledges. Testimonios can potentially
expose the projects of colonialism such as racial hierarchies, forced
migration, exploitation of land and bodies, and notions of knowledge
legitimacy. They disrupt the dominant narratives constructed around
them, offering an alternative narrative. Testimoniando thus requires
sociopolitical critiques of intersecting systems of oppression, such as
colonialism and imperialism, as well as participation in the reconstruc-
tion of the texts that aim to maintain these systems (Saavedra and
Nymark 2008).

In addition to the ways in which testimonio has been conceptualized as a critical literacy, it is also recognized as an embodied literacy
(DeNicolo et al. 2015). In other words, it is understood as a performative text that purposefully and strategically connects individual experiences to a collective story—voicing the silences of and exposing the
knowledge located within marginalized bodies (Elenes 2000). As an
embodied literacy, testimonio engages the body as a performative text.
Positioning testimonio in this way is similar to Elizabeth Johnson and
Lalitha Vasudevan's work in identifying how young people produce,
wear, critique, and consume literacies. These authors position the body
as text to move away from verbocentric notions of literacy and instead
argue that "students use their bodies to perform critical literacy—that
is, to respond to and convey their critical engagements with myriad
texts" (2012, 35). When we attend to this expansive notion of literacy
and situate testimonio within this discussion, the body becomes a site
where literacy is performed and produced—a mode where testimonio

emerges. Recognizing testimonio as a literacy practice requires deep consideration of how the knowledge we carry within and on us shapes the ways we exist in the world and how we enact those knowledges through our bodies.

Chicana/Latina feminist understandings of the body as a holder and producer of knowledge (Moraga and Anzaldúa 1983) is central to my understanding of testimonio as an embodied literacy. Through this theoretical lens, I see testimonio as a literacy practice that reveals the ways in which the body is located within the messy and complicated relationships to colonialism and imperialism and how it engages with the reproduction of colonial texts—how it internalizes, navigates, and resists them. It is a literacy practice that not only engages the embodied knowledge of the testimonialista but touches the bodies of others as well. In this way, others are affected by the knowledge and performance being conveyed. Such a literacy practice disrupts the mind/body split and instead engages the whole self in the production and engagement of multiple texts. Testimonio methodology, thus, moves me to consider and attend to what is unseen and unspoken and to pay close attention to how students' embodied knowledge surfaces in their meaning making and textual compositions.

Within literacy educational research, testimonio has the ability to lend itself to a process of voicing, healing, and making sense of realities for students of color. It carries the potential to engage students in a process of theorizing from their own experiences of oppression and marginalization (Delgado Bernal, Burciaga, and Carmona 2012). Serving as a tool that acknowledges embodied knowledge, testimonio comes with the possibility of moving students toward realizing their fullest humanity by producing knowledge, toward realizing and affirming their epistemological maps. From a Chicana/Latina feminist sensibility in literacy education, we offer a different standpoint from which students can deconstruct the ways that systems of racism, patriarchy, sexism, and heterosexism have affected their personal lives and communities at large (Ybarra 2020). With that offer, we challenge education research to acknowledge the powerful ways in which students have negotiated, lived, and resisted with(in) these systems of oppression. In other words, this standpoint to research requires a sensibility that exposes the agency practiced by youth even in the most confining and conflicted spaces (González Ybarra 2020).

In taking up a methodology of testimonio within literacy educational research, our students become testimonialistas—powerful voices in articulating educational realities for the marginalized and holders of sacred knowledge. Moving toward transformative research in education, Cruz argues that understanding these histories of marginalization and oppression as imprinted on the body "is fundamental in the reclamation of narrative and the development of radical projects of transformation and liberation" (2001, 657). For the educational researcher, in particular those of us who ground our work in community/ student-engaged scholarship, understanding these lived historical realities for our students is key in considering our methodological strategies for research. This sensibility has the ability to decolonize educational research in a way that repositions senses of validity and legitimacy. This strategy, for a Chicana/Latina feminist researcher in literacy education, is only the beginning of the reclamation for social change. Creating critical practices that, like methodologies, call upon the body for knowledge and the production of radical subjectivities leads us closer to that reclamation (González Ybarra and Saavedra 2021).

Testimoniando: Process, Product, and Praxis

As the Latina Feminist Group describes, testimonio is the "result of conscious relational politics and of collaborative testimonio, face-to-face theorizing and production" (2001, 6). It is the act of making sense of papelitos guardados, giving voice to personal, political, and social realities, in a way that reveals our other(ed) epistemologies. Testimoniando, sharing and analyzing our stories, is a way we come to understand more of who we are. As such, the product and process, a methodology, of testimonio are inseparable (Latina Feminist Group 2001, 8). It is through this process that we can consider the implications of testimoniando as a Chicana/Latina methodological approach for literacy education research. In my work in literacy education, I have taken up testimoniando (Latina Feminist Group 2001; Huber and Cueva 2012), or the process of telling, writing, and reading/witnessing testimonio, with Latinx youth. Generating testimonio within these projects has become a methodology that consists of oral sharing, recording, listening, and writing narratives that are lodged in the memory of the mindbodyspirit.

In our work with third-grade Latinx youth in the Midwest, for example, Christina DeNicolo and I (DeNicolo et al. 2015) began to think about what this process looks like in the classroom and how it facilitates this cyclical practice of sharing, witnessing, and writing. In this third-grade bilingual language arts classroom, students and I shared and witnessed each other's experiences of being bilingual Latinx children. In preparation for this project with the third graders, my mentora, Christina, created space for me to write my testimonio of language loss and reclamation. This testimonio included my relationship to Spanish and my language journey as a bilingual Chicana—how, for me, language is deeply connected to my family, my culture, and schooling. This testimonio gave the third graders an insight into my feelings of shame when I entered predominately white schools and my moments of pride and joy when I understood who I was and my language as powerful.

Third graders made self-to-text connections with my testimonio as well as with those of other Chicana/Latina graduate students in this study. These third graders documented their experiences with language, their struggles with navigating English-only discourses, and through their writing and oral sharing they demonstrated how these narratives were part of a larger collective struggle of bilingual Latinx in the United States. The process of testimoniando became a process for the third graders to understand their lived realities in relation to their community, building on connections through narratives for survival and resilience. As a methodological tool, testimonios (the texts) and testimoniando (the praxis) became integral to data collection and to better understanding the experiences of bilingual Latinx children.

Understanding testimonio as a Chicana/Latina feminist methodology requires a shift in conceptualizations of valued research and the ability to engage in a process that is collaborative and founded on reciprocity and love. In the sections that follow, I highlight necessary considerations when employing testimonio as a methodology, in particular the process of testimoniando as a form of data collection and theorization. In reflecting on the process of testimoniando, the Latina Feminist Group states, "With careful nurturing and reflection, our process evolved into un engranje de deseo, respeto, confianza, y colaboración—a meshing of desire, respect, trust, and collaboration" (2001, 9). For Chicana/Latina feminist researchers, our goals in academia are never neutral; rather, they come about through our desires to reclaim knowledge production and produce transformative research for what many of us consider to be our communities (Cervantes-Soon 2012).

Destabilizing Roles in Research

Testimoniando as a method has the potential to reframe authoritative power and how we understand legitimate research because it challenges who can "do research" and who is being researched. Testimonio calls into question the concept of the "informant" because, as Monica Russel y Rodriguez points out, it acknowledges that participants are "capable of their own political analysis." She suggests that testimonio reframes the author's "self-story" to a story that "moves in and between data gathering and analysis" (2007, 97). Understanding relationships and reciprocity as central to the methodology of testimonio allows researchers to cocreate a process that examines and recenters the personal as political across and within the research process. Testimonio, then, comes with the possibility of inviting participants to be coresearchers.

In my work with young Chicana/Latinas in a migrant (immigrant) housing community (González Ybarra 2018), I witnessed how youth made sense of the testimonios that emerged in their families and their community and how they connected them to collective sociopolitical injustices. In this project, youth engaged in the process of testimoniando with members of their community, specifically around immigration and migrant labor. In analyzing the connections across the testimonios, Karisa and Lilia, two mujeres in this study, crafted a composite narrative—a testimonio with fictional characters based on the actual events of the families within their community. They documented this testimonio on a PowerPoint slide with carefully selected images of the border, a local tree farm, their housing community, and a Mexican colonia. The text on Karisa and Lilia's slide reads:

> Juan caminaba lentamente guiando a su familia. Todos arrastrabran sus piernas tras la arena, la ague desaparece rápidamente y el calor del sol no se iva. Siete dias bajo el sol, iban a los estados unidos en búsqueda de oportunidades para ellos mismos. Su pobreza en monterrey no mejoraba y decidieron cruzar la frontera. En el octavo dia medio galón de agua faltaba. La esposa de juan falleció el se quedo solo con sus 2 hijos. En el décimo dia juan logro cruzar con sus dos hijos, su destino era Colorado. Encontró trabajo en el tree farm en donde multiples compañeros vivian en casa de la esperanza. Decidió aplicar, Juan y sus hijos vivieron en un alberque por alrededor de un mes hasta que su aplicación fue aceptada. Casa de la Esperanza le dio buena educación y ayuda a sus dos hijos.[2]

This narrative includes the testimonio of Juan, an (im)migrant traveling by foot across the desert with his family toward the United States. In the testimonio, the young women highlight the hardships and traumas of migration while also demonstrating and documenting the resiliency of (im)migrants. In crafting this testimonio, these young mujeres revealed the power of testimoniando as they engaged

---

2. Juan walked slowly, guiding his family. Everyone dragging their feet in the sand. Water quickly disappeared, and the sun was everlasting. Seven days under the sun, they were making their way to the United States to look for better opportunities for their futures. The poverty in Monterrey was worsening, and they decided to cross the border. On the eighth day, they had only a half gallon of water left. Juan's wife passed, and he was left with his two children. On the tenth day, Juan was able to cross the border with his children, making his way to Colorado. He found a job at the tree farm, and many of his coworkers lived in Comunidad Miravalle. Juan decided to apply for housing. In the meantime, he and his children lived in a shelter while they waited for the application to be processed. Comunidad Miravalle provided wonderful academic opportunities for Juan's children.

in this practice with families and members of the community. Karisa and Lilia also demonstrated how roles between researcher and participant, testimonialista and interlocutor, shift in the process. Karisa and Lilia became the researchers in this moment and highlighted very real events that unfolded in the testimonios of their community members. In doing so, they called attention to the realities of immigration, migrant labor, and the power and support within migrant communities.

Listening and Witnessing

Testimoniando moves us to listen and reflect, continuously pushing the soul toward an emotional shift charged by political intent. It demands an audience to critically listen and witness. To be the listener of a testimonio is much like receiving a gift: "The listener unwraps the testimonio to reveal the heart of the matter" (Delgado Bernal, Burciaga, and Carmona 2012, 368). In this exchange, it is possible to see inside another's world, to open our souls in a way that invites action and solidarity. As such, testimonio calls on a particular type of listening that moves us to hear from the heart, to participate in "radical listening" (Cruz 2012, 463). For a Chicana feminist researcher, radical listening within the process of testimoniando means continuously repositioning oneself in a way that transcends hierarchies and varied experiences and transitions to being with the testimonialista as an ally. Radical listening, particularly for the researcher, means listening for "what is being said and what is being left unsaid" (Cruz 2012, 470) and cocreating a space where what has been deemed invisible is seen (Dillard 2000). This is how we begin to facilitate the ongoing process and product of a testimonio methodology. As researchers, our obligation is to listen with love through a vulnerable state, which becomes open to a reciprocal emotional and epistemological exchange.

When testimonios emerge, they create moments for witnessing and cultivating solidarity. In my work with Latinx (im)migrant youth, for example, testimonios created moments for us to consider our lived experiences in relation to each other and larger sociopolitical contexts. As a third-generation Chicana, I continuously consider how my testimonios exist differently from those of my students, who come from mixed-status families, whose parents are exploited daily in (im) migrant labor, and who are undocumented. My citizenship status as well my class and educational privilege shape my narratives and ultimately the way I listen and witness the testimonios of my students. In reckoning with these privileges and the very material differences that exist between me and the youth and families I work with, I understand that even though positioned as allies in a process of testimoniando, we can only partially understand, feel, and access what is being illuminated.

Even in creating spaces for life stories to be witnessed, as Elizabeth Dutro argues, we also invite an "overwhelming sense that we can't know or hear or tell all stories that reside in any space where people exist together" (2013, 308). In other words, acting as a witness of testimonio comes with fear of what has been silenced, unspoken and unheard, and what that means for a process of reciprocal exchange. Testimonio, calling on the mindbodysoul to engage on behalf of the witness, has the ability to elicit visceral responses. In conceptualizing critical witnessing, Dutro suggests that our "visceral unsteadiness" is the entire point (2013, 310). In bearing witness to testimonio, we are moved to "estar con el hablante" (Cruz 2012, 462), or be with(in) the moment of the testimonialistas as they share their stories of trauma, oppression, and marginalization. Hearing someone's pain has the ability to disrupt our thinking and our bodies' balance and sense of stability. Our visceral responses to these stories are what move us to engage in the "moral imperative of critical witness" (Dutro 2013, 301).

In testimoniando, the researcher and participant have the potential to be testimonialistas. If truly reciprocal, a testimonio methodology positions both as witnesses. This is when we, as researchers, face the contradictions of our roles and allow the stories to speak for themselves and contain the visceral reactions that come with radical listening (Cruz 2012). This process comes along with recognizing that we, as witnesses, cannot fully grasp what is being shared with us. Acting as a critical witness requires an ability to reflect on what solidarity truly means when we have not lived what is being told to us. Testimonio, then, demands that critical witnessing be a part of a shift in those willing to participate as listener, storyteller, and researcher, whether working from solidarity or conflicted spaces.

Centering Experience: The Role of Testimonio and Pushing Boundaries in the Academy

In my experience, testimonios have played a critical role in mentorship because they have been used to share knowledge, cocreate knowledge, and make space for the dialogic process of experiential exchange. The practice of testimoniando is about voicing and learning from experiences and collectively rethinking what knowledge production might look like within the academy. Chicanas/Latinas, alongside Blacks, women of color, and Third World feminists, have been leaders in methodological shifts. They have paved the way for junior scholars to continue theorizing and seeking out humanizing methods that reflect the knowledge, culture, and linguistic resources of the communities with whom we work. It is through testimoniando that Chicana/Latina feminist scholars have healed from reviewers' and critics' questioning of the validity, rigor, and overall legitimacy of our contributions to the field. Through testimoniando, mentoras have shared, listened, and witnessed personal histories, engaging in reciprocal, vulnerable relationships and pushing against the rigid individualistic boundaries of academic institutions. Testimonio has functioned as a form of mentoring literacy and has been a foundational practice to cultivate what Ana Milena Ribero and Sonia Arellano articulate as comadrismo (see chapter 1). Through this collective narration of experiences, we are able to push boundaries of research and begin to document other(ed) methods and approaches to mentorship.

Testimonio allows Chicana/Latina feminist scholars to consider other(ed) possibilities for how to engage in research. In the examples provided throughout this chapter as well as in learning from the work of mentoras, testimonios are critical to voicing and unpacking educational experiences within a historicized and politicized context. Through my work with youth, in particular, I have learned how testimonio becomes a way for young people to recognize and value their negotiation and resistance in the systems that continue to marginalize them. A methodology of testimonio within educational research allows for a collaborative process in which my students become researchers and their stories become the entry points to theorizing from experience. Testimonio is thus a method for centering these marginalized voices, narratives, and epistemologies within the academy. In doing so, we can consider how literacies and knowledge are situated within the body and how they can move us toward disrupting colonial reproductions of inquiry while emphasizing their legitimacy and value within educational research.

References

Anzaldúa, Gloria. 1983. "Speaking in Tongues: Letter to Third World Women Writers." In *This Bridge Called My Back: Writings by Radical Women of Color*, edited by Cherríe Moraga and Gloria Anzaldúa, 165–74. New York: Kitchen Table, Women of Color Press.

———. 1987. *Borderlands / La Frontera: The New Mestiza*. San Francisco: Aunt Lute.

Brabeck, Kalina. 2003. "IV. Testimonio: A Strategy for Collective Resistance, Cultural Survival, and Building Solidarity." *Feminism & Psychology* 13, no. 2: 252–58.

Calderón, Dolores, Dolores Delgado Bernal, Lindsay Pérez Huber, María Malagón, and Verónica Nelly Vélez. 2012. "A Chicana Feminist Epistemology Revisited: Cultivating Ideas a Generation Later." *Harvard Educational Review* 82, no. 4: 513–39.

Cervantes-Soon, Claudia G. 2012. "Testimonios of Life and Learning in the Borderlands: Subaltern Juárez Girls Speak." *Equity & Excellence in Education* 45, no. 3: 373–91.

Cruz, Cindy. 2001. "Toward an Epistemology of a Brown Body." *International Journal of Qualitative Studies in Education* 14, no. 5: 657–69.

———. 2012. "Making Curriculum from Scratch: Testimonio in an Urban Classroom." *Equity & Excellence in Education* 45, no. 3: 460–71.

Delgado Bernal, Dolores. 1998. "Using a Chicana Feminist Epistemology in Educational Research." *Harvard Educational Review* 68, no. 4: 555–83.

Delgado Bernal, Dolores, Rebeca Burciaga, and Judith Flores Carmona. 2012. "Chicana/Latina Testimonios: Mapping the Methodological, Pedagogical, and Political." *Equity & Excellence in Education* 45, no. 3: 363–72.

DeNicolo, Christina Passos, Mónica González, Socorro Morales, and Laura Romaní. 2015. "Teaching through Testimonio: Accessing Community Cultural Wealth in School." *Journal of Latinos and Education* 14, no. 4: 228–43.

Dillard, Cynthia B. 2000. "The Substance of Things Hoped for, the Evidence of Things Not Seen: Examining an Endarkened Feminist Epistemology in Educational Research and Leadership." *International Journal of Qualitative Studies in Education* 13, no. 6: 661–81.

Dutro, Elizabeth. 2013. "Towards a Pedagogy of the Incomprehensible: Trauma and the Imperative of Critical Witness in Literacy Classrooms." *Pedagogies* 8, no. 4: 301–15.

Elenes, C. Alejandra. 2000. "Chicana Feminist Narratives and the Politics of the Self." *Frontiers* 21, no. 3: 105–23.

Huber, Lindsay Pérez, and Bert María Cueva. 2012. "Chicana/Latina Testimonios on Effects and Responses to Microaggressions." *Equity & Excellence in Education* 45, no. 3: 392–410.

Johnson, Elisabeth, and Lalitha Vasudevan. 2012. "Seeing and Hearing Students' Lived and Embodied Critical Literacy Practices." *Theory into Practice* 51, no. 1: 34–41.

Lara, Irene. 2002. "Healing Sueños for Academia." In *This Bridge We Call Home: Radical Visions for Transformation*, edited by Gloria E. Anzaldúa and AnaLouise Keating, 433–38. New York: Routledge.

Latina Feminist Group. 2001. *Telling to Live: Latina Feminist Testimonios.* Durham, NC: Duke Univ. Press.

Menchú, Rigoberta. [1984] 2010. *I, Rigoberta Menchú: An Indian Woman in Guatemala.* New York: Verso.

Russel y Rodriguez, Monica. 2007. "Messy Spaces, Chicana Testimonio, and the Un-disciplining of Ethnography." *Chicana/Latina Studies Journal* 7, no. 1: 86–121.

Saavedra, Cinthya M. 2011. "Language and Literacy in the Borderlands: Acting upon the World through 'Testimonios.'" 2011. *Language Arts* 88, no. 4: 261–69.

Saavedra, Cinthya M., and Ellen D. Nymark. 2008. "Borderland Mestizaje."
In *Handbook of Critical and Indigenous Methodologies*, edited by Nor-
man K. Denzin, Yvonna S. Lincoln, and Linda Tuhiwai Smith, 255–76.
Thousand Oak, CA: Sage.

Saavedra, Cinthya, and Michelle Pérez. 2014. "An Introduction: (Re)envi-
sioning Chicana/Latina Feminist Methodologies." *Journal of Latino/
Latin American Studies* 6, no. 2: 78–80.

Ybarra, Mónica González. 2018. "'Here, I Already Feel Smart': Exploring
Chicana Feminist Literacy Pedagogies with Youth in an (IM) Migrant
Housing Community." PhD diss., Univ. of Colorado, Boulder.

———. 2020. "'We Have a Strong Way of Thinking . . . and It Shows
through Our Words': Exploring Mujerista Literacies with Chicana/
Latina Youth in a Community Ethnic Studies Course." *Research in the
Teaching of English* 54, no. 3: 231–53.

Ybarra, Mónica González, and Cinthya M. Saavedra. 2021. "Excavat-
ing Embodied Literacies through a Chicana/Latina Feminist Framework." *Journal of Literacy Research* 53, no. 1: 100–121.

Afterword

A Letter of Solidarity for Junior Latina Scholars

Christine Garcia, Genevieve Garcia de Müeller, Aja Y. Martinez, and Laura Gonzales

Abstract

This afterword is written by four junior Latina scholars who share stories about their journeys navigating the academy. Designed with the goal of "exposing stereotypes and injustice and offering additional truths through a narration of the researchers' own experiences," these counterstories are "composite dialogues," where "characters are written as composites of many individuals" that "do not have a one-to-one correspondence to any one individual the author knows" (Martinez 2020, 17, 25). The purpose of bringing these counterstories to life is to illustrate how intentional coalition building among junior Latina scholars can foster community and survival in and beyond the academy.

Introduction

March 15, 2019, Pittsburgh, Pennsylvania

Scene: a crowded karaoke bar filled with Latinx academics who have come together after a conference. Alejandra, Bianca, Tina G., and Gabriela stand around a wooden table looking at each other in silence until they begin to speak at a near scream so as to be heard over the music.

"NO. I can't believe this."

"I've been meaning to tell you."

"I should have known."

At a conference in 2019, a group of untenured Latinas in academia who work at different institutions came together to discuss yet another instance of racism and persecution inflicted upon us by someone we thought was on our side. As we stood in a crowded room surrounded by our Latinx colleagues following several days of having to engage in the academic performativity that comes with many conferences, we talked, laughed, and cried as we shared with each other the enraging ironies that often accompany the terms *mentor* and *leader*.

Who are our mentors?

Who can we trust?

Who is actually trying to lift us up?

Who is just pretending?

Performing "wokeness" and allyship is a thing. And this thing is NOT accompliceship (crunkadelic 2016).

As untenured Latinas in academia, we continuously have to balance our desire to succeed professionally with our own gut feelings about who we can and cannot trust. We often come into situations where someone claims to mentor us while simultaneously doing everything possible to uphold academic structures that were intentionally built to exclude us.

In that crowded karaoke bar in Pittsburgh, we told stories, shared receipts, our papelitos guardados (Latina Feminist Group 2001), and in many ways relived traumatic experiences that we've faced in our relatively short time in the academy. We decided that in this collection about leadership, mentorship, and Latinidad, we can't conclude without addressing the fact that "Latina leadership" looks and feels different for us as contemporary, relatively junior Latina scholars. Part of processing violence and building solidarity, we've found, requires us to come together to discuss not only the successes and accomplishments we've had but also the struggles and obstacles that are continuously placed before us.

As our many Latina elders and real mentors have documented time and time again, the only thing we have is the power of our stories, nuestros testimonios. Sharing our stories and being honest about our experiences are the only things we can do to make sure that our experiences are acknowledged, valued, and remembered. To this end, in this afterword, as we look back on the chapters in this collection and reflect on our own career paths, we want to offer a letter of solidarity for other upcoming Latina scholars who may read a collection about Latina leadership and mentorship while also experiencing deep pain and isolation. You are not alone, and these stories are for you.

A Letter of Solidarity for Our Hermanas

Hermanxs,

Your feelings are valid.

That pit in your stomach that deepens as you walk into the academic department that told you repeatedly that you don't belong. To quote our profe, la gran Anzaldúa (1987), the "remolinos" on fire that your body produces in an attempt to suspend you off your feet and into safer ground—they are real.

People will tell you you're overreacting. That you should be "grateful" to be included, even if this inclusion actually means people are stealing your ideas and claiming them as their own.

People will tell you to tell them your stories, to share your pain, to "speak your truth" in a "safe space" that they have created. A space within their own research agenda that leverages your pain for their benefit.

Cuidado con las víboras; las más brillantes a veces muerden.

Academia ain't no safe space, and the only safety we have is what we build with each other.

Trust yourself. Your abuelitas and madrinas and tías and mamas taught you the power of listening to your body. No te olvídes.

Tina G.: Ponte lo que te dé la gana

One of the first lessons I learned as a young chola was the proper way to measure out the perfectly drawn eyebrow. The secret? Take your eyebrow pencil, align it next to each side of your nose, and mark out the width of each brow. Next, round or square them out to the thickness you're feeling that day: thin and arched if you're all business or full and fluffy if you're being all romantic. To complement the firme eyebrows, dark-lined or blood-red lips work well. Waterproof mascara? Check. Also, there is a set of hoops for every occasion, preferably gold and/or with nameplates. These are the sacred beauty rites of my borderlands culture, and I perform them proudly because I value and appreciate the land I come from and the people who raised me. *Órale.*

What we wear and how we wear it are a form of social, material rhetoric that can be performed in order to promote human agency— we become ourselves through fashioning how we look (Hernandez 2020). When I perform fashion by wearing a style that resonates with me, by adopting the look of my culture or subculture, or by modeling the dress of those I admire or aspire to be, I am using fashion rhetorically. I am making a fashion statement that consists of unspoken but clear codes of who I believe I am and who I want to appear to be to others. In the academy, the fashion codes are high stakes, especially for junior faculty. If we can appear to fit into a department or into the greater university atmosphere, our chances of being hired, renewed, and tenured are bolstered. But what if our identity markers, those very important fashion statements that code who we are, do not align with the academy's expectations?

People of color have been especially subject to codes and standards that position their identity expressions as deviant or in need of regulation. A contemporary example of this is the ban on natural Black hairstyles in schools and workplaces across North America. Gender-queer and gender-fluid people are also faced with overt policing of their identity expressions by means of dress codes that identify appropriate "male" and "female" fashion and are then used to force gender conformity. In such instances, fashion can be weaponized against us, used as a mechanism of control, as a way to weaken us by diminishing our agency.

At the heart of this process are the gatekeepers, who set out to exclude and control identity expression under the guise of propriety. These gatekeepers, sometimes acting under the guise of "mentors," seek to obscure the presence of differences and create a uniform identity template that reflects their concept of acceptability—a template

272 Garcia, Garcia de Müeller, Martinez, and Gonzales

that often aesthetically reflects the gatekeeper. Chicana and Latina feminist scholars Ana Milena Ribero and Sonia Arellano touch on this when they argue that the assumption of a white middle-class mentoring model leaves the needs of women-of-color academics unattended. They explain, "Mentoring can often seem bent on shaping the scholar to the white-dominant academy and not on transforming the institution into a space that values minoritized ways of knowing and being in the world" (see chapter 1 in this volume). We do not want to be mentored into a heteronormative white middle-class model because we are not those things and we do not strive to be those things. We are happy and confident in our skin and identity expressions. This audacity to fully be who we are is a threat to the chokehold whiteness has on academia, and this is a lesson I learned personally.

After successfully defending my dissertation, I attended a meeting with a "mentor" who had agreed to support me on the market with a letter of recommendation. I was proud of the work I had done throughout my PhD program and excited to get my job market search off to a running start. After a brief pat on the back for my successful defense, I was handed an envelope, which I thought was a sneak peek at my letter of recommendation. I can still remember the emptiness I felt, sitting in my car in the student parking garage, reading the letter I had been handed. Instead of a recommendation, I was faced with a list of critiques about how I styled myself, including makeup, dress, and behavior, all of which my "mentor" deemed unprofessional. Following these critiques were specific recommendations about how I should dress and act—recommendations that would erase my culture and upbringing and instead allow me to perform whiteness without question.

Though I was deeply hurt by this person's opinions of me written in that letter, I knew better than to trust the advice to whitewash myself in order to land a tenure-track position. What was I supposed to do, Mighty Morphin White Woman myself into some strange persona for the interviews but then show up to my new position all hoops and eyebrows? I don't think so. After speaking with a few close friends and confidants, I decided to push back and hold space for all nonnormative folx in academia. I did not enter the job market that year; instead, I put together a new team of letter writers and mock interviewers. I met with true mentors who counseled me in ways of remaining authentic to my identity performance, while also fine-tuning it for the campus interview. Because I was mentored into realizing my potential and speaking my truth, my job market experience was a success. I felt comfortable and respected during my campus visits, and in turn I was able to put others at ease. I felt confident in my teaching demos and research talks because I was performing my authentic work, not an imitation based on a standard that was set without my permission or consultation.

Bianca: No te calles, no te rindas

Mi mami taught me always to respect my elders, to do what I am told, and to smile and nod politely when my elders speak. This worked well for me as a child at holiday gatherings, when a tía would inevitably comment on how much weight I had put on over the summer; at school, when a Latina teacher would say something negative to someone else in Spanish, not realizing that Bianca the güera could understand; and in other public spaces, where I could hide the fact that although I was told that I "look American," I still couldn't speak English.

"No les hagas caso, hija. No te preocupes. Sigue con lo tuyo."

My mami's policy of respecting everyone and smiling politely in the face of ignorance has deep roots in the Latinx immigrant experience within the United States. We can't speak up, be loud, combative, or too different because these behaviors will only make us fall deeper into the stereotypes that gringos already have of us. And if you have white privilege, the lesson passed down is to lean into this privilege and stay even quieter so that nobody finds you out.

Although this may be a common story in many families, you would think that respectability and politeness politics would be looked down upon in academia—that supposedly liberal, social-justice-screaming performative space. Why would we smile politely and stay quiet when we are supposed to be advocating for justice and change? Why would we discourage each other from taking risks and doing what we believe in?

In my short time as an academic, what I've learned is that respectability politics continues to govern academic dynamics, particularly when Latinx scholars are involved. Even in my own privileged position, the loudness of my presence and the perceived difference in my voice have been consistently challenged, reprimanded, and eventually kicked out.

Yet I cannot and will not be a quiet white feminist; yo soy una malcriada.

I started grad school as a twenty-six-year-old newly divorced immigrant who had spent her late teens and twenties working at a grocery store while also teaching writing full-time. For me, making the decision to go get a PhD in 2013 was a huge leap of faith, and it was also the first time I got to "go away" and focus on school without also having to maintain a household and work multiple jobs. Mi hermanito had recently graduated with his bachelor's degree and moved out of our home, and my first marriage had collapsed. I was ready for a change, and, more importantly, for the first time in my life I *could* make a change.

When I got to my PhD program, I was on fellowship, which meant that I didn't have to teach any courses my first year and could focus entirely on my coursework. I came into this privilege after spending three years teaching four writing-intensive courses per semester while also working full-time as a cashier. So I did what any immigrant trabajadora would do: I kept working. I used my experiences to develop a research agenda, and I benefited immensely from senior mentors who took me in and allowed me to learn from and with them. In fact, one of my favorite early memories of grad school is that during orientation but before we even entered the building, I asked our department chair where I could file my application for the institutional review board.

I share these things not to compliment myself (in fact, writing them down is kind of embarrassing) but rather to illustrate the fact that our roots cannot be extracted from us as Latinas once we enter academic spaces. In my case, the immigrant work mentality and orientation to labor, the consistent pressure always to have to prove that I do indeed belong, did not just exit my body and mind as soon as I signed a fellowship agreement. I wanted to keep pushing forward because that's the only thing I knew how to do. I wasn't always right in pushing, and I didn't always go in the right direction, but I continue to follow my heart when it comes to making life decisions and speaking up for what I know is right. As our mamas and tías and abuelas teach us, our hearts always know what to do.

In grad school, the fact that I was in a "top-tier program" doing "important research" did not erase the fact that I was also making less money in a PhD program than I did as a writing instructor and grocery store worker. Being in a privileged academic position does not erase our other academic, family, and community responsibilities.

I considered quitting my graduate program many times, mostly owing to financial pressures, but I also saw another option. At the end of my second year in grad school, I decided that I wanted to graduate early and go on the academic job market. I had spent two years publishing and learning and extending the teaching experiences that I brought into the program. My gut told me I could get a job.

Upon making the decision to graduate early and go on the academic job market in my third year of grad school, I thought I would be met with support and encouragement from mentors who had seen something in me when I first applied to my grad program. I was fortunate enough to have the support of many people who knew I could do it or who were at least willing to support me along the way and catch me when I fell. However, I was also met with a lot of resistance from people who told me I was "undercooked," that I "would make the program look bad," that I was "lazy," that I should leverage the pain I was feeling over not being able to financially help my loved ones by "writing about transcontinental guilt," and that I would undoubtedly "be at the bottom of all the job application piles" because "nobody would take me seriously."

I applied to ten jobs that year, and I received seven offers for tenure-track positions at Research 1 institutions. Graduating early is not something I could ever have done alone, nor would I recommend it for everyone. What happened with me is something that will likely resonate with other Latinx and marginalized scholars writ large: my community came together and saved me. My peers, mostly those who are also from marginalized communities, reviewed my materials, scheduled practice interviews with me, listened and supported me when I went on campus visits. As always, what we have in times of stress and crisis is each other. No te olvídes.

Alejandra

My mom always told me, "You rise to the occasion. They set a bar, and you meet it and exceed it." And she's not wrong.

Drake's song "Started from the Bottom" is definitely an anthem and motto in my life. And what it speaks to is my potential. I can't think of an instance in my life in which I've ever just walked through the front door—especially the kind of front doors that others hold open for you. No. My route has always been through the side, maybe the back, winding my way through the basement, on sneak mode (for my gamers out there), crouched and on my toes, walking as if I'm on tissue paper, slowly, quietly, soundlessly, making my way up the basement stairs, into the main room, and then BAM! I appear! And all those who were genially ushered in the front door are startled and surprised at my sudden (to them) appearance in the house. "Where did she come from?" they ask each other—completely unaware of the darkness, the muck, the depths I have had to traverse to access the same room they arrived in, albeit by a very different path.

Yet here we all are.

And because I didn't just get ushered through the front door, I'm tough. I bear scars from the journey. I bear them with pride. With defiance.

And guess what? I brought friends. I made sure I showed them the path through those same side doors and basements because that's what the tricksters, the bridge builders, the cabrones, the adelantes did before me. And did for me. We all show up. A squad. Comadres. Ready.

Benevolence in the guise of mentorship is only gatekeeping. It's as old as the colonizers. They see us, and with pity in their eyes and a mournful expression on their caras they shake their heads in consternation and say, "We're telling you not to do [fill in the blank] for your own good." Colonizing gatekeepers think they always know what's best for us. They've convinced themselves that they are our best custodians. They enact their self-professed charity by "helping" us poor lost souls who would be positively destroyed by the academy if it were not for their benevolence. "What would they do without us?" they must ask themselves.

Nevertheless, *we do, we move, we survive, we thrive, and we exist,* not because of them but despite them—sometimes in spite of them.

GET. OUT. OF. OUR. WAY.

Move or be moved.

We found another way in. We will support each other. We don't need your paternalistic *care*. It's not useful, and you do not see us clearly. Wipe that mournful expression from your face, direct those pitying eyes elsewhere, and GET. OUT. OF. OUR. WAY.

We'll rise to the occasion on our own—juntxs. It doesn't matter if we have to start from the bottom. Estamos juntxs.

We got this, and we got each other.

Gabriela

I started my PhD program as a twenty-nine-year-old widow with an eighteen-month-old son. I was potty training him. On the first day of class, as I was waiting for my dad to pick him up, my son turned to me and said, "Mama, I need to go potty." I took him to the closest bathroom on campus, but it was too late, and I had urine all over my shoes. I held back tears because I didn't want my son to think he had done anything wrong. My dad picked him up, and I ran to class. I spent my first seminar as a graduate student with urine-soaked shoes. This is one of the stories I never told anyone. The moments, a decade ago, I was ashamed of. Shame is constructed, and in my program it was overwhelming and powerful. I am no longer ashamed.

Also in that first seminar was the only other Latina in my grad program. We looked at each other and knew then that we would be scoping each other out for the next few weeks to make sure we were both down. We needed each other in that university. In our lives. To survive. By the end of the semester, we were collaborating. We approached our professor and proposed a project on the lack of Latina representation in publications. The white woman professor laughed and said, "Racism doesn't exist in academia."

A few years later I told a mentor that I was a widow, to which he replied, "You should have said that sooner. People will make assumptions about you." Although this mentor himself had obviously made "assumptions" about me, which I am reading here to mean moral judgments on single motherhood, I was now given a "pass" because I had been married, which allowed for my existence within the academy. Motherhood, in particular single motherhood, in academia places women in a liminal space. Realizing the limited spaces to which I was relegated by some academics prompted me to add language to my syllabi that openly welcomed motherhood and in fact all parenthood into my classroom. A paragraph in every syllabus I make states, "If you are a caretaker of a child, please note that they are always welcome in my class. If you are having an emergency, need to leave early, or must bring your child to class for any reason, notify me, and we can make arrangements. Your parenthood will not hinder your progress in my classroom." Sometimes your experiences cultivate empathy with your students.

One morning last year, a man walked into my class and asked what I was doing using the computer. As soon as he saw my students, he apologized and said, "Oh, sorry, you didn't look like a professor." If this had happened eight years ago, I would have begun to ask myself, "What does a professor look like? Why don't I look like one? What do I need to change to look more like a professor?" Instead, my gut reaction to his comment was, "You don't look like a professor with your bad opinion." Sometimes your experiences cultivate a sense of belonging despite being told otherwise.

In the process of writing this, I couldn't help but think about the question Jose Orduña asks in his memoir *The Weight of Shadows*

(2016). Orduña, who migrated to the United States when he was two years old, describes heading into the Mexican side of the Sonoran Desert and passing out water and food to migrants as they cross. What must be true about the American mind, he asks, for this crisis to happen? For my gente to be here in this desert, what must be true about the American mind? I grew up in the Southwest and can't help but think of the desert as a place cultivated by state violence.

I think back on my graduate education as a time of cultivation: the act of cultivating the landscape of my identity, of trying to acquire or develop a quality or skill, and of working toward refinement of those skills in a place that seeks to assimilate rather than honor differences in this cultivation. It is a system in place, recognizable by some but experienced by all. What must be true about the academic mind? How do we cultivate our identities in places of violence? What is cultivation?

I am a Chicana, second generation on one side, third generation on the other. I'm also a mom, a woman, and a scholar. The intersections of these identities are a part of my intellectual assets. It took years of practice to understand how that can be so.

It's a tricky thing when you begin to understand how to articulate your trauma and process it through your work. When this moment happens, two paths diverge: ownership of your experience and deep knowledge on one path and whiteness trying to find a way to exploit your trauma for its gain on the other.

"Talk more about your widowhood. People will make assumptions about you."

"Why don't you write an article on being a first-gen student of color?"

"You should talk about the rhetorics of PTSD in Mexican communities. That's interesting work."

"You're a Chicana. Write about that."

"We need a woman of color on this diversity committee to meet the guidelines."

Last year I was the victim of a hate crime. I was sent death threats to my university email account. Within a few days after that, I had several emails from people asking me to contribute to special issues, book chapters, or conferences about what I experienced. I hadn't even stopped having panic attacks or fearing I was going to die, and white academia already wanted to profit from my trauma.

Take the other path. Never think you have to use your trauma for professional gain, but if you choose to write through the grief, through the pain, do it on your terms and for yourself and your community.

We want you here. We love you. We want to listen to you.

Our Shared Responsibility and Our Move to Pay It Forward

We share these stories with you as other junior Latinas in academia not because we think they are unique but because we *know* the experiences they relate are all too common. We know that if you are reading this as a junior Latina academic, you have likely experienced oppression and can relate to the stories we share here and those that many contributors to this collection also bring forward. We thus want to end this book with a note of solidarity and an invitation to continue sharing your stories. Speaking our truth is our biggest weapon, and our communities are our biggest source of protection. No te olvídes . . . we are here, and we got you.

In Solidarity.

References

Anzaldúa, Gloria. 1987. *Borderlands / La Frontera: The New Mestiza*. San Francisco: Aunt Lute.

Crunkadelic. 2016. "Get Your People." Crunk Feminist Collective, Nov. 9. At www.crunkfeministcollective.com/2016/11/09/get-your-people/.

Hernandez, Jillian. 2020. *Aesthetics of Excess: The Art and Politics of Black and Latina Embodiment*. Durham, NC: Duke Univ. Press.

Latina Feminist Group. 2001. *Telling to Live: Latina Feminist Testimonios*. Durham, NC: Duke Univ. Press.

Martinez, Aja Y. 2020. *Counterstory: The Rhetoric and Writing of Critical Race Theory*. Urbana, IL: National Council of Teachers of English.

Orduña, José. 2016. *The Weight of Shadows: A Memoir of Immigration and Displacement*. Boston: Beacon Press.

Contributors

Index

Contributors

Nancy Alvarez completed her PhD in English at St. John's University and teaches first-year writing and developmental writing at Bronx Community College. Her research interests include writing-center studies, writing pedagogy, digital literacies, language rights, and issues of access and equity for Latinxs in higher education.

Sonia C. Arellano is assistant professor in the Department of Writing and Rhetoric at the University of Central Florida, where she teaches courses on feminist rhetorics and visual/material rhetorics. Her research focuses on textile projects that address social justice issues, particularly at the intersections of migration and death. Her current book project examines the tactile rhetoric of the Migrant Quilt Project, which uses quilts to memorialize migrant lives lost while crossing into the United States. Arellano also engages in quiltmaking as a necessary part of her research. Her scholarship can be found in *Peitho* as well as in the edited collection *Rhetorics Elsewhere and Otherwise: Contested Modernities, Decolonial Visions* (2019).

Stefani Baldivia is an archivist in the Meriam Library Special Collections and University Archives Department at California State University, Chico, where she performs reference, instruction, and outreach activities. She established the Chico State Diversity Changemakers Oral History Project to illuminate the history of Chico State's diversity and inclusion efforts. Baldivia's research interests include diversifying the archives, flattening barriers to information literacy, and preserving social justice efforts in Chico, California, and beyond.

Blanca Gabriela Caldas Chumbes es una transnational indigenous/Latina scholar, catedrática en estudios de segundas lenguas y educación elemental en la Universidad de Minnesota–Twin Cities. She obtained su doctorado en la Universidad de Tejas in Austin en la especialidad de bilingual/bicultural education and Mexican-American/Latinx studies. Sus investigaciones están enfocadas en la preparación lingüística y académica y activista de future bilingual teachers, minoritized language practices y pedagogía crítica Freireana y Boaleana.

Raquel Corona completed her PhD in English at St. John's University and is a full-time lecturer at Queensborough Community College within the City University of New York system. Her research interests include Latinx literature, rhetoric, Black and Latinx feminisms, as well as the study of the Latina body in various media. Her dissertation is a rhetorical exploration of how transnationalism affects the dissemination and circulation of stories about the Latina body and sex.

Christine Garcia is an assistant professor of rhetoric and composition at Eastern Connecticut State University, Willimantic, where she teaches in the First-Year Writing and Freshman Experience Programs as well as courses in Chicanx and Latinx rhetoric and literature. She earned her PhD in rhetoric and composition from the University of New Mexico and holds both a BA and an MA in English language and literature from Angelo State University.

Genevieve García de Müeller is assistant professor and director of the Writing across the Curriculum Program in the Writing Studies, Rhetoric, and Composition Department at Syracuse University. Her research interests include examining intersections between race and writing program administration, critical pedagogy, the rhetoric of immigration policy, and the discursive practices of migrant civil rights activists. She has work in the *WAC Journal* titled "Inviting Students to Determine for Themselves What It Means to Write across the Disciplines" (cowritten with Brian Hendrickson, 2016). Her most recent project is a forthcoming book on the deliberative rhetoric of immigration policy.

Laura Gonzales is assistant professor of digital writing and cultural rhetorics at the University of Florida. She is the author of *Sites of Translation: What Multilinguals Can Teach Us about Digital Writing and Rhetoric* (2018), which was awarded the Sweetland Digital Rhetoric Collaborative /

University of Michigan Press Book Prize prior to publication in 2016 and the Advancement of Knowledge Award by the Conference on College Composition and Communication in 2020.

Mónica González Ybarra is assistant professor of bilingual education in the Department of Curriculum and Instruction at the University of Illinois, Urbana–Champaign. Her research examines the literacies and knowledges of Latinx/Chicanx (im)migrant young people through the use of Chicana feminisms, critical literacies, postcolonial and decolonial frameworks, and critical theories of race and citizenship. Drawing on scholarship across the fields of education and ethnic studies, her work is concerned largely with challenging and disrupting normative, colonial notions of knowledge production by centering the voices, experiences, and ways of knowing of youth of color.

Lorena Gutierrez is assistant professor of teaching in the Graduate School of Education at the University of California, Riverside. She received her PhD in curriculum, instruction, and teacher education from Michigan State University. Her research highlights the ways Latinx migrant and seasonal farmworkers thrive in their educational pursuits in spite of the inequities they face in K–12 schools. In her dissertation, "'Use My Name, They Need to Know Who I Am!': Latina/o Migrant and Seasonal Farmworker Youth at the Interstices of the Educational Pipeline" (2016), based on a three-year ethnographic study, she examines the schooling experiences of Latina/o migrant farmworker youth in K–12 schools and in a high-school equivalency program in the Midwest.

Michelle Hall Kells teaches courses in rhetoric and writing in the Department of English at the University of New Mexico. Her research interests include public rhetoric (civil rights and environmental discourses), language diversity, sociolinguistics, and community writing studies. Kells's scholarship centers largely on the public rhetoric of citizenship. Her most recent book is *Vicente Ximenes, LBJ's Great Society, and Mexican American Civil Rights Rhetoric* (2018). Her previous book was *Héctor P. García: Everyday Rhetoric and Mexican American Civil Rights* (2006). She was the lead editor of the collected volumes *Attending to the Margins: Writing, Researching, and Teaching on the Front Lines* (with Valerie Balester,

1999) and *Latino/a Discourses: On Language, Identity, and Literacy Education* (with Valerie Balester and Victor Villanueva, 2004). Kells's work has been featured in the journals *JAC*, *Written Communication*, *Journal of Reflections*, *Journal of Community Literacy*, *Praxis*, and *Rhetoric & Public Affairs* as well as in a number of edited books, including *Cross-Language Relations in Composition* (2010); *Dialects, Englishes, Creoles, and Education* (2008); *TESOL Encyclopedia of English Language Teaching* (2018); and *Who Belongs in America? Presidents, Rhetoric, and Immigration* (2006). She is currently working on a new book about women labor activists, environmental racism, and the landmark Empire Zinc Mine strike in New Mexico in the 1950s.

Cristina Kirklighter is a recently retired professor from Texas A&M University, Corpus Christi, and former editor of *Reflections: A Journal of Public Rhetoric, Civic Writing, and Service Learning*. She is the past cochair of the National Council of Teachers of English (NCTE) / Conference on College Composition and Communication (CCCC) Latinx Caucus (2009–14) and co-coordinator of the NCTE Writing and Working for Change Project, with a specific focus on documenting the histories of the identity-based NCTE/CCCC caucuses. With Diana Cárdenas and Susan Wolff Murphy, she coedited *Teaching Writing with Latino/a Students: Lessons Learned at Hispanic-Serving Institutions* (2007), the first book focusing on Hispanic-serving institutions within a discipline.

Kendall Leon is associate professor of rhetoric and composition, with a specialization in Chicanx/Latinx/@ rhetoric, in the Department of English at California State University, Chico. Her teaching and research interests include cultural and community rhetorics, professional writing, writing program administration, and research methodology.

Aja Y. Martinez is assistant professor of writing studies, rhetoric, and composition at the University of North Texas, where she researches and teaches rhetorics of race and ethnicity, including the rhetorics of race within both Western and non-Euro-Western contexts. Her monograph *Counterstory: The Writing and Rhetoric of Critical Race Theory* (2020) presents counterstory as a method for actualizing critical race theory in the research and pedagogy of rhetoric-and-composition studies.

Cristina D. Ramírez is associate professor of rhetoric and composition at the University of Arizona, where she directs the doctoral program. She specializes in archival rescue and recovery of work by Mexican and Mexican American female authors. With Jessica Enoch, she coauthored *Mestiza Rhetorics: An Anthology of Mexicana Activism in the Spanish Language Press, 1875–1922* (2019).

Ana Milena Ribero is a proud Latina, mother-scholar, and assistant professor of rhetoric and writing at Oregon State University. Her research and teaching focus mainly on the rhetorics of (im)migration, rhetorics of race, critical literacies, and women-of-color feminisms. Her book project explores "dreamer rhetorics"—the rhetorical productions of undocumented youth activism—during the Obama years. Her scholarship can be found in *Rhetoric Review*, *Peitho*, *Performance Research*, *Present Tense*, *Decolonizing Rhetoric and Composition Studies*, and *The Routledge Handbook of Digital Writing and Rhetoric*.

Index